Private Lives and Public Surveillance

Private Lives and Public Surveillance

Social Control in the Computer Age

James B. Rule

SCHOCKEN BOOKS · NEW YORK

To Sylvia

First SCHOCKEN edition 1974

Contents

List of Tables

List of Figures

Foreword

Seeing this study go to press, one cannot help drawing connections between its main ideas and recent events on the national political scene. The debacle of the Nixon administration, occurring after the completion of my research, seems as though designed to underscore many of its conclusions. The first explosion, as everyone now knows, came with the intrusion of White House agents into the headquarters of their political opponents, as they searched for sensitive or damning documents. The chain reaction spread with disclosure of the compilation of lists of critics of the administration, lists containing suggestions of personal indiscretions that might be used against them. Then there was an attempt to form a psychological profile of one political opponent—with data stolen from his psychiatrist—in the hope of using it to silence him, or at least to curtail his activities. These extreme measures represent nothing if not variations on the theme of this work—the use, by powerful agencies, of personal data on private individuals in order to control their behavior. Thus the Watergate affair hardly comes as a surprise. Rather, it represents the unhappy fruition of a number of possibilities which this book aims to probe.

Spokesmen for the dominant interests in America are already offering their reassurance that what we are witnessing is a crisis of men, not institutions. The Watergate Deluge, it is said, will at length recede, and the political landscape will be repopulated by descendants of the present species—uncontaminated, it is supposed, by the sins that brought on the original flood of censure.

But can we afford to accept this interpretation? The question of whether to ascribe blame in transgressions like these to men or to the system in which men act is absolutely crucial. To be sure, different men react differently to the temptation to unfair application of raw power against private individuals. But is it not obvious that changes in the kind of society in which we live have left private persons vulnerable in new ways to manipulation by powerful agencies? Is it not evident that electronic eavesdropping, psychiatric interviewing, and the array of other means of gathering and using personal data are distinctive products of our own times? Is it not clear that changes in the technology and social organization of surveillance over men's private lives have changed the character of important social and political institutions—in terms of their power position *vis à vis* the general public? True, any one atrocity is the work of specific men and thus attributable to their particular political morality. But ruthlessness in the use of power, though not a characteristic of all power-holders, is an ever-present ingredient in political life. What is new is not the appearance of ruthless men but the fact that modern social institutions have placed unprecedented levers of power in their hands.

This book is devoted to spelling out details of the collection and use of information on private persons by government and other bureaucracies. Many readers, I believe, will find the details of these practices intriguing and revealing, if not alarming. Nevertheless, *reportage* is hardly the first goal of this study. Disclosures contained here have already caused some public comment, but certainly there are better sources of shocking anecdote.

What this study does definitely aim to provide is an analysis of broad institutional trends—specifically, of the growth of institutions through which powerful bureaucracies use information on private persons in order to control their behavior. It aims to chart the social dynamics that have engendered and shaped the growth of this new form of power. The material has been drawn from institutions in America and Britain. But any complex society could have provided equally pertinent examples of such institutions, and the observations based on such material, I am convinced, would have been much the same. For the goals of a study like this are, more than specific revelations about particular men and events, generalizations about patterns of development that are being repeated in many different social contexts.

It is often said that institutions are in themselves nonpartisan or free of political content. In other words, the characteristics and capabilities of systems of information on people do not of themselves bring about abuse of power. Fundamentally, this argument is identical to the one that attributes the current scandals to men rather than to institutions. The statements are true as far as they go, but they hardly go far enough. Any analysis of the implications of institutional change must deal with men as they are, rather than as they ought to be. And this means taking account of all the possibilities of use of any particular institutional form. Institutions generally endure longer than the men who create them, and they typically take on aspects their founders could not have imagined. Thus it is no more than prudent to view new institutions in terms of their potential uses, rather than only in terms of the professed intentions of their founders or spokesmen.

The reader will no doubt recall that one of the ploys of the Nixon administration in its efforts to hound its antagonists was to use Internal Revenue files and auditing procedures against them. This incident strikes me as the most ominous of all the so-called "White House horrors," though it was hardly seen by most people as the most flagrant or most newsworthy of those events. But the implication of mobilizing for political ends the finely honed bureaucratic weaponry originally developed for more benign administrative purposes is grim indeed. The use of that system on a regular basis could subject far more people to direct political control than the attentions of a handful of espionage agents on the White House staff. That the founders of the Internal Revenue system may have intended nothing like these results is cold comfort under the circumstances.

Appreciation of this lesson—that it is not necessarily possible to resist the powers of institutions of social control once they are a fact—seems to have led to some heartening skepticism concerning their establishment. A case in point is the current resistance of some state governments to participating in the

FBI's centralized data bank on crime and criminals. How long this resistance can withstand some of the opposing forces portrayed in this study is unclear.

In concluding this book I wrote, "For the future, to maintain confidence in the indefinite forbearance of those who control these systems seems . . . to require a political and historical clairvoyance not given to men." Events since this was written only confirm the apprehension. The present information scandals will eventually be history, whatever political rearrangements they leave in their wake. But the problem of controlling personal information, as it is itself used to control men and women, is bound to remain and grow, and changes in personnel will hardly affect the broader issue. In the long run, this is a much more compelling ground for concern than any single conspiracy.

Stony Brook, Long Island
1 January 1974

Debate in the Commons on the Bill for Registering the Number of the People

Mr Potter brought in a Bill 'For taking and registering an annual Account of the total number of people, and of the total number of marriages, births, and deaths; and also of the total number of poor receiving alms from every parish and extra-parochial place in Great Britain'.

Upon this occasion, Mr *William Thornton* said:

'Sir; I was never more astonished and alarmed since I had the honour to sit in this House, than I have been this day: for I did not believe that there had been any set of men, or indeed, any individual of the human species so presumptuous and so abandoned, as to make the proposal which we have just heard ...

'To what end ... should our number be known, except we are to be pressed into the fleet and the army, or transplanted like felons to the plantations abroad? And what purpose will it answer to know where the kingdom is crowded, and where it is thin, except we are to be driven from place to place as graziers do their cattle? If this be intended, let them brand us at once; but while they treat us like oxen and sheep, let them not insult us with the name of men.

'As to myself, I hold this project to be totally subversive of the last remains of English liberty ...'

House of Commons, 30 March 1753

Preface

Any member of a modern, highly 'developed' society is apt to feel that he inhabits two worlds at once. One is the ordinary social world of events, people, relationships, and so on as they impinge directly on experience. The other is a 'paper world' of formal documentation which serves to verify, sanction and generally substantiate the former, experiential reality. At first thought, one might regard the documentary world as nothing but a highly imperfect copy of the first, wholly derivative from it and unable to subsist on its own. And it is true that documentation often falls ludicrously short of doing justice to the experiential world which it supposedly portrays. A marriage certificate can hardly capture the richness of any single marriage, or for that matter the essence of marriage in general. Nor, for example, do educational credentials often seem to bear much relationship to the experience of being educated. And yet there are times when the paper world stirs with life of its own, and comes to shape and dominate men's experiences. These are moments when the documentary tokens of birth or marriage, health or illness, good character or bad, weigh more heavily on men's lives than the 'reality' which they are supposed to represent. These two worlds coexist, but they do not coincide. Their relationship is a strange symbiosis, a sociological counterpoint whose two themes sometimes seem fittingly complementary to one another, at other times arbitrary and even absurd.

People feel, however vaguely, that this curious split between the documentary world and the world of 'reality' is somehow peculiar to life in modern societies. And in this they are correct. For the growing impact of personal documentation is nothing more than a manifestation of the increasing importance of bureaucratic process – of large organizations, precise rules and formal criteria for action. Bureaucratic organizations characteristic of modern, highly developed social orders thrive on and indeed require formal documentation as a basis for their activities. And as more and more junctures of men's lives come to involve participation of bureaucratic agencies, the reliance on authoritative personal documentation grows commensurately.

If systematic personal record-keeping is the medium of corporate attentions to the affairs of private persons, there is no question but that those attentions may be unwelcome and feared. One widely mistrusted aspect of such practices is their effects upon privacy. The application of the special powers of large organizations to data-collection, especially when implemented by impressive modern technologies, threatens to absorb all available personal information and more. Further, people fear that the collection of data about themselves will lead, in ways not always clearly envisaged, to the exercise of authoritarian controls over their lives. Thus, the growth of personal record-keeping may appear to jeopardize not only men's personal privacy, but their liberty as well. And yet, at the same time, the structures of modern society seem to rely so much on the exchange of authoritative personal information that one wonders whether it would be possible to dispense with it.

This book is devoted to unravelling the complex relationship between the systematic reliance on personal documentation and the growth of modern social forms. It particularly aims to examine the power conferred on large organizations by the use of such information, and the impact of this power on private persons. It is an empirical study, based on detailed investigation of five bureaucratic systems which rely very heavily on the systematic use of personal information. Three of these are British government agencies: the police criminal record-keeping system, the vehicle and driver licensing system, and the National Insurance system. The remaining two cases are from the United States, though the latter of these is increasingly worldwide in its operations. The first is the consumer credit reporting system, and the second is the BankAmericard system. Each of the five case studies examines in detail what information the relevant system collects, how it is stored and used, and what the effects of its use are on both the keepers and those depicted in it.

As with most people, my first sensitivity to these issues came on reading Orwell's *1984*. This is one of the rare books which one can call great and terrible without the slightest exaggeration; its influence on this study will be abundantly clear. A more strictly sociological interest arose on reading the literature on the development of modern social forms. Especially interesting to me were the changing mechanisms and patterns of social control associated with the growth of increasingly modern social structures. It seemed that personal documentation played an important part in these new forms of control, and this prompted an interest in the workings of bureaucratic data-gathering organizations like those studied here.

Thus there are at least three sociological literatures which bear on this study – those on modern social structure, on deviance and control, and on the workings of complex organizations. In addition, there has grown up, especially in the last few years, a considerable body of writing dealing with privacy and its fate in contemporary Britain and America. Perhaps some day someone will produce a comprehensive review of all these literatures as they bear on the use of personal documentation. This, however, is not such a study. My aim here has been to develop a specific series of questions, and then to amass and examine empirical material which bears on these. In so doing, I have forgone discussion of other writings on related topics to a very large extent. I have, to be sure, cited other studies where I have directly relied on them or where some comparative reference was obviously called for. But I have not gone out of my way to offer comments on others' writing simply for the sake of doing so. In pursuing the questions under study here I may unknowingly have made statements similar to those made elsewhere. I can only plead in advance that any such coincidence is purely accidental. Material presented without citation is my own, but there is no guarantee that the same ideas have not also been developed independently by others.

My first inquiries into any of these topics were made during the time of my doctoral research. But before the reader gingerly sets this volume aside, I must hastily explain that this study is not in any sense a version of a doctoral dissertation. With the partial exception of Chapter 5, all the material presented here was developed more recently than that, during 1970 and 1971. The data-gathering took place, as I have said, both in Britain and in the United States. Nevertheless, it would not be exact to describe this study as comparative in its aims. Rather, it is a *generalizing* effort, aiming at statements which hold true not just for these two societies and these five systems, but for similar societies and similar systems more broadly. It happened to be feasible to carry out the research in Britain and America, but I am convinced that equally pertinent cases for study could be found in any modern industrial society, and that the resulting generalizations would not be much different.

The topics dealt with in this research can be volatile and controversial; indeed, they have become distinctly more so in both Britain and America over the last several years. The sensitivity of the subject-matter has presented certain challenges for the pursuit of this research. Foremost among these has been the reluctance of those involved in personal record-keeping to disclose their practices fully, and the consequent difficulty in obtaining really reliable and suitably detailed material. Nevertheless, this reluctance did not prove to be an insurmountable obstacle. The five systems treated here were open to study through interviews with officials, through direct observation of record-keeping practice, and through the use of relevant documents. Each of the five case studies is followed by a brief description of the steps involved in gathering the data contained there. More detailed explanations of the techniques involved in gathering and verifying information presented in this book are to be found in the Appendix.

A second challenge inherent in the controversial nature of the material lies in its presentation in print. Because emotional reactions are inevitable, I have gone to particular lengths to present both facts and judgements even-handedly and fairly. This has meant neither retreating from controversial points because of their sensitivity nor emphasizing the sensational merely for the sake of doing so. Some readers, I am sure, will see this book as unjustly severe towards the organizations studied, while others will criticize it for failing to attack what they see as reprehensible practices. I am prepared to respond to either sort of criticism, but I ask that the book be read as a whole. Each chapter is one part of a comprehensive statement, and a number of the important strands of the argument are not finally brought together until the end. What may appear as implicit moral judgements early in the book, or as the lack of them, may assume a different aspect later on.

There must be some books which come into being solely through the solitary efforts of the author himself, without the involvement of any other persons or agencies. This is rather the opposite sort of work. From the beginning to the end of this study I have relied heavily on the support of others; without such support, this undertaking would have been not just impossible but unthinkable. The thanks which I now express cannot compensate for this assistance, and hence are no more than a token gesture. But they are deeply felt nonetheless.

Perhaps the most staggering debt is to those who have furnished information for the case studies. Information thus provided, mainly by members of the agencies under study, was the 'raw material' for this inquiry, yet I obtained it free of charge. If I had to pay the true cost of the countless hours taken from the working days of the several hundred officials at all levels of responsibility on whom I relied for help, this study would have been outrageously, prohibitively expensive. I never ceased to be amazed at the durability of my informants' good will in withstanding the attentions of an initially ignorant but incurably prying outsider. This sense of amazement turned into something less comfortable when I tried to imagine my reactions to an outsider's inquiries into my work. I am particularly grateful to those officials who went out of their way to help me even while realizing that the provision of controversial information could only complicate their lives. The willingness to extend assistance under these conditions was nothing short of noble. I only hope that those who helped will find this book worthy of their considerable pains on its behalf.

A second enormous debt is to Nuffield College, Oxford. By appointing me Research Fellow between 1969 and 1971, the College provided indispensable conditions for me to carry out this work. Not only did the College grant me a position with no responsibilities other than research, but it also added all sorts of invaluable support facilities such as secretarial assistance, an office, telephone, library and so on. In addition, the College provided major grants for such important requirements as the travel involved in gathering the material presented here. I am thus extremely grateful to the entire Nuffield College community – Warden, Fellows, students and staff – for making those two years both enjoyable and productive.

Other agencies have also made important financial contributions to the research. The United States Department of Health, Education and Welfare, and the Russell Sage Foundation provided support for some of the early work on consumer credit reporting. Later on, the William Waldorf Astor Foundation generously financed two trips from England to the United States. This travel was indispensable in preparing the material presented in Chapters 5 and 6.

I should also like to thank three teachers whose influence has meant a great deal to me. These are Professors Lewis Coser, George Homans and Charles Tilly. I am particularly in the debt of Professor Homans both for his energetic attempts to force me to clarify the ideas developed here and for his extensive practical assistance in getting the actual research under way. None of these three men, needless to say, has influenced the writing of this book so directly that he could remotely be held responsible for its shortcomings. But all three have set an example of sociological expertise and of dedication to the enterprise of scholarship which I have earnestly striven to follow.

Finally, it is a great pleasure to thank Sylvia Hewlett, to whom this book is dedicated. Her support took many forms, from moral to sociological, but her most important contribution was to make life worth living as this study was taking shape.

1

Social Control and Modern Social Structure

Why do we find the world of *1984* so harrowing? Certainly one reason is its vision of life totally robbed of personal privacy, but there is more to it than that. For the ugliest and most frightening thing about that world was its vision of total *control* of men's lives by a monolithic, authoritarian state. Indeed, the destruction of privacy was a means to this end, a tool for enforcing instant obedience to the dictates of the authorities.

And yet, such thoroughgoing, relentless social control represents nothing other than an extreme manifestation of one of the ubiquitous processes of social life. Ubiquitous, and actually vital. True, sociologists have generally accepted the argument that social life would be impossible unless men felt a measure of willing commitment to abide by its rules. The social order would collapse, according to this argument, if everyone felt free to lie, steal, rape or cheat whenever he or she could avoid punishment for doing so.* But social life would be equally impossible without special means for making disobedience difficult or unattractive. For men's willingness to obey the strictures of established social forms is never wholly automatic, never merely a result of their inner commitment to the established rules. No, such conformity depends as much on a host of specific mechanisms of social control, ranging from gentle reproof to mass execution, from locks on doors to driving licences. Without them, we would find our world both unrecognizable and unviable.

* This assumption is the stepping-off point for all the immensely influential work of Talcott Parsons. The key reference, of course, is *The Social System*, London, Tavistock Publications, 1952.

Social Control

By social control I mean all those mechanisms which discourage or forestall disobedience, which either punish such behaviour once it has occurred, or prevent those with inclinations to disobedience from acting on those inclinations. These mechanisms reinforce and sustain the most diverse social units. From the family to the state, from the most fanatical sect to the most hidebound bureaucracy, social bodies have their means of excluding those apt to break the rules, and their means of ensuring specific unpleasant consequences to those who disobey. Even lovers come both to recognize what each expects of the other and to be influenced by the unpleasant consequences of violating such expectations. Of course, the conspicuousness of the sanctions varies immensely. Some sanctions are informal and subtle, while others are flaunted as intimidating deterrents. But one may be confident that, wherever there are rules to guide men's behaviour and to constrain their selfish desires, there will also be mechanisms of social control to ensure that these rules are obeyed.

The workings of social control, and particularly efforts to impose or resist it, give rise to some of the bloodiest, most conflict-ridden chapters of social life. The growth of centralized states from groups of smaller, autonomous principalities, or the creation of an empire from a group of smaller states, represent cases in point. The efforts of the constituent elements to avoid subordination under a single system of control are bound to lead to serious tests of strength among them, and often violent ones at that.* Once the issue is settled and the predominance of the new authorities is evident, social control may proceed more routinely, without repetition of the violent contests necessary to instate it in the first place. Nevertheless, the fact that the state or any other social unit may sustain itself

* Struggles over the imposition of central social control in the growth of the modern state, and the tests of strength connected with this imposition, have formed the main preoccupation of the recent research of Charles Tilly. An excellent representative of his many papers on the subject is 'The Changing Place of Collective Violence', in Melvin Richter, ed., *Essays in Social and Political History*, Cambridge, Mass., Harvard University Press, 1970.

by inconspicuous, routine manifestations of control should not obscure the considerable forces of social control implicit in the existence of such units.

It would be wrong to imply that contests over the imposition of social control occur only in the context of politics. The same dynamics are evident in the development of a new, inclusive religious faith which incorporates or supersedes an earlier array of smaller, parochial sects. Or, in the attempt of powerful business interests to overcome or take control of their localized competitors in order to found a national or international monopoly. The underlying process in all such cases is the same. Where there have been a plurality of centres of direction and coordination – of control, in short – a single centre attempts to assert its domination over these elements or, by destroying the old structures themselves, over the people who had comprised them. It is through such struggles that new social units of all kinds are born.

If new social units come into being with the extension of social control, failure of control can lead to their death. The challenge of a provincial revolt against a centralized state, after all, is nothing if not an attempt to deny the centre its ability to maintain control. Should such a revolt succeed, the state dies, even though its constituent parts, the provinces, may remain. The growth and breakup of states, again, is only one example. The same process is evident in the splintering of a broadly-based political movement into a congeries of sects, or the dismantling of a corporate empire into its constituent firms. The point is, maintenance of some measure of control over any social unit is one way of identifying the unit as such. When social control fails, when the centre can no longer enforce its customary directives, the state, political movement, corporate entity or whatever loses its coherence and hence its identity.

Most social systems, in fact, have points of special vulnerability to failure in social control. These are points where disobedience is especially likely to occur, and where failure of control leads especially quickly to the unviability of the body as a coherent social unit. For an empire threatened by revolt, the salient problem might be the enforcement upon the provinces of customary obligations of taxation and military service.

For an established church facing a rash of heresy, the pre-occupation might be the enforcement of doctrinal or liturgical orthodoxy. In cases like these, the regime will also have other tasks of social control, other norms which it desires to see enforced. But first concerns are apt to go to these more pressing problems. An empire about to lose its grip on its territories, or a church about to lose its religious authority and hence its following, must concern itself with the preservation of these things before it can afford to be concerned about anything else. One can identify similar 'fault lines' in most social units, points at which disobedience is especially likely and the failure of control especially dangerous to the system. The leadership of such bodies, if it is shrewd, will not begrudge the attention necessary to assure compliance at these points, even at the cost of neglecting other forms of control.

Those who seek to maintain social control must accomplish two sorts of things. First, they must maintain what one might call *powers of control*. This means, for one thing, that they need to be able to apply sanctions, or inducements sufficient to discourage the sanctioned person from repeating his disobedient acts. The sanctions, of course, can be positive or negative, physical or symbolic, formal or informal, so long as they really do influence behaviour. Second, if the system is not to rely only on reward or punishment after the fact, it must possess means of excluding would-be rule-breakers from the opportunity to disobey, for example, by refusing in some way to deal with them. Many systems, including those studied here, can afford to be weak in the first respect, so long as they remain strong in the second. And many forms of punishment, such as execution and imprisonment, work both to make misbehaviour undesirable from the standpoint of the would-be deviant, and to insulate others from his behaviour.

Neither of these two powers does any good, however, without what is termed in this book a system of *surveillance*. In the first place, surveillance entails a means of knowing when rules are being obeyed, when they are broken, and, most importantly, who is responsible for which. In some instances these things may be easy to accomplish, e.g., a flagrant armed robbery by notorious criminals. In the case of other forms of disobedience, such as income tax evasion, it may be extremely difficult. A second element of surveillance, also indispensable, is the ability to locate and identify those responsible for misdeeds of some kind. Again, this may be simple in many cases; in cases like those studied in this book, however, it may be the most difficult condition of all to fulfil.

In practice, it is often very difficult to draw boundaries between processes of surveillance and the application of what had been termed the powers of control. In the cases studied here, for example, the same people and the same bodies are often engaged in the collection of information and in the application of sanctions. Nevertheless, when I want to emphasize those activities having to do with collecting and maintaining information, I speak of *systems of surveillance*. Where the concern lies more with the actual management of behaviour, through sanctioning or exclusion, I refer to *systems of control*. To designate the organizations, persons or interests seeking to maintain control, I use the terms *agency*, *regime*, or more broadly, just 'the system'. Finally, those from whom compliance is sought are called the 'clientele' of any particular system of control.

For the purposes of this study, a crucial fact about the maintenance of social control is that it entails *costs* to the agency of control. Sanctioning or isolating those who do not obey, whether this entails throwing them in jail or depriving them of their cheque-books, is time-consuming and expensive. Keeping track of how people behave, who breaks the rules, and where the rule-breakers can be found is no less so. These costs demand close attention both from the leaders of such agencies and from anyone else who seeks to understand the workings of these systems. To be sure, tasks of control vary enormously in the demands they make on the resources of the system. A mutinous army may engage all its officers' time and energies in putting down revolt; a spirited force, on the other hand, may obey with minimal prodding. Nevertheless, it is doubtful that any regime, over an extended period of time, can avoid devoting some of its resources to securing obedience from its people.

In any setting, excessive costs can render social control unviable, and bring about the death of the social unit involved.

This can happen even when the rules are finally enforced. If a department store must spend half its yearly budget guarding against shoplifting, it may be forced to close its doors, even if it succeeds in stopping the thievery. If an army can advance only under the guns of its officers, its viability as a fighting unit will be hopelessly compromised in advance. This issue of whether the results of enforcing compliance justify the costs is an endemic one, and it will figure centrally in the analysis of the five cases studied here.

The Staging of Social Control

Because of both cost considerations and other factors, rules enforceable in one setting may be quite incapable of enforcement elsewhere. It may be easy to enforce, say, a tax on the use of a particular road simply by erecting a toll gate and exacting payment from all who pass. Here the task of control is relatively simple and inexpensive; anyone who fails to pay is easily noted, apprehended and sanctioned. Much more problematic, however, is the enforcement of a tax on the distillation of whisky. For there the authorities have difficulty in knowing that the violation is occurring in the first place, and perhaps even more difficulty in determining who is responsible for the violation. Because of such tactical considerations, agencies of control often try to manipulate the social setting of the behaviour in question so as to gain the maximum advantage over their clienteles. In Britain, for example, international travellers may legally land and depart only from a limited number of recognized seaports and airfields, staffed by the 'Special Branch' or political police and immigration authorities for this purpose. Were this not the case, control over movement in and out of the country would be more expensive at best, and perhaps impossible in any case.

In this book, such tactical considerations in enforcement are called the *staging* of social control. More specifically, one might define staging as the relative advantage and disadvantage to system and clientele posed by the social structural context of surveillance and control. Thus the staging of any forms of control may be favourable to the system, in that it makes enforcement easy, or to the clientele, in that it facilitates evasion. Differences of this kind are a main concern of this study.

More than anything else, this book is concerned with the effects upon the staging of social control of changes in the *scale* of social life. Social scale is a concept sometimes used by sociologists and economists to describe the extent of interdependence among people in different social units.* The scale of any social unit is seen as proportional to the numbers of people comprising it, and to the intensity of relations among them. The unit itself may either be the whole of a society, or some smaller element of social organization, like a family or a bureaucracy. In the instance of whole societies, the smallest-scale cases would be the isolated, autonomous group of primitives, self-sufficient as a band of even a few hundred people. Few social groupings like this actually remain, but so far as one knows all men once lived in very small-scale units like these. Of middling social scale, by these criteria, would be loosely integrated, ancient states, where a single capital theoretically rules a considerable area, but actually impinges rather little on the lives of those in the province. England during feudal times is a tolerable example. Even when the nation was united under a single monarch, there was little in the way of central administration, and both local government and the balance of local social and economic life went on in considerable parochial autonomy.

By contrast, the large-scale organization of the modern nation-state both embraces very large numbers of people and orders their lives in very close dependence upon one another. The highly centralized, powerful polities of modern states, with their powers to tax the entire population, to raise massive military forces, and to maintain uniform legal systems throughout their boundaries are only one manifestation of this interdependence. Their closely integrated economic systems, where

* To the best of my knowledge, this concept was originally developed in Godfrey and Monica Wilson, *The Analysis of Social Change*, Cambridge University Press, 1945; see especially Chapter II. Another application is in Eshref Shevky and Wendell Bell, *Social Area Analysis*, Stanford, California, Stanford University Press, 1955.

the failure of one firm can immediately endanger the jobs of workers in a different industry thousands of miles away, is another. No less significant are the comprehensive, interdependent structures which dominate education, communications, religion or any number of other social activities. Indeed, the growth of the modern nation-state is very much the story of the destruction of old forms of local and regional autonomy, and of their replacement by social forms which bring the affairs of all the populace into closer coordination.*

All of this scarcely gives a rigorous definition to the notion of social scale. It leaves open, for example, the question of the relative weight given to the two elements of the definition, size of the social unit and intensity of its internal coordination. Thus, without further specification, there is no way of comparing the scale of a medium-sized, loosely coordinated social unit to that of a smaller, more tightly integrated one. Nor, for that matter, is there a precise rule for measuring the intensity of social integration or coordination. These problems are hardly insoluble, however, and different analysts will solve them differently according to their own requirements. For present purposes, it will not be necessary to create such exact conceptual tools. The notion of scale as defined above will serve well enough to convey the idea that social units vary both in the numbers of people participating in them and in the degree of involvement, coordination, loyalty, and so on that they demand of these participants. Seen in this light, the modern nation-state clearly represents an advance in social scale over its predecessors, no matter what the specifics of the definitions one chooses.

Certainly, too, this notion of scale calls attention to the fact that the process of modernization, reckoned in terms of the growth of scale, is hardly complete. For contemporary societies continue both to intensify their internal centralization and to

---

* This process is the theme of virtually all Tilly's recent work. It is also the main preoccupation of S. N. Eisenstadt in his monumental work on ancient political empires, which is in fact a study of the growth of social scale through the extension of social control. The reference is S. N. Eisenstadt, *The Political Systems of Empires*, Glencoe, Illinois, The Free Press, 1963.

join with other states in still larger units. The development of centralized systems of surveillance like those studied in this book and the growth of supra-national bodies like the European Economic Community represent cases in point. Without making any blindly evolutionary assumptions about the 'inevitability' of such change, then, it is fair to say that the growth of social scale has marked the development of the state throughout our recent past, and shows signs of continuing to do so in the near future. One wonders, in this connection, about the significance of the fact that the world of *1984* was divided wholly into three massively large-scale societies. ·

I have already suggested that the scale of different social settings has everything to do with the viability of different forms of social control, and specifically with the staging of control. Forms of behaviour easily controlled in small-scale social settings may be almost impossible to control elsewhere, and vice versa. Hence changes in the scale of social life have drastic effects on the relations between agencies of control and their clienteles.

Small-scale social units, whether they are primitive tribes, small towns, or something else, generally rely on highly informal but nonetheless effective means of social control. In such settings, after all, social behaviour is much more likely than elsewhere to be a public matter. Instances of thievery, an illicit love affair, or any other breach of commonly accepted rules are not apt to escape general attention. Moreover, given that people in such settings are apt to know their fellows through face-to-face acquaintance, the perpetrator is unlikely to escape the resulting sanctions of community disapproval. Gossip spreads the news of misbehaviour throughout one's entire social world, and one's past is thus virtually an open book. In more cosmopolitan settings, however, escape from one's past may be much easier. The simple fact that these societies comprise so many participants makes it impossible for everyone to know about everyone else. Nor are the standards of 'correct' behaviour so uniform. Given these differences in the staging of social control, one wonders whether the conformity often noted in small-scale settings necessarily stems, as many anthropologists have felt, from some special moral solidarity.* A more likely explanation, one suspects, is the effectiveness of specific mechanisms of social control.

By contrast, consider the position of the state or any other agency seeking to obtain compliance from a mass clientele in a large-scale social setting. Attempting to make the members of such a body pay their taxes, or obey the motoring laws, or refrain from subversive political activities, any regime automatically faces enormous problems of surveillance. No one person could possibly be acquainted with all members of such a public, still less keep track of them all at the same time. Nor is it easy to maintain surveillance over all points where disobedience might occur, so as to note violations of the rules. Faced with the problem of securing compliance from a mobile, anonymous public, any regime must do its best to develop techniques to replicate the functions of gossip and face-to-face acquaintance in small-scale social settings.

Still, means do exist to this end. The commonest solutions to the problem of mass surveillance in large-scale societies lie in the use of documentation. Whether in discursive prose, standardized data-sheets or computer records, the formal rendering of information about people comes to take the place of informal mechanisms of surveillance found in small-scale settings. The crucial function of such documentation is to link people to their pasts, and thereby to provide the surveillance necessary for the exercise of social control. Given the anonymity of large-scale societies, the mobility of persons within such societies, and the time lapses involved in encounters between agency and client, it is only through documentation that the former can keep track of who is who, and who has done what. Without passports, credit records, licences, and the host of other documents which link flesh-and-blood men and women to their past statuses, misdeeds, accomplishments or whatever, all sorts of critical relations would be impossible – including the

---

* More persuasive, in this context, are the arguments of Malinowski. See Bronislaw Malinowski, *Crime and Custom in Savage Society*, London, Kegan Paul, Trench, Trubner and Co., 1926; especially Chapter XI.

relations of control which subsist between the members of mass societies and their major institutions.

This book is concerned with the workings of systems of mass surveillance and control, systems which rely heavily upon documentation in order to deal with very numerous clienteles. All five of the systems studied in the following chapters have developed elaborate means of collecting, processing and maintaining pertinent data about their clients. All of them use these data to make decisions concerning the clients, decisions which serve to enforce rules with which the system must secure compliance. The content of the decisions is highly varied, but invariably involves determining who has complied with the rules, and in which cases some form of punitive or preventive action against clients is necessary. In these respects, present-day systems of mass surveillance and control like those studied here share many of the sociological qualities of the single massive surveillance system depicted in *1984*, though of course they are much less powerful and they do not necessarily pursue the same malevolent purposes.

Systems like these are distinctive products of the modern, large-scale societies in which they occur. Specifically, they are likely to develop under the following conditions:

1. When an agency must regularly deal with a clientele too large and anonymous to be kept track of on a basis of face-to-face acquaintance;

2. When these dealings entail the enforcement of rules advantageous to the agency and potentially burdensome to the clientele;

3. When these enforcement activities involve decision-making about how to act towards the clientele, e.g. whether or not sanctions are warranted against a particular client;

4. When the decisions must be made discriminatingly, according to precise details of each person's past history or present situation;

5. When the agency must associate every client with what it considers the full details of his past history, especially so as to forestall people's evading the consequences of their past behaviour.

These conditions are not predictive in an exact sense, but highly conducive to the growth of mass surveillance systems. One might expect to find systems of mass surveillance based on documentation in the absence of one or more of these conditions. But it is difficult to imagine how all five could be present without giving rise to a system like those studied in this book. Certainly all of these predisposing conditions led to the inception of the five systems studied here, as they presumably did to the system portrayed in *1984*.

Three of these five conditions have directly to do with the growth of social scale. The relationship is obvious with regard to the first condition, in that the number of participants in any social unit represents a defining property of social scale. But the fourth and fifth points also touch on matters related to scale, in that they involve the intensiveness of coordination or inter-relationship among participants, the second element of the definition of scale. The need of any agency to concern itself with the fine details of the lives of its clients implies a kind of relationship not found in less tightly integrated settings. It is one thing, for example, for a state to raise an army simply by rounding up every able-bodied young man in sight, or to collect revenue by extorting as much as it can from a captive populace. But a much finer form of social control, and a much more penetrating extension of state power to the lives of individual citizens, is necessary for the operation of a modern, bureaucratic system of conscription or income-taxation. The latter two cases require the agency of control to act towards each client on the basis of a discriminating reckoning of such factors as his age, family status, income, and so on, and to maintain forceful and effective ways of locating and apprehending him if he should fail his obligations. This *fine-grained concern* of agencies with the details of their clients' lives is a measure of the intensity of interaction between agency and clientele, and hence of the scale of the social units involved.

In any case, a moment's reflection should suffice to convince one that systems of mass surveillance are a fairly recent product of modern industrial society. All the five systems studied here have had their inception in this century, and most of them have attained their present scale of operation only within the last fifteen or twenty years. Moreover, it is difficult to imagine how any mass surveillance system numbering its clients in the millions could have existed in Britain or America before the turn of the century. In Britain, it is true, the State has kept virtually complete listings of births, deaths and marriages since the 1830s, but these have not been used directly for purposes of surveillance or control. Yet systems of mass surveillance have grown up explosively since their inception, so that they now monitor some of the most important junctures between private individuals and the major institutions of modern society.

The growth of mass surveillance and control, then, seems somehow bound up with the changing structures of modern societies. But just what is the nature of this association? And what new forms of social organization and control do further developments along these lines promise? Does the continued extension of mass surveillance promise the advent of more and more oppressive forms of social control? Is the association between rigid mass surveillance and authoritarian rule accidental or inevitable? Again, one recalls uneasily the very large-scale, very tightly controlled world of *1984*. Does the continued growth of mass surveillance draw us relentlessly into a world like Orwell's? Or will a closer, more analytical look at these developments yield a more complex and subtle set of predictions?

The Growth of Mass Surveillance

Since the mid-1960s, these developments have received increasing public attention, both in Britain and in America. Journalists, legislators, jurists and others have identified in the growing collection and use of personal information both the seeds of destruction of personal privacy and the beginnings of *1984*-style authoritarianism. The cause of the alarm has not only been the growth of mass surveillance in the sense used here, but also in the development of sophisticated eavesdropping techniques, data banks, census inquiries and other forms of intrusion into men's private lives. Such concerns have led to a good deal of writing on these topics, by both academics and other interested observers. These authors have generally decried the growth of such activities, offered grave predictions concerning their imminent effects, and proposed various solutions to avert such calamities.

Anyone concerned about the growth of mass surveillance, and about the moral and social issues which it poses, will be grateful for this response. The concern underlying such writings, concern over the possibilities for domination inherent in the growth of the new techniques, is of course one of those which has led to the research presented here. Nevertheless, I feel that the inferences drawn by these authors, even the most conscientious of them, have sometimes been excessively glib. This tendency is most serious at that delicate point where discussion moves from observed fact to inference and prediction.

A case in point might be drawn from the recent study by Malcolm Warner and Michael Stone. At one point the authors provide an interesting and useful discussion of data files, and the issues inherent in their centralization and confidentiality, only to have their imaginations run wild in conclusion. Commenting on the possibility of adopting a single number for the files of every individual, they write:

> Probably a unique number would mean that there would have to be an issue of identity cards – to be carried at all times so that the number could be quoted at all times. That seems harmless, but once you make any piece of paper obligatory it is a very easy step into tyranny – witness South Africa. If you haven't got it, it's a crime; if it is taken from you, you're stuck – you become a 'non-person'.*

Here one feels that the authors have stopped thinking critically, and instead are contenting themselves with playing to the grandstand of alarmed public opinion.

Even Alan Westin, whose book *Privacy and Freedom* is widely and justly regarded as the best review of recent developments on these topics, is not invulnerable to the temptation to make unhelpfully rash speculations. One passage in that book

* Malcolm Warner and Michael Stone, *The Data-Bank Society*, London, George Allen and Unwin, 1970; p. 77.

discusses the possibility of a universal credit system where no financial transaction would take place in cash:

... the life of [the?] individual would be almost wholly recorded and observable through analysis of the daily 'transactions' of 'Credit Card No. 172,381,400 ...' Whoever ran the computers could know when the individual entered the highway and where he got off; how many bottles of Scotch or Vermouth he purchased from the liquor store; who paid the rent for the girl in Apartment 4B; who went to the movies between two and four p.m. on a working day at the office; who was at lunch at Luigi's or the Four Seasons on Tuesday, September 15; and the hotel at which Mrs Smith spent the rainy afternoon last Sunday ... There would be few areas in which anyone could move about in the anonymity of personal privacy and few transactions that would not be fully documented for government examination.*

These two statements are representative of an extremely widespread trend among recent writings on these topics. Such statements are not factually incorrect; their speculative nature makes it impossible to submit them to proof or disproof. But they are unhelpful in that they carry speculation to such an extreme as to blur the distinction between concrete, verifiable trends and fancy. More seriously, they seem to take for granted precisely the questions which are most problematic and most challenging. *How* does the use of identity cards lead to tyranny? *How* does computerized credit accounting conduce to state control over persons' private lives? Is it *necessarily* true that the development of unique numbering for personal identification brings any society within 'a very easy step' to tyranny? Would universal reliance on credit *inevitably* and *inherently* lead to a situation where 'there would be few areas in which anyone could move about in the anonymity of personal privacy and few transactions that would not be fully documented for governmental examination'?

The most pressing need of all in these cases is to judge the real possibilities of such developments, to assess the concrete forces which conduce to or contravene the feared results. The installation of a central water supply for a large city may in

* Alan F. Westin, *Privacy and Freedom*, New York, Atheneum, 1967; p. 165.

itself open the possibility of poisoning the entire populace with a single lethal dose. But one's concern about such an event clearly turns on the concrete conditions which would make such an event likely or unlikely. So it should be with the development of mass surveillance.

Let me suggest that no approach to these problems can take us far unless it is in some way sociological. This is hastily not to say that only sociologists should address themselves to such issues, or still less that meaningful writing on the subject must be marked by the dead hand of sociological prose. But I believe that the underlying questions concerning the growth of mass surveillance to date, and the future which it portends, are inherently sociological. The compelling concerns on this topic are not just over the possible effects of this or that surveillance technique as such, but over the broad social trends which shape the customary uses of such techniques. In other words, we are interested above all in the role of surveillance in modern societies generally, and in the social forces shaping the continued development of such practices. In considering these questions, it does not suffice merely to cite the conceivable effects of possible future developments along these lines. What is required instead is close documentation of existing practices and painstaking analysis of their relations to their social contexts.

The research presented here is designed to meet these requirements. The strategy adopted has been to choose for study five present-day systems which most fully embody the organizational characteristics of fully-developed systems of mass surveillance and control. The assumption is that systems like these should provide the most direct clues to the effects of changing social scale on mass surveillance and control, and the most telling inferences concerning any totalitarian tendencies inherent in their growth. All five cases are very large in the numbers of their clients, with several of them running into the tens of millions. All face tasks of enforcing rules and ensuring compliance from these clienteles, the latter being scattered throughout the nations in which the systems exist, and, in one case, throughout the world. To effect such enforcement, each of the systems collects, stores and uses information on its clients in critical decision-making concerning them. By giving these five systems close study, it is hoped that the dominant trends in their growth, and in their relationship to their broader social contexts, will emerge.

Inevitably, selection on these principles means the exclusion of other interesting possibilities. This study neglects, for example, the growth of data banks and other repositories of personal information which are not evidently and regularly used for purposes of social control. It neglects certain other systems where data are used for control but where files are too dispersed to constitute a single system for the whole of a society. The British Inland Revenue is a near-miss in this respect, in that its record-keeping does serve the purpose of control, but yet remains relatively localized at this point. Finally, this study does not concern itself with activities of firms like detective agencies and other private investigators. For however much these bodies may inquire into the affairs of private citizens, there is as yet no single, massive system of control based on such information. None of this is to say that any of these topics is unworthy of attention, or to deny that these other practices affect the privacy and liberty of private citizens. But the concern of this book is with the effects of centralized surveillance practices on broad sectors of the populations of modern societies, and the relations of these practices to other social structural changes. To study this problem with a measure of thoroughness will more than absorb the writer's and the reader's attentions.

The nature of the task requires the development of parallel material on each of the five cases, and for this reason the organization of the case studies is relatively similar. Each of the five, for example, begins with a detailed exposition of the structure of the relevant surveillance system. First, this involves an account of the human organization of the bureaucracy or bureaucracies which carry out the surveillance. Second, it requires a discussion of the structure of the information kept in the system's files, with regard to both form and content. What data are filed, in what form, with what variation from file to file? Also important in this connection is the organization of the filing system itself. This includes questions of whether the data are stored in computerized or manual form, how centralized is their storage, and how readily the contents of any single file are accessible to those who use the system.

Following the discussion of organization, each case study examines what is termed 'Information Flow and Decision-making'. This entails, first of all, a careful tracing of the movement of data into the files kept by the system. Where does the information come from, how rapidly does it enter the files from its source, how frequently do various sources serve in these respects, and so on? Next it will be necessary to chart the movement of data. How does information make its way from the outside into the various repositories of filed information? How, and how often, is it subject to further transmission within the system, and for what purposes? Most importantly, how rapidly and how fully can filed data come to bear on decisions made for purposes of social control? What considerations bear in the decision-making based on these data, and how do different records lead to different decisions? The net effect of these discussions should be to define the limits to the capabilities of each system, to establish what the system can and cannot accomplish in terms of social control, given the resources at their disposal.

Finally, each of the case studies will note the major patterns of change within the relevant system. Some of the systems, undergoing considerable change at the time of writing, will require lengthy treatment; elsewhere, the discussions will be brief. These accounts, in any case, will avoid sweeping predictions of developments as yet far from realization, and will confine themselves to changes evidently in store for the immediate, foreseeable future.

In these three areas – structure, movement of information and decision-making, and patterns of change – discussion will necessarily remain quite close to the observed facts. But the nature of the task also requires something more analytical, something more abstract. It requires for each of the cases some assessment of the relationship between the facts on the system and the prospect of the fully-developed, authoritarian system of social control so freely predicted and so widely feared. In other words, there must be some means of comparing the realities of each of the five systems with the extreme possibility of what very large-scale, highly centralized, highly effective mass social control might be. To this end, let me sketch a model of the most extreme possible development of mass surveillance, an ideal type of a social order resembling the one portrayed by Orwell, though perhaps even more extreme. This I call a *total surveillance society*.

In such a world, first of all, there would be but a single system of surveillance and control, and its clientele would consist of everyone. This system would work to enforce compliance with a uniform set of norms governing every aspect of everyone's behaviour. Every action of every client would be scrutinized, recorded and evaluated, both at the moment of occurrence and for ever afterwards. The system would collate all information at a single point, making it impossible for anyone to evade responsibility for his past by fleeing from the scene of earlier behaviour. Nor would the single master agency compartmentalize information which it collected, keeping certain data for use only in certain kinds of decisions. Instead, it would bring the whole fund of its information to bear on every decision it made about everyone. Any sign of disobedience – present or anticipated – would result in corrective action. The fact that the system kept everyone under constant monitoring would mean that, in the event of misbehaviour, apprehension and sanctioning would occur immediately. By making detection and retaliation inevitable, such a system would make disobedience almost unthinkable.

One should never expect to encounter a real system like the one just described. That is just the point. The only usefulness of this paradigm is as a foil for comparison to real systems, as a case guaranteed to be more extreme than the real world could ever produce. True, some agencies may develop something like systems of total surveillance over very limited numbers of people, for short periods of time. Police may keep constant watch over a small group of conspirators, or the staff of a hospital may exercise something like total surveillance over those in the intensive care ward. But difficulties of staging, and especially prohibitive costs, rule out such techniques for larger clienteles over longer periods of time. No, the usefulness of the paradigm lies in its making it possible to compare systems of surveillance and control now in existence to this theoretical extreme, and to one another in terms of their proximity to this extreme.

All five systems under study here are readily susceptible to comparison with the total surveillance extreme. All, naturally, fall far short of it, but they do so to different extents in different respects. In other words, though the five systems are limited in their ability to maintain surveillance, these limitations are best reckoned in more than one dimension.

For example, any real surveillance system is limited in *size*. This means, for one thing, limitation to the numbers of persons whom it can depict in its files. Second, there is always a limitation in the amount of information with which a system can cope, the amount which it can meaningfully use in its decision-making on each person. Indeed, as the discussion will show, the amount of *usable* information is often less than that which is theoretically available on file. And such limitations on the amount of usable data kept per person correspond in turn to limitations in the amount of the subject's life depicted in the files. Third, surveillance systems also face limitations in what one might term the *subtlety* of their decision-making based on filed data. In the world of *1984* the authorities seemed to use information cunningly enough to know what their people were going to do even before they themselves did. The five systems depicted here are generally not that subtle in interpreting available information, but the five do differ considerably in how much they manage to get out of the data which they keep on file.

Second, real surveillance systems are limited in the *centralization* of their files. To be sure, the only systems considered for study here were at least somewhat centralized, but, as the discussion will show, some are more centralized than others. Centralization of data is extremely important in the staging of social control, in that it prevents clients from escaping the effects of their past by moving from one place to another. If the single central record can be applied wherever the fugitive goes, such movement does no good. Thus, to be fully effective, any system of surveillance should be able to collect information on a person's behaviour from any point in a society, and use it to enact measures of control on the same person at any other point. This development was complete in the total surveillance case, but not nearly so in the five systems depicted here.

Third, real systems fall short of the total surveillance extreme, and vary considerably among themselves, in terms of the *speed* of *information-flow* and *decision-making* which they exhibit. In Orwell's world, all misbehaviour presumably was registered with the authorities immediately, and resulted in immediate retribution when necessary. The systems studied here, by contrast, are not nearly so sophisticated. They are slow, for one thing, in their intake of information: relevant facts may be available for some time before the system can bestir itself to incorporate them in usable form. Moreover, these systems vary in the speed of movement of data once it is incorporated in their files, and in the application of such data to decision-making about people. Limitations like these make it easier for the individual to escape the effects of his past, for example, in cases where the agency of surveillance and control cannot bring its data to bear on a client quickly enough to act against him.

Fourth, and finally, real systems of mass surveillance and control are limited to varying degrees in what I term their *points of contact* with their clienteles. This again involves several things. First, existing systems are limited in the numbers of points at which they can incorporate information on the people with whom they must deal. Whereas in *1984* the authorities could 'tune in' on virtually every moment of every person's life, real surveillance systems restrict themselves to limited points of intake – for example, through the courts and a few other junctures in the case of police surveillance, and through credit-granting institutions, in the instance of consumer credit reporting. Similarly, existing systems are limited in terms of their ability to 'get back at' – to locate, accost and apprehend – those who have broken the rules. Unlike Orwell's world, modern societies provide many opportunities for those who wish to avoid the attention of the authorities simply to drop out of sight. To be sure, systems of mass control have their own ways of countervailing against these opportunities.

But the point is clear; systems vary in their ability to penetrate the anonymity of mass society so as to make the disobedient available for sanctions. A final and equally important element of contact between system and· clientele is the ability of the former to identify individual clients. In situations like those studied in this book, the position of the agency of control suffers unless it can quickly and unerringly link any single client to his record. Since clients themselves often wish to avoid such linkage, the strength of identification systems represents one of the important elements of the hold of the system on those with whom it deals.

These four forms of limitations of present-day surveillance systems, in relation to the total surveillance extreme, are at the same time criteria of their *capacity* or effectiveness. As any system develops along any of these dimensions, it improves in its ability to carry out the tasks of mass surveillance and control. Nor are the four criteria only theoretical toys, for, as the case studies will show, these same four issues are of immense practical concern to those who run systems of mass surveillance. And because surveillance systems vary considerably among themselves in these respects, the four criteria of capacity will serve as means of organizing discussion of the strength of each system, and of comparing it to other systems.

One further point, before concluding. Throughout this book, the terms 'mass surveillance and control' are used with a special meaning not identical to their use in everyday speech. As defined above, 'surveillance' means any form of systematic attention to whether rules are obeyed, to who obeys and who does not, and to how those who deviate can be located and sanctioned. 'Control' means the application of concrete measures to forestall or discourage disobedience. 'Mass' is used to refer to situations where single institutions address themselves to very large, impersonal, anonymous publics. 'Mass surveillance and control' is thus not meant to carry a pejorative connotation of continuous, close and malevolent monitoring. The closeness and the friendliness with which the systems studied here attend to their clienteles is a matter for study, not something to be assumed in advance.

Objectives of This Study

Perhaps the reader has noted that none of the four criteria of surveillance capacity is in itself overtly political. None, that is, deals with the political significance of rules enforced through mass surveillance, or with the political effects of behaviour subject to control. Nor, for that matter, is any of the five systems studied here primarily political in its objectives. This may seem strange in a book which aims, among other things, to explore possible totalitarian trends in the growth of mass surveillance. But the primary interest of this study lies with the social and organizational *form*, rather than the political *content*, of mass surveillance and control. My concern, in other words, lies with the structures and processes through which agencies of control, in very large-scale social settings, enforce compliance from anonymous, scattered, mass clienteles. It lies with the techniques and practices which enable such agencies, whatever their purposes, to penetrate the anonymity of mass society and to extend discriminating powers of control down to the level of the individual. These new mechanisms of social control, I suggest, demand attention from all those interested in the emerging patterns in the growth of modern industrial society, and in the dynamics of conformity and deviance, quite apart from the content of the rules enforced.

This is hardly to forswear the interest expressed above in the possibility of totalitarian trends inherent in the growth of mass surveillance. But the 'assumption is that political control is no different from other forms of mass social control, in that it requires specific organizational mechanisms for enforcement. There is no point in anticipating the advent of an Orwellian state unless one can be certain that structures of social control exist to sustain the power of such a state. Thus the research presented here concentrates its attention on the mechanisms of social control, in hopes that this will shed light on the changing relations between mass publics or clienteles and all kinds of agencies of control.

To these ends, the last three chapters of the book will attempt to build upon the observations in the case studies to answer some more far-reaching questions on the growth of mass surveillance. The first of these questions has to do with the present capabilities, or capacity, of mass surveillance, and the probable directions of its future growth. Just how far does the 'reach' of these five systems, and of others like them, extend? How much can they know about people, and what are the forces limiting such knowledge? What rules can they enforce, and what considerations limit such enforcement? What portions of people's lives are now and will in the future be subjected to the attentions of surveillance systems? Finally, what are the broad directions of change in all these respects, and how rapidly is change occurring?

Secondly, the concluding chapters will draw upon the case studies to assess the social context of mass surveillance. This will require an appraisal of the interests which have fostered the growth of these systems so far, and which are likely to do so in the future. Who benefits from mass surveillance, in other words, and will these same interests continue to sponsor the further perfection of these systems? Similar analysis will apply to the forces countervailing against the development of these systems. In both cases, discussion will touch upon forces both internal and external to surveillance systems – both the demands of running the systems themselves, and influences impinging on the systems from the rest of society. Throughout these discussions, considerations raised earlier in this chapter will figure importantly: the costs of maintaining surveillance, the staging of social control, and the results of failed control.

The final question is the most interpretive of all, and the most important. This is the question of the relationship between the growth of social scale and the development of totalitarian forms of control. I have already expressed my reservations about the tendency of other writers to assume that the present direction of change points unambiguously to a *1984* world. To what extent such tendencies are inherent in present developments is precisely what this research seeks to explore. But having said this much, I must also note that some of the available signs are disquieting. It does appear that the growth of more and more effective forms of mass surveillance and control are the trend of the times, along with the growth of social scale. For the immediate future, neither shows signs of abating. It is at least reasonable to wonder whether the relation between increasing social scale and more effective mass surveillance and control is one of necessity, such that one requires the other. And, if so, whether the form to be taken by this social control is bound to be oppressive, no matter how benign the systems presently exercising it may be. In short, is closer and closer social control the inevitable price of 'progress', a necessary concomitant of the continued development of modern social forms? If this study can shed light on such important questions as these, the efforts involved will be amply repaid.

2

Police Surveillance in Britain

Probably most Britons realize that the work of the police involves some measure of record-keeping on members of the public. People are aware, for example, that conviction for a crime is apt to result in a 'criminal record', and that the police exert vigilance for persons designated as 'wanted'. But beyond these points, there seems to be little general understanding of the forms taken by police surveillance, or of the institutions and practices which have been developed to carry out such surveillance.

In fact, like any other agency facing a task of social control over an anonymous and scattered mass clientele, the police have had to develop a system of considerable complexity and scope. The Criminal Record Office and the Fingerprint Office of London's Metropolitan Police, which together represent the nerve-centre of police record-keeping in Britain, are major operations. The former employs more than four hundred police and civilians, the latter another hundred. The two together occupy more than a floor of the modern headquarters of the Metropolitan Police at New Scotland Yard, working closely with one another in collecting, compiling, storing and disseminating information on crime and criminals. The Criminal Record Office operates twenty-four hours a day every day of the year to provide such information to all police forces in Great Britain and Northern Ireland, through direct telephone and telex links. Together the two offices maintain information on more than two million persons; and since the overwhelming majority of these are adult males, the files must depict a substantial proportion of that part of the populace. Nor do these two offices comprise by any means the whole of police surveillance activities; they merely stand at the top of a much larger pyramid of information exchange. That pyramid broadens to include ten pairs of regional criminal record offices and fingerprint offices, which together probably employ as many staff as the London offices, and the entire structure of local police enforcement, which acts as the 'consumer' of the information provided by the national and regional offices.

This chapter provides a description of the organization and workings of this system, and an analysis of it in terms of the concepts and questions set out in Chapter 1. It begins with a close look at the everyday routines of police surveillance, even where this means granting attention to what first appear as obscure bureaucratic details. Even then, considerable selection of subject-matter will be necessary. This system comprises not just a single repository of records, but a series of them, linked in varying patterns of connection and exchange with one another. The task will be to devote most attention to the aspects and elements of the system most pertinent to the questions at hand. After a review first of the main structures, and then of the basic processes involved in British police surveillance, the discussion turns to analysis. Here I shall try to show the strengths and weaknesses of police surveillance in Britain, and to note the likely directions for further change. This should make it possible, in conclusion, to appraise the *capacity* of the police surveillance system, and, later on in the book, to compare this system to others studied here.

The Development of British Police Surveillance

The advent of central record-keeping on crime and criminals in Britain has been relatively recent. This is not in itself surprising since, as the first chapter stressed, there were few mass surveillance systems anywhere before this century. Perhaps more remarkable, however, is the recency of centralized and uniform police institutions themselves in Britain, which still of course has no national police force.

Today the Home Office in England, and the Scottish Office in Scotland, exercise certain forms of regulation over police affairs, and the Metropolitan Police Force plays an intangible role of first among equals in relation to the other police forces in Britain. But there was no police force as such for London until Robert Peel's legislation of 1829; nor did some rural parts of England and Wales establish police forces until as late as 1856. And the process by which the various police forces came to be susceptible to a measure of central control was slow and uncertain. With the legislation of 1856, the Crown was empowered to appoint Inspectors of Constabulary, who were to visit the various provincial forces and to report on their efficiency. This move itself seems to have been regarded as a flagrant imposition of central power upon the country, even though the only power of the Inspectors was to recommend, rather than to require, changes in police practices. Perhaps more important in establishing a measure of conformity to the wishes of the central government was the policy, also dating from 1856, of making grants to offset the expenses of those police forces regarded as suitably efficient. The maximum amount of this subsidy grew steadily, and along with it the powers of persuasion of the central government. In 1874 it became the policy to contribute one half of the expenses for pay and clothing of those forces, in both the Metropolis and the provinces, considered to meet minimum standards. In 1918 this became nearly one half of total costs. This arrangement has continued up to the present, with Inspectors of Constabulary from the Home Office still carrying out their duties of review over the activities of the various forces and of liaison between them and the central government. Since the institution of the various police forces, conditions have gradually been standardized among them, so that today there is a considerable uniformity of police practice and organization from one force to the next.

The growth of police surveillance must be seen in this light. There was nothing approximating the central listing and dissemination of information on crime and criminals until 1869, when the Habitual Criminals Act required the Metropolitan Police to keep a register of persons convicted for crime in England. This act provided the impetus for founding the organizational ancestor of the present-day Criminal Record Office, which continues to be maintained by the Metropolitan Police on behalf of police throughout Britain. It is significant that, other than this initial legislation, there is very little specific legal authority for the maintenance of police surveillance in the way described in this chapter. This is not to say that these activities are illegal, but simply that there is very little stipulation as to what information must be collected, and how. Decisions on these matters therefore rest very largely in the discretion of the police and of the Home Office.

The first index instituted under the Habitual Criminals Act was the listing of convictions of particular criminals, the immediate predecessor of what the police call their 'Criminal Record Files'. These are now probably the most important, and certainly the most extensive, files kept at New Scotland Yard. In 1901 the police instituted their fingerprint files, and began to rely routinely on fingerprinting as a means of identifying criminals. The Fingerprint Office at New Scotland Yard is now organizationally separate from the Criminal Record Office, but works in the closest cooperation with it. The most recently instituted of the major indices in the Criminal Record Office itself is the wanted and missing persons index. As the name implies, this is a listing of persons wanted for arrest and for questioning by the police, and of those reported missing from home. There are also a number of other indices of somewhat less interest here, and they will receive only limited attention in the course of this chapter.

All the various indices kept in the two offices have grown substantially since their inception. The number of fingerprint files in the main fingerprint collection, for example, has virtually doubled every twenty years since 1910. The press of requests for information from these offices has grown commensurately, and the result has been a chronic case of growing pains for the two offices themselves and for the users of their services. One particular difficulty for the latter was the fact that, given the extent of demand for service from Scotland Yard, responses to inquiries were often very slow. Thus many provincial forces were chagrined to find that even information which they themselves had 'deposited' in the system was unavailable to them when needed.

The result was the institution during the 1950s of an inquiry into the role of central record-keeping in police practice. This led to the creation in 1952 of ten pairs of regional record offices, including one pair each in Glasgow and Belfast, to serve the needs of provincial forces. This regionalization – a step away from the steady centralization which has marked the drift of change in the other surveillance systems studied here – made it possible for the forces of a given area to obtain more rapid and complete service than they previously received from the London office. The precise relationship between the regional and central offices is complex, however, and requires more detailed treatment below.

Up until the 1970s, then, one might see the organization of police record-keeping in Britain in two qualitatively distinct stages – first the period of centralization, and then the period of limited decentralization, in which the regional offices supplemented the activities of the London offices. Looking ahead, one can anticipate a third period, to begin sometime in the near future, one based on centralized computer record-keeping. At the time of this writing, the central authorities are installing their Police National Computer, which they hope will bring about a more powerful and more efficient centralization than had prevailed before. The planners of the computerization programme in fact expect it greatly to reduce, and perhaps to supplant, the limited regionalism which has prevailed since 1952. The likely structure and scope of this new system will also receive discussion at the end of this chapter.

Police Record Systems: Content and Organization

The task of making a portrayal of police surveillance both balanced and accurate is bound to be a little daunting. The problem is not just one of the complexity, but also of the inter-dependence of the subject-matter; description of any one element of the whole threatens to require simultaneous treatment of its relations to the rest. But since it is neither possible nor desirable to discuss everything at once, this chapter relies on a principle also followed in the other case studies, the separation of structure from process. This section is devoted to the organization and content of the various police files, and to the social organization of the various bodies involved. The following section then goes on to trace the movement of information within and among these structures, the decision-making based on use of that information, and its results in terms of social control. The remarks in this section on the organization of police record-keeping should be understood to apply to the central offices at New Scotland Yard. The limited differences between these and the regional offices will be explained at the end of the discussion.

The 'Criminal Records'

In employing the terminology used by the police themselves, one must resign oneself to some confusing anomalies. The first of these is that, although all the record systems are in one sense 'criminal records', the police themselves use this term to refer only to a single set of records. These are the files which list the details of persons' criminal careers – the offences for which they have been convicted, the courts in which the convictions took place, the dates of the convictions, and other pertinent data.

These files make up the most voluminous and discursive, and in many ways the most important, records kept by the police. Their maintenance is probably also the task requiring the greatest expenditure of resources, in terms of staff time and amount of space. Entered in large manila folders, filed numerically according to the sequence of their creation, and shelved very nearly from floor to ceiling in row after row of racks, they give the distinct impression of the stacks of a closed-access library. Continuously plying these stacks are the staff of civil servants of the clerical grades. Like their counterparts in a library, they receive a constant flow of slips requesting specific files for use outside at the 'Main Desk', and an equally predictable flow of used files to be returned to their correct places. Circling around and through the stacks is a system of trolleys, which move the files from the stacks to their destinations and return used files, and requests for new ones, to the staff.

The fact that the files are organized by number rather than by name makes it necessary to keep a nominal index, to link the one with the other. This nominal index serves the same purpose as a library card catalogue. It consists of small slips, filed in loose-leaf binders according to the surname of the criminal.

These list the criminal's full name, any aliases or variants of his name, his date of birth, and his 'CRO Number', representing the key to the location of his file within the 'stacks'. At the beginning of 1971, there were approximately 3,000,000 entries in the nominal index at New Scotland Yard, a number considerably exceeding the total of 2,500,000 criminal records. The discrepancy stems from the fact that many of those whose files appear have also passed through the system under different names, all of which must be linked to the single criminal record file.

What of the contents of the files? They consist mainly of three documents found in nearly every file, plus a few others occurring much more rarely. Examples of the three basic forms appear on pages 52-5. The first of the three is a sheet itself called the 'criminal record' file. The 'criminal record' in this narrowest sense is the straightforward listing of the individual's criminal career, conviction by conviction, from the first to the most recent. It notes the courts, the sentences, the offences for which the convictions took place, and the dates, along with the name and CRO number of the criminal.*

The second of the three main documents making up the criminal record is what is often termed the 'descriptive form', or more simply the 'DF'. This detailed data-sheet is made up for every occasion when charges are brought against a man, and retained in the files every time there is a conviction. It gives a complete description of the individual, the circumstances of the arrest, the arresting officer and police force, as well as his name, his current address and the date. It will also include a photograph in all but a very small minority of cases. The most recent example of this form will thus provide the police with useful

* Entries in this file are not made for absolutely every conviction, but for all convictions for what the police term 'scheduled' offences, that is, those appearing on the police 'schedule' of indictable offences. This is a listing of virtually all the more serious crimes, excluding only the less serious driving and parking offences, and a few other very minor infractions. It is interesting that, although great pains are taken to make every record complete, a long listing of convictions is not the norm. Although many criminals do accumulate the proverbial record 'as long as your arm', the police report that between fifty and sixty per cent of all criminal records list only a single conviction.

information about the criminal, should they want to locate him at some time subsequent to his last listed conviction.

The third main document contained in the criminal record folder, unlike the other two, is not made out according to any set form. This 'antecedent history' sheet is always in discursive prose. In the event of a defendant's conviction, the courts require presentation of a statement from the police concerning his background and circumstances. This is in addition to the listing of his past convictions, which the courts also require. The contents of the antecedent history sheets vary considerably, according to the habits of the police force and the requirements of the courts, but certain inclusions are standard. It will almost always provide some description of the defendant's family life and place of residence. Equally predictable are some mentions of his employment history, financial situation, and customary associates. The original purpose of this sheet was to aid the court in setting an appropriate and reasonable sentence for the crime, but it is also a matter of routine to file copies of it in the criminal record. Like the descriptive form, this sheet can be useful in subsequent attempts by the police to contact the individual.

Although these three forms represent the standard, key entries in the criminal record file, there are others. These are difficult to describe very fully, because their inclusion is at the discretion of the police, who are often chary about discussing them. But if the criminal comes under suspicion for a subsequent crime, the police will very likely turn to his past record for information on his description and whereabouts. Notes stemming from this investigation are apt to be entered in the file. If, for example, he is found to have a new address, this will be noted, or if he has been wrongly confused with another suspect, this will likewise be recorded. Some criminal record offices make it their practice to file stories on or photos of the individual as they encounter them in the press. Many police forces will want to record word of new habits or associates if this comes to their attention. These recording practices, I am convinced, vary greatly from one police force or criminal record office to the next. Thus some offices may use criminal record files extensively as repositories of up-dated information on their 'clients', while

EASTERN REGION: CRIMINAL RECORD

E. Reg. No. 684.8/60

C.R.O. No. 1234/62. FILE NAME . MUGGINS, William Horatio.

Aliases, Nicknames, etc: "Bongo Bill"
Date of Birth: 25.3.1945.
Place of Birth: Midchester.
Height: 5'7½" 5'9½" 5'10"
Complexion: spotty, fresh.
Hair: dk. brown.
Eyes: brown.
Accent: Eastern.
Peculiarities:
Broken nose.
Right ear pierced - sometimes wears small gold earring.
Is a heavy drinker.

Occupation: Labourer. / Van driver's assistant.

Marks (left)
Fingers H.A.T.E.
2" scar on cheek.

Marks (right)
Fingers L.O.V.E.
Forearm – "Death before Dishonour"
"A.C.A.B".

Modus Operandi Index

Sex:	Fraud:	Viol:	Other:	Tatts:
		√65	Description Ht.	
		Aff	3.3.68	

Photo No.

Note: Juvenile Convictions - See Sec. 16 C. and Y.P. Act, 1963

Sentence	Court (Committal Court and M.P. Station Code)	Date	Offence	Release date	Name in which convicted
Probation for 2 years.	Midchester Juv.Court.	22.8.60.	Stealing money. (3 offences considered).		William Horatio MUGGINS.
1 & 2. Fresh Prob. Order made for 2 years with condition of residence for 1 year.	Midchester Juv.Court.	16.1.62.	1. Housebreaking (2 cases). 2. Stealing money (i.e. original offence of 22.8.60).		" "
1 & 2. Borstal Training (conct). 3. 1 days impt.	Midshire Quarter Sessions, (Midchester Mag.Court).	28.9.63.	1 & 2. Burglary (2 cases). 3. Housebreaking (i.e. original offences of 16.1.62).	26.8.65.	" "
Fined £10 in each case.	Midchester Mag.Court.	3.10.65.	Larceny from shop display, (2 cases).		" "
12 months impt.	Midchester Assize. (Midchester Mag.Court).	2.11.66.	Robbery with violence. Sec.23,Larceny Act, 1916. (With accomplice, entered shop, assaulted shopkeeper and stole £18 from till).	1.8.67.	" "

Continuation of CRIMINAL RECORD

C.R.O. No. 1234/62.

FILE NAME: MUGGINS, William Horatio.

Sentence	Court	Date	Offence	Release Date	Name in which convicted
Fined £5.	Aylingham Mag.Court.	1.12.67.	Common Assault. Sec.47 Offences against the Person Act, 1861.		William Horatio MUGGINS.
Fined £20 in each case.	Rushborough Mag.Court.	6.4.68.	Indecent assault (2 cases). (Accosted young woman in public park and committed offence). (Sec.14. Sexual Offences Act, 1956).		"
6 months impt.	Midchester Mag.Court.	28.11.69.	Burglary (shop).		"
	At Midchester Quarter Sessions on 14.12.69 appealed against above conviction and sentence. Appeal against conviction dismissed but appeal against sentence allowed - Varied to 6 months impt. suspended for two years.				"
1. 6 months impt. 2. 1 month impt. (conct). 3. 6 months impt. (consec).	Midchester Mag.Court.	10.1.70.	1. Malicious wounding. Sec.20 Offences against the Person Act, 1861. 2. Theft (shoplifting). Sec. 1 & 7 Theft Act, 1968. 3. Suspended sentence of 14.12.69.		"
1. Fined £20, Disq. for one year. 2. Fined £25. To pay £38 compensation.	Alton-on-Sea Mag.Court.	11.3.71.	1. Take conveyance (m/car). Sec.12 Theft Act, 1968. 2. Obtain pecuniary advantage by deception. Sec.16 Theft Act, 1968. (Stayed at Hotel with female companion and left without paying).		"

1. A plausible but entirely fictitious 'criminal record sheet' as kept in the 'criminal record file'.

C R I M I N A L   R E C O R D   O F F I C E
Form to be typed and sent with Finger Print Form to Finger
Print Branch for Search
(or to C.R.O. if finger prints NOT taken)

1 Force   MIDSHIRE   Div. MIDCHESTER   Station. Tele. No. 123456

2 Arrested/~~Summoned~~ 3.15 ~~a.m.~~/p.m. on 7.11.69 ~~and appearing~~/remanded on bail/
   at Midchester Magistrates Court ~~on~~/until   28.11.69   ~~in custody~~

3 Offence(s) (Briefly)

                    Burglary (Club)

4 Date, time and place   About 2-30 p.m. 7.11.69 Midchester Football Club

5 Method (In detail for M.O. see overleaf. If cheque used give Bank,
                             Branch and Number)
   Broke and entered Midchester Football Supporters Club by smashing glass in rear
   window releasing catch and climbing through. Internal door to bar forced by
   kicking in a door panel. Stole bottles of spirits and cigarettes.

6 Admits/Is suspected of other offences (Give type, locality and approx.
   Does not admit and is not suspected of other offences.   date)

7 Unidentified property

8 Name in which charged/summoned (show maiden name) William Horatio MUGGINS
9 Current Address: 123 Castle Street, Uptown, Midchester.

10 File Name: William Horatio MUGGINS   C.R.O. No. 1234/62

11 Circulated in P.G./C.R.O. Infos.: _   Case No. _ Dated _
12 Date and place of birth Midchester 25.3.45.   Occupation: Van driver's mate.
    Height: 5 ft. 10 in.   Build: _   Comp.: Fresh
    Face: _   Hair: Dark Brown   Hair on Face: None
    Head: _   Forehead: Eyebrows: Bushy
    Eyes: Brown   Nose: Broken.   Mouth: Large
    Lips: Thick   Teeth: Natural, disco- Chin: Cleft
    Ears: _   hands: _   loured Voice: rough, Eastern
13 Marks and unusual features: (if man of colour state race)   accent
       Love and Hate on Fingers. RFA 'Death Before Dishonour' A.C.A.B.
       Noticeable scar on left cheek.
                                      "A" Address for reply to be sent

14 Dress: Rough working clothes or suits with
           coloured shirts and flashy ties.
                                           Superintendent
                                           Midshire Constabulary
15 Frequents: Midchester and neighbouring towns.   Midchester
16 Officer arresting John Campbell   No. L 126   Midshire.

17 Date: 8.11.69

2. The 'descriptive form' as discussed on page 50. A photograph
of the accused normally accompanies this form.

NAME: MUGGINS William Horatio   C.R.O. No. 1234/62
                         123 Castle Street.
                         MIDCHESTER.

William MUGGINS is appearing before the Midchester Magistrates' Court on 28th
November 1969 to answer a charge of burglary.

MUGGINS was born at Midchester on 25.3.45 and is therefore 24 years of age.
He is a single man living with his parents in a corporation owned house at the
above address. He is the eldest of six children, two of whom have married and
are living away form home. The home circumstances are fair. His father has
not been in regular work for some years. His mother is employed as a part-time
cleaner.

He received an elementary and secondary education at schools in Midchester.

Since leaving school he has had several jobs of an unskilled labouring type
interspersed with periods of unemployment and imprisonment. None of the
employments have lasted very long and the defendant states that he left most
of them of his own accord. At the time of his arrest for the present offence
he was employed as a van drivers' mate by Midshire Carriers Ltd. and is still
so employed. (Verified)

His average weekly pay is £18. per week out of which he allows his mother £8.
for his keep. He pays £2.75p. per week on outstanding Hire Purchase Agreements.
He is the Registered Owner of Austin motor van ABC 1234 and holds a full driving
licence issued by Midshire County Council.

He is personally known to:-   David EVANS   Detective Sergeant
                                       John CAMPBELL   Detective Constable
                                       of the Midshire Constabulary.

3. A typical but fictitious 'antecedent history' sheet as prepared for
the courts and filed in the 'criminal record file'.

others may only add information to these files on being notified of a new conviction.

The Fingerprint Indices

Like other systems of mass surveillance, police record-keeping works to associate people with their past behaviour. More than many of its counterparts, however, this system often faces especially energetic efforts from its clientele to forestall this association. The work of the police in this respect would be all but impossible except that every person's fingerprints are unchanging and unique, and that fingerprints are subject to classification and indexing, so that single prints can be matched or placed systematically within even large collections. Police identification procedures are predicated on these facts, with the result that criminal record offices, both in London and in the provinces, work in the closest cooperation within their associated fingerprint offices. The pattern of this partnership is highly predictable. The Criminal Record Office compiles details of crimes and criminal records, while the fingerprint staff specialize in linking both crimes and criminal records to specific persons. Thus the establishment of positive identification is virtually the whole of the task of the Fingerprint Office. Like the Criminal Record Office itself, this office organizes its activities around a series of different files:

The Nominal Index. Like the Criminal Record Office, the Fingerprint Office of the Metropolitan Police relies upon a small file to link people's names to the file locations of their fingerprints. Here, too, the nominal index consists of small slips filed according to surname. Each slip also lists any variants or aliases of the person's name, the Criminal Record Office number, and the classification number corresponding to the set of ten fingerprints.

The 'Mains' Collection. This is the core of the fingerprint collection, corresponding roughly to the criminal record files in the Criminal Record Office. For the great majority of criminal record files there should be an entry in this collection, consisting of a full set of ten fingerprints taken by the police.* On 1

---

* The exception lies in certain limited categories of crimes and criminals for which no fingerprints are taken during the course of

January 1971, there were approximately 2,154,000 of these sets on file. Each set is arrayed on a large, loose-leaf sheet, much like those used in photo albums, filed according to the classification in which the set belongs, and bound with other prints belonging to the same classification. Besides the full set of prints, each sheet also contains the individual's name and CRO number.

The 'Singles' File. There are many occasions when the Fingerprint Office must check an incoming print to determine whether it matches any print in their collections, without knowing whose print it is or which finger it comes from. For these and other purposes, it is necessary to maintain a file of fingerprints contained in the 'Mains' collection, with each individual print filed separately according to its fingerprint classification. This index does not comprise all prints contained in the 'Mains' collection, however, but only those of persons convicted of breaking offences, motor vehicle theft, and crimes of violence. The classification system used by the police merely allows the assignment of each fingerprint to a category, without locating it within that category. Thus, searching for fingerprints from well-represented categories in this index takes much longer than for prints from rare groupings.

The 'Scenes of Crime' Index. The fourth main index, unlike the preceding two, consists of prints taken from the scenes of unsolved crimes, rather than from criminals as they are processed by the police. Scenes of crimes investigators become highly skilled at locating and salvaging such prints. Although they are never so clear as those taken by the police under optimal circumstances, many are good enough to provide the basis for positive identification. The 'Scenes of Crime' file, composed of these fingerprints, obviously lacks any reference to person's names. It consists of the fingerprints, filed according to their classification number, each with a reference to the unsolved crime with which it is associated. There were approximately 54,000 such prints on file at New Scotland Yard at the beginning of 1971.

---

police processing. The most numerous of these are crimes committed by juveniles, where the police generally do not take fingerprints, and certain crimes deemed to be of lesser seriousness, like minor traffic violations.

The Wanted and Missing Persons Index

This index, maintained by the Criminal Record Office, is considerably less complex in its organization and contents than the criminal records. Basically, it is a comprehensive, central listing of persons wanted for arrest, detention or questioning by the police and other agencies throughout Britain. It is of special interest for this study in that it enables the police to extend the net of their surveillance to apprehend persons well outside the locales in which they are wanted. It consists of a large number of small file cards – numbering approximately 65,000 at the beginning of 1971 – filed alphabetically by surname of wanted person, listing for each a brief description, date of birth, the agency by which the person is wanted, and the circumstances under which they are sought. Located next to the array of twenty telephones used for this purpose, the index is constantly under interrogation, as police from both London and the provinces check the status of persons they encounter in the course of their work. It is the never-ending flow of inquiries to this index which requires around-the-clock staffing of the Metropolitan Criminal Record Office.

Some Other Indices

Although the preceding discussion has dealt briefly with all the indices kept in the Fingerprint Office, several varieties of records kept in the Criminal Record Office remain to be discussed. Perhaps the most noteworthy is the listing of persons disqualified from driving by the courts; the main use of this file, as one might expect, is for police checks of persons detained while driving. Another is the Stolen Property Index, most notably the part of it dealing with stolen automobiles. This index lists identifiable stolen property for limited periods of time – usually twelve months – after it is reported stolen. The aim is the identification of such property and its use as evidence against those responsible for stealing or handling it. There are also two 'Modus Operandi' indices, one for known criminals and another for unsolved crimes. These are organized according to the professional habits and techniques of the criminal, as a means of associating crimes with their perpetrators. Finally, there is the 'Distinguishing Marks File', organized according to distinctive qualities of speech and appearance of known criminals. Reports of witnesses and victims of crimes often lead to identification of criminals through this index. None of these indices is as important for present purposes as are those discussed in the preceding sections, and limitations of space prevent fuller treatment of them here.

The Regional Offices

Since 1952, the activities of New Scotland Yard have been supplemented by a series of regional clearing houses for police surveillance, each including both a criminal record office and a fingerprint office. The purpose of these ten pairs of regional offices is to help serve the surveillance needs of the police forces which comprise the region, and these forces jointly bear the offices' expenses. The regional offices are located in or near the police headquarters of the largest force within the district, and generally work in particularly close conjunction with that force, often sharing staff and office space with it. In many respects, they serve as links between the surveillance activities of the various local forces and the Metropolitan CRO and Fingerprint Office. As such, they observe a fairly uniform set of procedures in handling information on crimes and criminals, procedures agreed upon by the Association of Chief Police Officers in conjunction with the Home Office.

It would be a serious oversimplification to state that the regional offices function as miniature versions of their London counterpart. Nevertheless, the statement is true as far as it goes. Each of the CRO and fingerprint files described above for the central office has its direct counterpart in the regional offices. Indeed, entries in the regional criminal record files, the fingerprint files, and the wanted and missing persons indices are largely duplicates of the equivalent material filed in New Scotland Yard. It is true that the regional offices frequently experiment with different techniques of *organization* of filed material – especially with respect to fingerprint files, whose effectiveness often depends more on organization than on content. But every *variety* of information filed at New Scotland Yard has its counterpart in the regional offices, and the similarity even extends to the physical appearance of the installations. The bank of telephones, the telex machine, the rows of filed cards in the nominal and wanted and missing indices, and the library-like archives of the criminal records file are equally distinctive of the regional offices and of New Scotland Yard.

The key difference between the national and regional offices, however, is that the latter mainly restrict their activities and attentions to crime and criminals within their respective districts, while the former attempt to cover all of Britain. The criminal records, the wanted and missing index, the fingerprint files and all the rest list primarily persons who reside within or who have committed crimes within the district covered by the regional offices. Files pertaining to crimes rather than criminals, such as the scenes of crimes index in the fingerprint offices, restrict themselves to materials from crimes committed within the region. There are, however, exceptions. Under some circumstances, both crimes and criminals are filed from well outside the region; the same applies to fingerprints.

All of this raises a number of questions. For one thing, what circumstances govern the occasional breaches of the regional principle? Perhaps more importantly, given the desire of criminals to escape the net of police surveillance, what prevents them from evading the effects of their records simply by moving their operations outside the region which maintains their records? And how, if New Scotland Yard maintains 'master' listings for the whole of the country, do the regional offices serve any useful function at all? These questions are highly pertinent to any conclusions about the capacity of police surveillance. To answer them, however, the discussion must turn to the movement and use of information within the system, as distinct from its structures.

Information Flow and Decision-Making

The effectiveness of any surveillance system does not depend in the first instance on the amount of information held in its files. More important is its ability to generate relevant information to the appropriate persons at the appropriate time to enable them to make pertinent decisions concerning the application of social control. This section concerns itself with the marshalling of available information for purposes of police surveillance. It deals first with the means and mechanisms of information exchange among the police. Next, it takes up the actual patterns of information flow among and within the various indices and repositories described in the previous section. Finally, it deals with the use of information for social control, particularly with respect to the day-to-day decision-making practices of the police.

Methods and Routines of Information Exchange

It is impossible to understand the workings of police record-keeping without first considering the several broad categories of inquiries which make up the bulk of its business. Perhaps the most important of these is the 'stop check', in which the policeman on his beat checks the names of persons he encounters against listings in the regional or national criminal record office. Such inquiries are part of the basic routine of policing, learned as such by all policemen in the course of their training. Thus, whenever a policeman on patrol encounters someone who, by appearance, manner, whereabouts or whatever, appears suspect, he is apt to detain him long enough to check his status with the nearest criminal record office. In most parts of Britain, the constable has no legal power to hold any person against his wishes without arrest, although it is safe to assume that the police do not emphasize these facts to those whom they accost. In any case, most Britons submit to these procedures without much fuss, to such an extent that anyone who refuses such an inquiry is apt by so doing to subject himself to still further attention.

At one time, it was necessary for the policeman making the inquiry to locate a telephone box and to place his inquiry from there to the nearest criminal record office. Now, however, most 'stop checks' are entered initially from the small personal radios which virtually all patrolling policemen carry, or from police auto radios. Such inquiries go to the nearest police radio receiver, and from there are relayed to the nearest criminal record office; the response is then relayed back to the inquiring policeman. The result, for the criminal record offices, is a constant flow of telephone inquiries, and a considerable investment of resources in processing such inquiries. The Metropolitan Criminal Record Office maintains a battery of twenty telephones for such inquiries, ten apiece for requests from London and from the provinces. The typical regional office has four or five telephone lines for such requests, and both the Metropolitan and some regional offices are equipped to answer inquiries directly by radio. One of the most predictable features of any criminal record office is the steady ringing of telephones and the movement of staff plying back and forth between the phones and the files.

In some cases the teleprinter or telex, found in every criminal record office, serves as substitute for the telephone. Every police force, and some individual police stations, possess a teleprinter which, although used much less frequently than the telephone, figures importantly when the message is urgent or when a written record of the exchange is required. Through the use of the teleprinter every police force in the country can be notified within as little as ten minutes of urgent matters like the flight of a dangerous criminal.

For other purposes, much information exchange takes place in writing. This is especially true with respect to communications of the detail of persons' criminal records, in connection with court appearances. There most communication takes place via the standard series of 'criminal record' forms discussed above. As the following discussion will show, forms are made out by the local police and passed back and forth at prescribed stages during the prosecution of accused persons. These forms, whose processing accounts for one of the major expenditures of resources by criminal record offices, do not pass through the mails, but travel daily back and forth between the local police and the criminal record office by police courier.

A third trunk line of communication in police surveillance is what are termed 'police informations'. These are the small bulletins circulated internally among the police. The largest and most widely circulated of these is the *Police Gazette*, published six times per week by New Scotland Yard, and distributed in quantity to every police force. It contains information on crimes and criminals throughout Britain, especially in those cases where action by police outside the area where the crime occurred is deemed necessary. Thus there are listings of stolen property, wanted and missing persons, and serious unsolved crimes, as well as routine cancellations of previous notices where crimes have been solved, property recovered, wanted or missing persons located, and so on.

Each regional criminal record office likewise publishes its own police 'information', much like the national publication but proportionately smaller. These appear five or six times per week, and are circulated in quantity to the police forces within the region, as well as to all other criminal record offices. By the same token, every local force circulates a still more modest police information, listing crimes and criminals of local interest for the benefit of its own members and of neighbouring forces. Their frequency of publication varies according to the force, but is usually once or twice per week.

These police informations – national, regional and local – are one of the main paths of information flow to the wanted and missing persons indices and the stolen property indices. A basic routine in all criminal record offices is the perusal of such sheets and the clipping of relevant bits of information for the files. Names of wanted or missing persons, or notices of stolen or recovered property, for example, are added to or deleted from the relevant index. For the regional criminal record offices, listings in the national *Police Gazette* are authoritative, in that they are listed regionally without question. More discretionary, however, are the listings in the regional and local police informations, which may or may not be added to the regional or national files, according to the nature of the crime or criminal.

The Criminal Records and Fingerprint Files

The next few pages trace the flow of information to and from the criminal record files of the national and regional offices, and, in so doing, also describe the fuctioning of most of the fingerprint files. Although the combination may at first seem strange, these several bodies of information work so closely with one another that it is virtually impossible to discuss one without the other.

Let me begin at the beginning, which in this case is the point at which the police bring charges against an individual for one of what they term 'Fingerprint Schedule Offences'. In the routine processing of such a person, one of the major tasks is to determine whether he is wanted elsewhere by the police, and whether he has a criminal record. The first is relatively easy to accomplish, by checking his name against the wanted and missing index. This will be done either against the regional index, if the crime of which he is suspected is minor and if he is a resident of the region, or otherwise against the national index. The second involves a more complicated routine.

Once arrested, accused persons must be brought before a magistrate within twenty-four hours. If the charge is especially serious or the accused considered likely to flee, the court must consider the matter of whether to grant bail, and this often requires a check into the criminal history of the accused. If the police are doubtful that bail should be granted, they will request a check of the wanted and missing persons index and of the criminal records. Such a check should reveal for certain whether the individual has a history of serious crime and whether he is wanted for arrest or questioning anywhere in Britain. These two factors have much to do with the likelihood of the court's granting bail.

The information normally required by the local police at this point is the most recent three convictions on the criminal record of the accused, and his or her status on the wanted and missing persons index. New Scotland Yard cannot make a conclusive check of its criminal records without fingerprints, and the demands for inquiries to the wanted and missing index are such that every additional telephone or telex inquiry represents an irksome burden. On the other hand, the regional record office is in a position to answer both requests relatively quickly, usually within the day of receipt; moreover, the likelihood of finding significantly fuller information in the London offices is usually considered slight. Thus in the majority of cases, where there is no special reason for suspicion, this first check goes only to the regional offices. The results, whether from the regional or national centre, are usually relayed back to the local police by telephone or, more rarely, by telex.

Once this hurdle is surmounted, the police must get to work with the more ambitious project of assembling the full version of the defendant's criminal record. The first step is for the local police – who have made the arrest, and who will carry out the prosecution – to fill out the descriptive form illustrated above, giving the defendant's physical description and the circumstances of his arrest. This they forward to New Scotland Yard, along with a full set of the individual's fingerprints, also obtained in the course of their routine processing of the suspect.

The initial destination of the file at New Scotland Yard is the Fingerprint Office. There the first step is to check the name given by the accused against the nominal index. In approximately fifty-two per cent of all cases, the name matches an entry in this index, and the entry corresponds to prints in the Mains collection matching those of the accused. When this occurs, the fingerprint staff note the defendant's CRO number on his records, and pass them on to the staff of the Criminal Record Office.

If the check of the nominal index reveals no fingerprints filed under the name given by the accused, the police can scarcely afford to let the matter rest. For there is every possibility that, through either accident or design, the defendant has given a different version of his name from the one he gave at the time of his previous conviction. For this reason, every incoming set of prints not identified immediately through the nominal index is also checked against the Mains collection as a whole. This is not so difficult as it may sound, for the organization of this index makes it possible to check an incoming set against it relatively quickly. The exact time required depends on the commonness of the fingerprint classification of the relevant set, but the mean time at the Metropolitan Fingerprint Office is reported to be thirty-five minutes.

There is one other routine search, as well, to which all incoming sets of prints are subjected. This is the comparison of the defendant's prints to the entries in the scenes of crimes file. Every set of incoming prints is matched against this file in hopes that this will lead to the identification of persons responsible for these unsolved crimes. Such expectations are by no means

fanciful; during 1970, this practice resulted in 4,690 identifications by the Metropolitan Police alone.

Once processing by the Fingerprint Office is complete, the
documents move on to the Criminal Record Office. There the
staff routinely check the names of all accused persons against
the wanted and missing persons index, with the frequent result
that the accused is found to be wanted for other crimes, or for
questioning, elsewhere. Then, if the Fingerprint Office has
reported 'No Trace' on the accused, his papers go directly
back to the local police with notation to that effect. Otherwise,
where the search of the fingerprint files shows that a criminal
record for the defendant does exist, that office will pass the
documents on to the Criminal Record Office with a citation of
his CRO number. Using this key number, the staff will obtain
his criminal record and copy it out in full detail on the back of
the Descriptive Form. This will then go back to the police
prosecuting the charge.

The police then hold the criminal record in readiness
throughout the trial, along with the antecedent history sheet,
which they will have prepared themselves, perhaps building on
previous versions of the sheet held in the criminal record file.
Under the law, the police are not to disclose even the existence
of a previous criminal record during the course of the trial,
although they may reveal information of the sort contained in
the antecedent history sheet. If the trial results in conviction,
however, the police are asked to read out the detail of any
previous convictions, as well as to present the 'antecedents'
material verbatim. This information will then figure in the
court's deliberation over sentencing.

In the event of conviction, the scene is already set to enter the
appropriate records in the individual's criminal record, or to
create such a record if this is the first offence. The record of
conviction, including the charge, the court, the date and the
sentence, will be added to the descriptive form, and that form,
along with the copy of the antecedents sheet, will go via the
regional office to New Scotland Yard. Travelling the same route
will be the individual's photos and fingerprints. The new data
will be copied and entered in the appropriate regional files, as
well as in the national repositories. The system does not work

perfectly in this respect, and some convictions go unrecorded. But David Steer reports in his paper 'Recorded Convictions' that ninety-six per cent of 624 convictions in his sample did make their way to the Metropolitan Criminal Record Office, and the remaining four per cent were largely for relatively minor offences.*

In the event of acquittal, the police generally destroy the data which they have developed in the course of their preparations. Some criminal record office spokesmen have gone to great lengths, in their conversations with me, to insist that no form of 'black mark' remains in their records as the result of acquittal. Other criminal record offices do retain certain information generated in prosecutions leading to acquittals, and practices vary considerably among the various offices. Some CROs, for example, retain photographs of acquitted persons, if such persons already possess criminal records whose photos are out of date. Elsewhere, information may be retained after acquittal if the charges have involved matters considered by the police especially serious or especially likely to be repeated – sexual offences being the prime example. And, of course, many criminal record offices do not hesitate to update their records whenever they can, so that current address and other information generated in the course of unsuccessful prosecutions will find its way into the criminal record file.

The criminal record file, then, is a living creature, constantly undergoing additions, inquiries and deletions. Table 1 summarizes the information flow into and out of the Metropolitan criminal records during 1970:

Table 1. *Metropolitan Criminal Record Files, at 1 January 1971*

Number of criminal records in file	2,500,000
New files added during 1970	197,000
Number of convictions recorded during 1970	500,000
Number of files deleted from criminal records in 1970	46,000

Source: The Metropolitan Police. All figures are approximate.

I have largely neglected, thus far, the division of labour

* David Steer, 'Recorded Convictions', University of Oxford Penal Research Unit, mimeo, 1971, pp. 8a–8c.

between the regional offices and New Scotland Yard. This is an important point, because it holds implications for the capacity of police surveillance, especially with respect to the possibility of criminals' evading accountability for their past misdeeds.

As stated above, the key difference between national and regional files has to do with the coverage of criminal clientele. Although the documents kept in the two repositories are very similar, and indeed often identical, the regional files contain information mainly on crime and criminals from within the region. This segregation comes about cumulatively, as documents on persons being tried within the regions, but no others, pass through the regional record offices *en route* to London. This pattern obviously tends to develop a backlog of data on persons convicted within the region, to the exclusion of others.

Equally obvious, however, is the fact that not all criminals are scrupulous enough to commit crimes entirely within any single police region. Regional offices do attempt to compensate for this by copying criminals' full lists of convictions into the regional files, as records pass through the regional centres. Nevertheless, it is evident that offences from outside the region will not enter the regional file through this procedure until the criminal is arrested again within the region. Then, too, all regional criminal record offices are supposed, as a matter of routine, to notify other offices when a criminal from the second region is convicted in the first. This should make it possible for both sets of files to be kept up to date. Officials from regional offices report, however, that this practice is not strictly adhered to, especially given the difficulty of determining a criminal's place of residence. In the light of all this, it is certain that the regional criminal record files sometimes fail to represent, or to represent fully, the criminal histories of persons apprehended within the region, although it is impossible to say just to what extent this occurs.

Why, then, maintain the regional centres at all? What can their inherently fragmentary records offer, against the comprehensiveness of those maintained centrally? The answer lies in the strains upon the national centre resulting from their enormous accumulation of information and ever-increasing demand for service. The full processing by London of a set of fingerprints and a descriptive form submitted as described above now requires at least a week, and often more, from the dispatch of the materials from the regional record office to their receipt there. In many cases, persons are arrested, brought before a magistrate, tried, convicted, and sentenced in less time than this, and in such cases it is obviously useless to rely on the London offices for the necessary data.

There are also other difficulties involved in relying on New Scotland Yard. Even requests by telephone or teleprinter are subject to long delays, when all lines to the London headquarters are engaged. As I have said, these delays make it difficult even to obtain the basic data necessary for the defendant's first court appearance. And one regional official even reports obtaining 'No Trace' reports on persons known with certainty to have criminal records, suggesting that the frustrated staff of the London offices have simply refused to check the files as requested. By contrast, most regional offices can, when necessary, supply the full written report necessary for sentencing within one working day. Under these circumstances, it is not difficult to understand why recourse to the regional office is usually preferable in urgent cases, and in those cases where the crimes involved are less serious.

Nor is this to suggest that the national pool of information is in every sense more complete than that maintained by the regional offices. The preceding discussion has shown how regional record offices and fingerprint offices continually select only the more urgent listings in their various indices for inclusion at the national level. This means that the regional offices maintain fuller coverage of regional crimes and criminals, overall, than does the national centre. This represents another reason why local police, the actual users of the information, often prefer to rely on their nearest regional office, instead of on London.

Nevertheless this reliance on the regional source does entail risks. Theoretically, the defendant may be wanted for arrest elsewhere, and thus liable to disappear if freed. Or, he may have a record of fairly serious crimes to his credit in other regions, unknown where he is arrested. Although the police cannot obviate these risks altogether, they do take steps to minimize them. Concretely, they do not bypass the national centre in those cases where they suspect the defendant of having a record outside the region, or where the crime involved is relatively serious. Those accused of murder, arson, rape or armed robbery, for example, will always receive the full check, as will those persons known to reside outside the region, or believed to circulate a good deal in the course of their criminal activities. It is difficult to say how much evasion results from the reliance on regional files, which obviously depends very largely on informal judgements on the part of the police of the persons who pass through their hands. About the most one can say is that available research supports the police contention that most crime is local, and that the police themselves are satisfied that they very rarely lose from these techniques. What is certain is that the limitations of the present police surveillance system give little choice but to adopt some such expedient.

So much for the 'lives' of criminal records. What of their 'death', the point at which they are destroyed? This question is of considerable interest to those who view police record-keeping as a threat to liberty, and who fear the recording of crimes as an indelible mark against the offender. The police do have policies governing the 'weeding' of files, however; the trouble is that it is difficult to be certain how rigorously these are carried out. In the Metropolitan Criminal Record Office, for example, there are a series of rules for culling files after they have ceased to show any activity for a given period. The criminal records of juveniles, for example, are reportedly culled after ten years, if there is only a single offence in the record. For adults, the stated practice is to retain files for twenty years on only one conviction, or until age seventy if the criminal record contains more than one entry. After that age, files are discarded if they show no convictions for ten years. An exception, according to the official rule, is made for sexual offences, which remain in the files until the offender reaches age seventy. Offenders' fingerprints are reported to be destroyed simultaneously with their criminal records.

During 1970, the Metropolitan Criminal Record Office deleted approximately 46,000 criminal record files and, with them, the fingerprints of the persons to whom they refer – evidence that weeding processes do certainly go on, at least in that setting. It is very difficult to know, however, the extent to which the CRO staff can weed out all the files which should be excluded, by the lights of official policy. For it is very hard to determine the whereabouts within the criminal record repository of files eligible for exclusion, except, to some extent, by checking the oldest records in the CRO library. The same holds true for the regional offices. Their weeding procedures in any case have had little test, since the offices themselves have existed only since 1956. In general, it is difficult to see how either the national or regional offices can spare the manpower necessary to search systematically for files due for exclusion. Probably the staffs exclude superannuated files as they encounter them, but little more. The proportion of files eligible for exclusion which are actually weeded thus remains difficult to determine.

The Wanted and Missing Persons Index

As noted above, this index is a comprehensive listing of persons whom the police want to contact or apprehend. Its main use is in connection with the 'stop checks' which make up such an important part of the policeman's daily routine. It would be wrong to think, however, that the only names in this file are of persons wanted by the police for arrest and of missing persons, though these are important categories. Also included, in both national and regional listings, are persons wanted for questioning by the police; absconders from borstals, approved schools, and mental institutions; prison escapees; deserters from the armed forces;* and persons wanted by the courts for non-payment of fines. Missing persons, as distinct from those wanted for arrest or for return to some institution, cannot under the law be detained by the police, but only informed of the concern about their whereabouts which led to their being reported missing. Likewise, of course, persons wanted simply for questioning are not subject to arrest, although it is safe to say that, if they should refuse to be questioned, they are apt to become the subject of further attention from the police.

* As this chapter was nearing completion a change in policy occurred concerning the listing of deserters from the armed forces. In the future this index will not include such listings, but this information will be available to inquiring policemen directly from the armed forces.

The slips comprising the wanted and missing index list only the briefest, most circumscribed information, in keeping with the need to rely on them for the quickest possible exchange of data. The index is arranged by surname of the wanted person, and additional slips are usually filed for each known alias. Each entry contains, in addition to names and alias, space for the person's date of birth, his national or regional record office number, a brief description, the police force or other agency by which he is wanted, and the reasons for his being listed. Significantly, the responsibility for decision-making based on this file lies with the officer confronting the suspect, not with the criminal record office maintaining the listing. It is the policeman himself who, on the basis of the name, the date of birth, the description, and the circumstances of his encounter with the suspect, must decide whether or not to arrest or detain him.

It would be misleading to leave the reader with the impression that the 'stop check' inquiry necessarily entails only a check of the wanted and missing file. True, this is probably the most important check which any policeman will want made, and may be the only one if he or the office staff are under pressure of time. But in most cases the policeman will also want to know whether his suspect is 'known to' the police, and this will require recourse to the nominal index and possibly the criminal records, as well. For the police often place the greatest importance on linking a suspect with his past record, as a means of determining how to deal with him in discretionary situations. Thus several record offices, although not the Metropolitan, maintain their nominal index in the same file with the wanted and missing file. The two kinds of entries are easily distinguishable, of course, by their different format and content. But joint filing makes it possible to tell in a single operation both whether the suspect is wanted and whether there is a criminal record in his name.

Police feel that they need information on suspects' criminal records in order to determine how much and what kind of surveillance to apply to them. Thus, if a stop check on a suspect reveals that, though not wanted, the person does possess a record, the policeman will want to know the details of that record. If it consists of a recent series of burglaries, for example, the suspect will almost certainly find himself under very close surveillance as long as he remains within the area, both from the original policeman who interviews him and from others. A record of disorderly conduct convictions far back in the past, on the other hand, will probably not spur the police to much further action. In all of these cases, the discretion of the police is enormous, so much so that it is impossible to predict positively what results this or that criminal record will have for the treatment of a suspect. Perhaps the only certainty is the general principle that past record will affect future surveillance, even in the absence of any entry in the wanted and missing index. Indeed, in some cases, it may even make the difference between making an arrest and letting someone go, as when a person with a past record of sexual offences against children is found illegally loitering near a playground. The police will generally want to arrest a person with such a record if they can, provided that he is indeed breaking a law, whereas they would be very unlikely to make an arrest under these circumstances in the absence of such a record.

The police confront the same problems of overloaded files, and consequent need for division of labour between regional and national offices, in the wanted and missing index as elsewhere. The listing for the Metropolitan Criminal Record Office, which of course serves the needs both of London and of the provincial forces, comprised some 65,000 listings at the beginning of 1971 – an unwieldy figure, from the standpoint of manual operation.* And yet, in this index as much as the criminal records files, there is an obvious premium on comprehensiveness.

The solution adopted by the police in this connection reflects the same sort of thinking as those adopted with respect to the provision of information to the courts. The extent of listing of wanted and missing persons turns on a joint appraisal of the seriousness of the circumstances in which the person is

* Besides acting as the central repository for all of Britain the Metropolitan Criminal Record Office and Fingerprint Office act as regional offices in relation to the police forces of Greater London and the environs.

wanted and the likelihood of his circulating outside the region. Thus persons wanted for such serious crimes as murder, rape, armed robbery or the like will certainly be listed with every criminal record office in Britain. Someone wanted for disorderly conduct, on the other hand, will ordinarily be listed only in the region in which the offence occurred. Likewise, if the person is believed apt to travel, his listing will be circulated. If he is known to reside in another region, then his name may be listed only there and in the region where the crime took place. Similarly, prison escapees are listed nationally, whereas juvenile absconders from approved schools receive only regional circulation. By the same token, missing persons receive only regional listings, unless there is reason to believe that they are apt to come to some harm or to travel to a specific area outside the region. Missing persons thought to be prone to suicide or amnesia, for example, receive national listings, but such wide listing of missing persons is in fact quite rare.

Policemen must observe the obverse of all these principles in making inquiries about the status of persons whom they accost in the course of their work. The great majority of 'stop check' inquiries go simply to the nearest regional criminal record office. And indeed the strains on the capabilities of New Scotland Yard make it difficult at many times to get an inquiry processed there in any short space of time. But there are cases in which a suspect seems almost certain, to the policeman, to be wanted somewhere, or to be from outside the region. For these cases of 'foreign' suspects, or for suspects whose actions or circumstances give ground for particular suspicion as to their status, the police will attempt to check their names against the national listing.

Again, decisions about where a wanted or missing person will be listed are highly discretionary. The head of each criminal record office must decide in his own right whether any one person should receive listing outside his area. If he decides affirmatively, he need only request New Scotland Yard for a national listing, and other offices, including the Metropolitan, add the entry automatically. Publication of the listing carries with it the responsibility to publish a de-listing when the person is apprehended or for some other reason no longer wanted. But the fact that the instructions of the regional office receive automatic cooperation from the other offices should not obscure the fact that the latter resent requests for listings which they consider unjustified by the circumstances. Such listings result in extra work for those who carry them, and the entire system, as the reader has no doubt gathered, operates on a principle of economy of effort.

What about the 'death' of entries in this file? Much more so than the criminal records, the wanted and missing persons index is a dynamic repository of information where, at least theoretically, any given file remains only for a short time. Thus, files should either result in police contact with the person in question, and thus be de-listed this way, or be culled automatically after a given period of time. For the most part, these principles work in practice. As a general rule, listings are removed after three to five years with no arrest, depending on the criminal record office involved. There is an option for renewing the listing at the insistence of the police force originally requesting it, but generally this is not exercised. Some police officials express an attitude that, if a suspect has remained outside police attention for this length of time, he perhaps should be forgiven his misdeeds in any case.

The Scenes of Crimes Fingerprint Collection

Like all the other indices discussed here, the Metropolitan scenes of crimes collection has its exact counterpart in every regional office. There are two forms of information flow involved in its workings. First, there is the routine checking of every incoming set of prints against this index, in hopes of associating persons arrested with other previous crimes which remain unsolved. This can happen, of course, even where the accused is ultimately acquitted of the first set of charges. At the same time, every new mark bound for the scenes of crimes collection is checked against the full singles collection before it is filed, in hopes that it will match the print of someone already known to the Fingerprint Office. These practices result in their share of identifications, as the following table shows:

Table 2. *Metropolitan Scenes of Crimes Fingerprint Collection*

Total entries, January 1971	54,000
New entries during 1970	17,150
Identification during 1970	4,690

Source: The Metropolitan Police. All figures are approximate.

In addition to the 4,690 identifications reported from the national scenes of crimes file, one imagines that there must have been several times as many from its regional counterparts. When the police succeed in making an identification, they bluntly confront the suspect with the accusation that he was responsible for the given crime – sometimes adding '. . . and we know you were responsible for others, too'. The flabbergasted defendant, with no idea of how the identification was made, usually admits the crimes in question, and perhaps others. The police prefer these 'voluntary' admissions. For one thing, they save the time and work which would be necessary to prove the identification in court. For another, fingerprint officers almost universally prefer to avoid the publicity stemming from court appearances, which, they feel, helps to increase the awareness of their techniques within the criminal community.

As with all other files, there is constant pressure to minimize the costs of operating the scenes of crimes index, and to obtain maximum results from limited investments of time and money. Thus the same kinds of constraints apply here as with the other files, concerning the extensiveness of listings and the length of time a given item is kept in file. In general, fingerprints remain in this collection no more than two years, and more often just a single year, the exact duration depending on the policy of the fingerprint office involved. The debilitating effects of expansion of the total collection are especially dramatic here, because such expansion automatically lengthens the time required to search any incoming print against the collection. The same consideration affects the filing of scenes of crimes marks outside the regions in which they occur; such 'foreign' listings are guided by the same sorts of rules as the listing of wanted and missing persons. Fingerprints from the scenes of more serious crimes, and those from crimes which, like the theft of art objects, are associated with mobile criminals, receive national listings. Elsewhere, the print remains in the regional file only.

Other Forms of Police Surveillance

This concludes discussion of information flow within the various police record systems studied here. It would be wrong, however, to leave the reader with the impression that these are the only kinds of police surveillance. For the police also maintain a number of other forms of surveillance of a much smaller scale. Indeed, local police forces, and even subdivisions of the local force, regularly generate, record and use information on local criminals and suspects strictly on their own.

Every police force has its own Criminal Investigation Department, whose responsibilities include both the investigation of specific crimes and the maintenance of broader surveillance in the sense used in this book. These duties regularly lead to the development of discursive written notes on the activities of persons thought liable to commit crimes, whether or not they possess criminal records. In some cases, CID materials include photographs of persons of interest. It is also common for CID staff to consult local vehicle licensing files in order to identify drivers of vehicles involved in suspect activities. Another CID function is to maintain surveillance over a particular place, like a public house, where suspect persons congregate. In all of these matters, the CID are apt to rely closely on their nearest criminal record office, and some regional record offices share quarters with the Criminal Investigation Department of the local police.

Nevertheless, interesting as these practices may be from other standpoints, they do not in themselves represent systems of *mass* surveillance and social control. Although the CID staff may develop lengthy and detailed written records of persons whom they subject to surveillance, these records do not generally circulate in such a way as to lead to social control by agencies in other places. They are relevant to the surveillance needs of the local force, but no more. Nor can these practices ever serve to cover more than a relative handful of persons at any one time.

These limitations stem, for one thing, from the fact that CID record-keeping sacrifices the *extensiveness* of a mass surveillance system in favour of *intensity* of surveillance over small numbers of persons. It may be true, as I have said, that something like total surveillance can prevail in settings like a maximum security prison or the intensive care ward of a hospital, and it is likewise true that the police can and do exercise very intense surveillance over the affairs of suspects whom they regard as especially and imminently dangerous. But to maintain this sort of surveillance *ipso facto* means diverting attention away from the great bulk of other crimes and criminals. There are many reasons why, from the CID standpoint, such a sacrifice may be worthwhile. But it is the sort of sacrifice that rules out mass surveillance.

In much the same way, these purely local forms of surveillance sacrifice easy *accessibility* and *transmissibility* of information for *voluminousness* and *discursiveness* of content. Unlike nearly all criminal record office files, the CID notes are lengthy, unstructured sheets of comments and observations by members of the Division on the day-to-day progress of their surveillance. These files are highly evanescent; they outlive their usefulness in a matter of weeks, and are destroyed as they become outdated by events. This unstructured, discursive quality and the absence of any indexing make this information all but inaccessible to other police agencies which might desire to use it. If these files were to become part of a national system of information flow, they would have to be more uniform in their structure and content – in other words, more like criminal record office files. Again, the police find this sacrifice worth making, especially given that the subjects of this form of surveillance are usually of primarily local interest. But it is worth noting again that a sacrifice is involved.

Access to Files and Exchange with Other Organizations

Both the origins and present organization of police surveillance reflect above all the requirements and practices of law-enforcement agencies. Virtually all the structures and processes described above have developed in order to meet the needs of the police and the courts, who are at once 'producers' and 'consumers' of information. And yet, it should be obvious that all sorts of other organizations, both public and private, share a deep interest in the content of police files. The resulting pressures for access to these data weigh heavily upon those responsible for police record-keeping, particularly because public opinion is so volatile on this subject.

Virtually all of the material presented in this chapter derives from the police themselves – either from the Metropolitan Police staff or from provincial officials concerned with criminal record-keeping. Seeking some information on the broad policies governing the communication of criminal record data to non-police agencies, however, I did pay a visit on 12 February 1971 to the Home Office Police Department. The two Assistant Secretaries whom I met on that occasion were anything but forthcoming on these topics. But, more seriously, one of the few explicit statements which they did make proved seriously inaccurate in light of facts uncovered in this search.

Specifically, when questioned about the provision of criminal record data to government agencies, one of the officials denied that such provision occurs, except 'very rarely' and 'under exceptional circumstances', circumstances which he declined to explain. And yet, standing instructions from the Home Office Police Department require local police forces to communicate as a matter of course the details of convictions of members of a number of broad categories of the British populace. Record of convictions of such persons goes routinely to employers in government agencies, and to certifying professional bodies in other cases. Table 3 shows the detail of these practices.

Nor is this listing exhaustive, although it accounts for the majority of reports. Among the more obscure categories of persons reported on are: drivers and conductors of public service vehicles; applicants for employment with the post office; candidates for the various military constabularies; and others. In general, responsibility for making these reports lies with the Chief Constable within whose jurisdiction the conviction occurs. Action taken on receipt of information is naturally determined by the receiving agency, but it is difficult to imagine that the effects of such reports are beneficial to the person reported on. Apparently anticipating some measure of

Table 3. *Reporting of Convictions by Police to Outside Agencies*

Persons on Whom Convictions Are Reported	Nature of Convictions Reported	To Whom Reported
civil servants and employees of the Atomic Energy Authority	all convictions, except minor traffic offences	Civil Service Dept. for transmission to employing department
justice of the peace	all convictions	Lord Chancellor's office
solicitors or solicitors' clerks	any offence involving money or property	The Law Society
teachers	'offences of a nature which may render them unsuitable for teaching or care of children'	Home Office
registered medical practitioners		General Medical Council
state certified midwives	all offences for which the *maximum* penalty is imprisonment for one month without the option of a fine or greater	General Midwives Board
registered dental practitioners		Dental Board of the United Kingdom
state registered nurses, enrolled assistant nurses, student nurses, and pupil assistant nurses		General Nursing Council

Source: Home Office Circular Number 151/1954; Number 77/1955; Number 11/1961 and Number 4/1969.

dissatisfaction from the latter, one memo from the Home Office to Chief Constables in this connection notes: 'An undertaking has been obtained from the Government Departments and all other authorities concerned to indemnify the police against any liability which may be incurred by the police authority or by any individual police officer as a result of the submission of a report.'

Another point which the Home Office spokesmen pressed quite strongly at the time of our meeting was their insistence that employers are unable to obtain information from the police on the criminal records of prospective employees. The research has shown this assertion, too, to be faulty, although here the picture is more mixed. It is very common for employers to seek information from criminal records so as to exclude former criminals from employment, especially if the nature of the job is such as to make criminal behaviour by employees especially troublesome. The police, for their part, are quite varied in their attitudes towards such entreaties. Some police officials report providing such information readily under certain circumstances, while others flatly disclaim all such disclosure. Such variations no doubt correspond to differences of opinion concerning the ethics of such disclosure, with different members of the police following various policies under various circumstances.

It is by no means rare, for example, for the police to provide advice concerning job applicants to administrators of children's homes, or to headmasters of schools. This advice may entail merely a recommendation not to hire in specific cases, or it may involve more detailed disclosure of an applicant's past record of crimes against children. Police are probably more likely to cooperate here than elsewhere, because of special repugnance concerning these sorts of crimes, and because of their knowledge that persons with tendencies in this direction often actively seek employment in such institutions.

Perhaps less widespread is the provision of information to other employers at special risk from theft or other criminal activity on the part of their employees. Some forces and criminal record offices routinely review lists of seasonal employment applicants at resorts and holiday camps in order to screen out those with convictions for larceny, breaking and entering, and the like. Similar requests for advice come regularly from banks and other firms whose employees must look after highly valuable and portable property. These, too, are honoured unevenly, and it is difficult to put any definite figure on the frequency with which the firms succeed in obtaining directly the information they seek.

There is reason to believe, however, that no employer with resources and patience need go without information of this kind. The police record-keeping system is, after all, an enormous bureaucratic mechanism designed to provide information on people's criminal records, a mechanism with numerous exits through which such information can flow. It is very difficult to prevent such a mechanism from working for unofficial as well as official purposes. Criminal record offices, for example, answer hundreds of telephone requests each day – the figure is in the thousands for the Metropolitan Office. The routine response to these requests is a report on some person's status in the wanted and missing index, and often a summary of his criminal record. It is impossible to prevent in all cases the dissemination of such information to non-police callers, even though criminal record office staffs may do their best to do so. Virtually anyone familiar with the telephone number of the regional office and the routines for making such requests can eventually obtain the information he seeks; if not on the first try, then sooner or later.

The vulnerability of these offices is especially great to former members of the police, who are invariably well versed in the techniques of making such requests. Industrial firms employ retired policemen in large numbers as security officers, precisely because of their familiarity with police routines in these and other matters. In many cases, too, the personal ties between these private security officers and their former colleagues make it possible for them to obtain services which would be denied to others.

Another pertinent question on the outside circulation of police information, one which particularly tends to worry civil libertarians, is its use for political purposes. This is a sensitive matter, and hence a difficult one to study and report on. It is known, however, that the Special Branch or political police do enjoy full and unquestioned access to all criminal record files, and that most police forces comprise one or more of these officers, who act in close coordination with the Special Branch of the Metropolitan Police. In at least one regional record office, Special Branch officers routinely review all criminal record files in the course of their transmission between that office and New Scotland Yard. And the police of foreign countries – though presumably only those of 'friendly' nations – are provided with criminal record information on request.

A similar discrepancy between the official and actual workings of the criminal records system has to do with the categories of people on whom records are kept. This is not in itself a matter of disclosure, but is nevertheless worth discussing here. Many police officials emphasize that criminal records are kept only on persons who have actually committed and been convicted for crimes. The earlier parts of this section should make it clear that this is no more than a partial statement of the matter. It is true that the files which the police themselves term 'criminal records' very rarely come into existence unless there has been a conviction, though there are some cases in which information generated in prosecutions leading to acquittal may be retained. But in other police indices, the decision to include an entry may have little to do with a man's past record. Obviously, persons wanted for arrest or questioning are listed regardless of their record of past convictions. Moreover, persons suspected of criminal inclinations, whether or not they have been convicted in the past, may be depicted in the 'police informations' circulated among the various forces. Finally, CID documentation can depict anyone whose activities interest the police, again without regard for past histories of criminal convictions.

None of the preceding remarks on compilation and disclosure of criminal record data is meant as commentary on the ethics of the practices involved. I feel that the ethical issues involved are far from clear-cut, and this book does not take up those issues directly until the final chapter. But an understanding of the flow of information between the police surveillance system and other persons and agencies is crucial for analysis of the place of such systems within the social structure, and hence indispensable here. Whether the official or the actual workings of the system in these respects are more justifiable is a matter for discussion later on. The interests of thoroughness, however, make it necessary to point out that the two are by no means identical.

Computerization

It is essential, in a book like this, to avoid the historian's fallacy that the present represents the final and inevitable result of cumulative past developments. Far from having reached their ultimate and finished state, the surveillance systems studied here are changing so rapidly that they scarcely sit still for their portrait. On the other hand, one wants to avoid deriving prophecies of revolutionary change from tentative and untried innovations in the social organization or technology of surveillance. In the light of these two considerations, the task of dealing with the advent of computerization in police surveillance requires a steady touch. Computerized record-keeping will certainly be an important part of police surveillance by the mid-1970s, and its growth clearly represents a continuation of trends and forces already noted. But the more closely I have studied the computerization programme as the police themselves are pursuing it, the more reserved I have become in offering predictions as to its long-term results. Consequently, in the brief discussion which follows, I try to avoid the more sweeping predictions of both the police and their critics, and to concentrate instead on the more concrete developments which the new system will bring, and their relation to present trends and practices as described above.

The most obvious impetus to computerization plans has been the galloping increase in demand for the services of police surveillance. Table 4 shows the growth in numbers of entries in the 'Mains' collection of fingerprints, which may be taken as

Table 4. *Entries in the 'Mains' Fingerprint Collection of the Metropolitan Fingerprint Office, 1910–70*

1910	150,000
1930	400,000
1950	1,138,000
1970	2,154,000

Source: The Metropolitan Police. All figures are approximate.

representative of the growth in numbers of criminal records in file, though the totals of the latter are slightly larger.

The institution of the regional record offices in 1956 was supposed to mitigate the effects of this growth. To a large extent, it has done so. The service now provided by the system would be impossible without them; but the volume of business facing the national centre has nevertheless continued to grow. Some police in fact feel that the increased availability and visibility of surveillance services have themselves prompted demands for more and more use of the system. The undesirable results of this growth have been apparent in the preceding discussion – the length of time required by the national centre for full processing of criminal records, the delays and blockages of telephone and telex inquiries, and the occasional 'No Trace' reports on persons known to have criminal records.

Nor are these the only difficulties inherent in the present limited decentralization of police surveillance. The regional offices, as the discussion has shown, involve a considerable amount of duplicated effort, with their own versions of criminal records and fingerprints also held in New Scotland Yard. Moreover these regional repositories fall short of the comprehensiveness of the fully centralized system, with the occasional result that persons escape accountability for information recorded on them elsewhere.

Since the 1960s preparations have been under way for the computerization of police record-keeping. The essence of the plan is simple in its ambitiousness: to convert all records, regional and national, from criminal record offices and, ultimately, fingerprints offices, to computer storage in a single central location. The point of centralization is to be the Police National Computer in London, which is to serve all police forces throughout Britain. To oversimplify only slightly, the announced aim of the system will be to provide the same qualitative services now provided by the national and regional record offices, but to do so much more quickly and efficiently from the single computerized centre.

Storage will be on discs, rather than tapes, so that the police can interrogate their files and update the information kept there immediately. Access is to be through terminals maintained in the headquarters of every police force in Britain, and, ultimately, in many local police stations as well. Plans provide for two kinds of terminals. One is to be a keyboard console, combined with a screen or visual display unit. Inquiries would be tapped into the central record with the keyboard, and responses would appear on the screen. The other terminal would resemble a telex machine, with inquiries typed in and responses typed out. One of the most important benefits of the system, according to the planners, will be the speed with which the machine can respond to queries; responses are predicted to be forthcoming to either terminal within ten seconds of submitting the request. Thus the constable on the beat or in his patrol car would radio a stop check request to his nearest terminal, and from there to the central file, and back again. The most optimistic predictions from the police envisage that the policeman making the request will be answered in less than half a minute.

As I have said, the long-term assumption has been that all criminal record files ultimately will be susceptible to computer storage. There are even plans for computerized storage of fingerprints, and for programming the machines to sort incoming prints against the entire collection. There are, however, considerable obstacles in the way of computerizing the more discursive, voluminous files like the criminal records themselves. It is very difficult to say when the computerized storage of these materials in their full form will be operational. The final computerization of fingerprint files will also require at least several years from the time of this writing. On the other hand, there are concrete and realistic plans for prompt computerization of some of the simpler indices. The computer itself is being delivered at the time of this writing in 1971, and its initial experimental operations should begin in 1972. As one of the planners explained to me, the first goals will be to make operational the index of stolen vehicles; then the wanted and missing persons index, including the listing of disqualified drivers; and then the nominal index, the latter to enable the police to determine whether persons are 'known' to them. The computerization of other indices is to follow once the first three have become successfully operational.

If these remarks have seemed guarded concerning results of the computerization programme and the speed of its realization, it is no accident. Those charged with the implementation of the programme have changed their plans from time to time in the course of pursuing the project, and other police officials express considerable doubt about the feasibility of many aspects of it. They point out, for example, that the initial allocation of only one terminal to each police force is apt to create serious bottle-necks in information flow, with 'stop check' requests having to 'queue' before being relayed to the computer. This could in fact prove serious, since many such checks can occur simul-taneously within a single police force during busy periods. And yet, without rapid access to the computerized file, the new system would provide little help to the ordinary constable attempting to identify a suspect. There are a number of other points of scepticism concerning the ultimate workability of various aspects of the system, points pressed most strongly by the local police forces which ultimately will represent the 'con-sumers' of the computerized service. This is not the place to pass judgement on these misgivings, nor am I able to predict in any detail the ultimate form of the computerization of police surveillance. Probably no one can safely make such predictions. I raise these points merely to emphasize that these matters remain subject to question even within the police fraternity itself.

Still, there is no question but that the first stages of com-puterization will be in operation by the mid-1970s. Nor is there any doubt that computerization of the more succinct indices, like that of wanted and missing persons and dis-qualified drivers, is ultimately workable, whatever the initial difficulties. And when this service is perfected, it will certainly extend the capacity of police surveillance by making a national, central file accessible to policemen throughout Britain. This step alone will represent a significant advance over the limited regionalism of the present system.

There is one other feature of the police computerization pro-gramme which, in closing, deserves special attention. This is the venture of cooperation with the Ministry of Transport, whose efforts at centralizing and computerizing car and driver licensing are discussed in the next chapter. The police have a deep interest in vehicle and driver licensing, since much of their work has to do with traffic control and with crimes associated with the use of vehicles. Under the present system, vehicle and driver licensing procedures are highly dispersed, in the hands of some 183 local government offices; under the coming scheme of things, however, all information on the status of drivers and the persons registered as 'keepers' of motor vehicles will be maintained in a computerized repository in Swansea.

The police and the Ministry of Transport are planning a system of information exchange between Swansea and the computerized police surveillance system. I have already mentioned that the police expect to include, in their computerized version of the wanted and missing index, a listing of disqualified drivers. Swansea is to provide this information daily to the police computer as it is added to Ministry of Transport records. In addition, there are plans to retain in the Police National Computer the name of the keeper of every motor vehicle registered in Britain, thus providing the police with quick identification of drivers and a reliable way of determining whether a vehicle is stolen. There will also be a comprehensive list of vehicles reported stolen. All this information is available now to the police, but only through much slower channels. The police can, for example, obtain the name of the keeper of any vehicle from the local licensing office. Regional record offices, likewise, list disqualified drivers from their own regions in their files, as well as recording the details of stolen vehicles. But the new system will reportedly be able immediately to provide any of this information to any British policeman requesting it. In return, the Swansea office will receive from the police daily information on vehicles reported stolen so that these can be prevented from being re-registered. This symbiosis between the two surveillance systems represents a significant example of the increase in capacity of such systems through their use of another's information, and it is a matter which will be discussed further in following chapters.

The Capacity of Police Surveillance

The portrayal of the structure of police record-keeping, and the analysis of its functioning, are now virtually complete. It remains, however, to draw together the material presented above, in terms of issues and questions central to this book as a whole. Specifically, this means reviewing police surveillance with an eye to appraising its *capacity*, in the sense of that term developed in Chapter 1. If this chapter has succeeded, the reader will already have these issues much in mind. For the attempt throughout this chapter has been to portray police surveillance so as to show what it can and cannot accomplish, where it succeeds and where it fails. Thus it should already be clear how the tension between what the police would like to achieve in these respects and what their resources actually enable them to achieve shapes the day-to-day workings of this system. The description of this tension in terms of the criteria of surveillance capacity should simply serve to formalize points already made, in such a way as to facilitate comparisons between this system and others.

The first criterion of capacity, as noted in the first chapter, is the *size* of the system. This is, of course, subject to reckoning by a number of different standards. In terms of the numbers of persons depicted in its files, the police system is rather small, at least by comparison to the others studied here. Probably all criminal record offices in Britain together contain files on no more than a total of 2,500,000 persons. Certainly this does not approach the total surveillance extreme of watchfulness over everyone, and even the yearly increases in numbers of files currently experienced by the system seems to be straining its capabilities. It must be remembered, however, that the police face a particular problem, in comparison to other agencies of social control, in that members of their clientele provide minimal cooperation with the controlling institution. Thus, though the clientele may be relatively small, the police face the special problem of identifying and apprehending their especially unwilling clients from the public at large.

Another aspect of the size of a surveillance system is the amount of useful information stored for each client. Precise comparisons on this dimension are impossible, and police files vary considerably in this respect, but in general police records are substantial in comparison to others studied in this book. Much

of the information recorded in criminal record files is brief but
highly succinct, serving to provide positive identification and
helping to enable the police to locate the criminal when they
need to do so. But the information held in the 'antecedents'
sheet in the criminal record is more voluminous, more discursive and also more *subtle* in the decision-making which it
affords. The antecedents sheet often provides a brief biography
of the criminal, touching not only on matters connected with
his crime, but also depicting a number of other important areas
of his life. An experienced police officer, on reviewing an
antecedents sheet richly supplied with these kinds of information, can often form highly sophisticated judgements of the
criminal's likely future movements and activities. Likewise, the
police use information generated in the course of 'stop checks'
in subtle ways that can involve highly discretionary decision-
making. The details of past convictions, for example, may make
the difference between arresting a suspect or bidding him good
evening, according to the circumstances in which the police
encounter him. It is true, of course, that the *original* purpose of
the voluminous criminal record files was to provide certain very
circumscribed factual information for use in sentencing by the
courts, and this is obviously still the official *raison d'etre* of
the criminal record files. But there are many occasions when
the police also use these files in a more subtle, discretionary way.

The matter of *centralization*, another criterion of capacity,
has already come in for much discussion. British police surveillance, it is clear, is but imperfectly centralized; moreover,
as David Steer has pointed out, some highly pertinent information is lost in the course of processing and never reaches the
central repositories. Information can flow from any one part of
the system to any other, given the proper signals, and the
records kept at New Scotland Yard in some respects come close
to comprehensiveness. But the maintenance of the regional
repositories does compromise the principle of centralization.
And it is clear how this limitation does enable an undetermined
number of persons to evade accountability for information
recorded about them elsewhere. In the hypothetical total surveillance situation, the full version of all information would be
available instantly from a single central location; the police hope

to move in this direction with the introduction of the new computerized system.

The third criterion of capacity is the *speed* of information flow and decision-making within the system, the rapidity with which the system can bring relevant information to bear on its clients once it has them in hand. This involves both the speed of entry of relevant data into the system's repositories, and the speed with which members of the system can gain access to it. Certainly police surveillance does not embody anything like the instantaneous reckoning of persons' behaviour and the immediate response depicted in *1984*. True, at its most rapid, the input of certain kinds of data can be virtually instantaneous, as when the particulars of a wanted person are circulated urgently to all criminal record offices throughout Britain, and there held in readiness for 'stop check' inquiries. But such rapid information flow is exceptional, and even then subject to frustration by the overloading of telephone or telex lines. At the other extreme, the flow of information relating to the criminal records fingerprint files can be quite slow. In most cases, data on a conviction, including fingerprints, require at least a week to make their way from the court, via the regional record office, to entry at New Scotland Yard. By the same token, this information requires at least a week for access in its documentary form, and the frustrations inherent in this delay are the main reason for the potentially risky reliance on the regional record offices.

News of wanted and missing persons, where speed is probably of the greatest essence, ordinarily travels more rapidly than criminal record data. Police 'informations', the usual medium of transmission for this kind of material, usually reach their destinations by police courier the day after their preparation. On the other hand, concerning *access* to wanted and missing persons data, when instantaneous communication may be at a premium, it is clear that policemen often encounter frustrating delays in checking the status of suspects. Police surveillance is especially vulnerable in this respect, in that it becomes increasingly difficult to detain persons with the passage of time. And if the provincial policeman desires to make his check with the central file in London, the likelihood of delay is even greater.

Again, the planners of the computerization scheme suggest that the new system will both speed inquiries considerably and provide policemen throughout Britain with access to a central, comprehensive file. But it appears that, at least until a very large number of computer terminals are available, the problem of speed of access will continue to trouble police surveillance.

The last of the four criteria of capacity is what I have called the *points of contact* between the system and members of its clientele. There are several aspects of this notion. One part of it is the ease and certainty with which clients can be identified, and here the police are, in one respect, unusually fortunate. For the police can often rely on fingerprinting, perhaps the one virtually foolproof means of identification. Because of this, there is almost no chance of a criminal's being associated with someone else's record, nor is there any chance of the system's failing to take note of his record, unless the hard-pressed fingerprint staff simply fail to look for it. On the other hand, this form of identification is time-consuming, with searches of incoming prints and sets of prints taking several days at the Metropolitan Fingerprint Office.

The luxury of identification through fingerprinting is in any case out of the question when it comes to that most important form of contact between the police and their public, the stop check. There the individual policeman, on whom responsibility for accurate identification rests, must rely only on the name and known aliases of the suspect; a brief physical description; and his date of birth. If the suspect refuses to provide his correct name and date of birth, identification can be very difficult indeed. In theory, all policemen are supposed to 'familiarize themselves' with the contents of all police informations, and to remain vigilant for wanted persons publicized there. But this is practically impossible, given the large numbers of national, regional and local informations published every day. Thus the ability of the police to single out and identify those wanted for arrest or questioning is uneven, dependent on chance and on the judgement and memory of the individual policeman. In a total surveillance situation, of course, wanted persons would be instantly identifiable to the authorities, wherever they might be. A system of numbered identity cards would take Britain a step farther along in this direction, and vastly facilitate police checking for wanted persons. But such a measure appears politically unpalatable to the British public.

Closely related to the question of identification is the matter of the points at which the system can acquire useful information on its clients. An agency of total surveillance would continuously monitor the whole of the behaviour of all its clientele, but any existing system of mass surveillance is bound to be limited to a relatively few points of intake. The police, in fact, must restrict themselves for the most part to collecting information on persons during the time the latter are actually undergoing police processing. Fingerprints, photographs, physical description, current address, court actions and even the more discursive details kept in the 'antecedents' sheet – all these data derive from those limited periods when the criminal is actually in police hands. However pertinent this information may be, the fact that it is available under such restricted circumstances does represent a limitation. True, there are a few other points of information intake. Some offices do add supplementary information to their criminal record files on occasions other than the conviction of the criminal for an additional offence, e.g., the criminal's return to the region after release from prison. And, of course, CID files may develop information through day-to-day and hour-to-hour attention to the movements of persons not in police custody at all; but these activities are not connected with *mass* surveillance in the sense intended here. In general, then, mass surveillance as practised by the police does restrict itself to the acquisition of information at limited points of contact between the system and its clients. And it suffers from not having more extensive information at its disposal on many occasions when it wishes to bring itself up to date on the activities of its clients.

All of this takes us to the final aspect of contact between system and clientele, the ability of the system to place itself in contact with and to apprehend those whose behaviour is unsatisfactory. In the world of *1984*, after all, the authorities responded immediately and forcefully to any citizen who disobeyed. But real institutions have a much more difficult time in locating those who want to avoid attention. The whole routine of stop checks, after all, represents an effort to bring the police surveillance apparatus into contact with as many persons as possible, in hopes of accosting in this way those towards whom action is necessary, in the light of their records. The strengths and weaknesses of the stop check system in this respect should be apparent from the preceding discussion. Of course, there are other ways of apprehending someone besides merely looking out for them in public places, and the police often prefer to go directly to where they expect their suspect to be. When trying to reach someone for arrest or questioning, the police will naturally consult the criminal record file for information on address, place of work, and other places frequented by the criminal. But this information may very likely be out of date, leaving the police with nothing more than the informal channels of community gossip or police informants as tools for locating and apprehending the person. If, as is the case in many continental countries, every police force kept a register of persons resident in their districts, or if there were some other form of expanded information intake on persons available to the police, their tasks of apprehension would be easier. But such measures appear offensive to the libertarian conscience of the British public at present.

THE DEVELOPMENT OF THIS RESEARCH

The material in this chapter was gathered between April 1970 and December 1971. The main sources of information were the Metropolitan Police and several regional criminal record offices. There were approximately seven visits to officials in the former, all of them men with special acquaintance in criminal record-keeping activities. The visits to regional offices numbered about ten. There were also two visits to the Home Office Police Department, and a number of conversations with outsiders to these organizations who nevertheless possessed special knowledge of police practice. These various encounters ranged in length from less than an hour to virtually a whole working day.

As in the other case studies, the material was gathered mainly through extended interviews and direct observation of record-keeping practice. I spent long periods in various criminal record offices simply observing the flow of work and asking questions of those engaged in it. Many officials were extremely generous in providing me with a wealth of statistical and documentary material. I am much in the debt of the police, both the Metropolitan and the various provincial forces, for the support which they have provided for this study. Especially impressive has been their willingness to deal candidly and helpfully with subjects which are bound to be volatile and difficult to treat.

My experience with the Home Office was much more mixed. Certain officials of that body, at the beginning of this study, authorized the Metropolitan Police to assist me in this research, and later provided permission for the release of certain statistics included in this chapter. I am very grateful for this assistance, which obviously was essential to the development of this research.

On the other hand, other Home Office actions did no credit whatever to that body. One particularly unacceptable act was the denial, by senior Home Office officials, that the police routinely report criminal record information to outside agencies. Those who made this denial certainly knew better, and the discussion on this point has made it clear that the provision of such information is both routine and extensive.

Other actions from the Home Office, subsequent to this denial, were also highly unsatisfactory. On 5 March 1971 a Home Office official wrote to me to ask for a copy of this chapter 'so that we can read and if appropriate comment on it before it goes to a publisher'. I replied that I intended to provide such an advance copy, and I repeated this assurance orally several times to other figures in the Metropolitan Police and the Home Office. I then sent such copies to the two agencies at the beginning of September 1971, with a request for comment on the draft. There was no acknowledgement of receipt of these manuscripts from the Home Office, though I did hear indirect reports of considerable chagrin over the chapter. Nor was there any response to my subsequent inquiries about the chapter on 21 September and 1 November 1971, until I received a letter dated 17 November. This letter came from the very top of the Civil Service hierarchy in the Home Office, several tiers higher than anyone with whom I had communicated before, in the person of Sir Philip Allen, GCB. Sir Philip's remarkable letter deserves quotation in detail:

... there is so much in the chapter – in content, in emphasis and in your speculative paragraphs – with which I disagree that it would be possible to meet my points only by leaving out substantial passages and making fundamental changes in others . . . Also, although naturally

I have not the slightest objection to your expressing your own views and making your own guesses as to what might or might not be the position on a particular issue, I cannot help feeling, if I may say so with great respect, that some of the speculative sections which are not based on any hard evidence do not fit in all that well into a work of scholarship, and they certainly make assumptions which I for one could not possibly accept.

I am afraid that you will think that we are being less than helpful, but I have come to the conclusion that there would really be no advantage in my commenting in detail.

A subsequent letter from me reiterating my request for comments received an equally negative response.

There is simply no justification for a response of this sort. I had gone to some lengths to provide drafts of this chapter, as the Home Office had requested, and my expressed purpose in doing so was to take advantage of any advance comment or criticism. Other agencies depicted in the case studies found no difficulty in commenting in detail on similar drafts, even when they disagreed sharply with points which I had expressed. Discussion of these disagreements, in every other case, led to an exchange of information which ultimately resulted in improvements in the final version. Under the circumstances, the actions of the Home Office can only appear as an attempt to conceal embarrassment over the findings in the chapter.

Fortunately, there were other opportunities to obtain authoritative comment on the same advance version of this chapter. The same manuscript received a reading from four other persons in several different organizations, including the police, which were actually engaged in the activities under study. These four made suggestions for change in matters of detail, but otherwise pronounced the work basically sound. The chapter has subsequently been revised in light of their suggestions, incorporating recommended changes. I only regret that the attitude of the Home Office makes it imprudent to thank by name or affiliation those who have provided these conscientious commentaries.

3

Vehicle and Driver Licensing in Britain

This chapter is the second of the five case studies of systems of mass surveillance and control. The subject is Britain's system of registration and licensing of motor vehicles and drivers. In 1970, this system was charged with keeping track of some 17,520,000 drivers and 14,950,000 vehicles, with maintaining records on the status of drivers, vehicles and the 'keepers'* of vehicles, and with enforcing the law governing their registration. The responsibility for these tasks is in the hands of a far-flung organizational system operating from some 183 offices throughout England, Wales, and Scotland.

On the face of it, these activities scarcely seem to involve social control in the obvious and forceful sense of police surveillance. The business of registering one's car or of licensing oneself to drive may seem more a bureaucratic formality than a significant manifestation of state control over the affairs of the citizenry. To some extent this reaction is reasonable. As this chapter will show, the 'grip' of this system on its clients is looser than in the case of the police, and the sanctions which it administers generally less serious, though not always so.

But it would be a mistake, in a study like this one, to choose cases only in terms of their dramatic appeal. True, the licensing system does not usually involve such forceful measures of social control as does the police system. Nor, for that matter, is it so complex in its internal organization or in the patterns of information flow within it. But these considerations should

---

* 'Keeper' is the precise term for the person who has charge of a vehicle and whose responsibility it is to register it. In practice, the keeper is usually the owner.

scarcely exclude it from interest here. For the vehicle and driver licensing system is on every count an authentic example of the phenomenon under study – a system dealing with millions of persons, committed to compiling information about them for the purpose of discriminating decision-making, and using that decision-making apparatus to enforce compliance with certain rules. The rules, of course, are the laws governing who may drive and which vehicles may be on the road. In the case of vehicle registration, moreover, compliance with these rules involves the payment of a tax which many motorists are naturally tempted to avoid. And, finally, the system is at the time of writing undergoing changes in organization and technology which hold a very special interest for the purposes of this book.

Organization of the System

Vehicle and driver licensing activities in Britain operate under a division of responsibility between national and local government. Legislation governing these activities is uniform throughout Britain, and the Department of the Environment is the national body responsible for implementing it. But the actual record-keeping and enforcement activities involved in licensing are delegated to local government. The one hundred and eighty-three local licensing offices are all located in buildings owned or leased by local councils and staffed by local government personnel. Every driver and every keeper of a vehicle is expected to license himself or register his vehicle in the office of the local government body in whose jurisdiction he lives. The Department, however, specifies the practices followed by these offices so as to maintain virtual uniformity among them – a necessary uniformity, since they must cooperate readily and exchange information extensively amongst themselves. The Department of the Environment wholly underwrites the expenses of these offices.

As I write, the structure of this localized but intercommunicating system is undergoing drastic change. The delegation of responsibility to local government and the dispersion of documentation is coming to an end, to be replaced by a single centralized, computerized installation.* This new system will carry out most of its business by post, retaining about eighty locations for over-the-counter transactions between staff and the public. Located in Swansea, the new centre will be directly under the responsibility of the Department of the Environment, and the staff of even the outlying offices will become national civil servants. Despite the drastic change in organization and the increase in surveillance capacity which it will bring, the basic information stored in the new system and the rules which it will aim to enforce will remain very much the same, at least for the immediate future. This chapter, then, begins with a description of the system as it is constituted at present, then goes on, in the final portion, to describe the detail and significance of the imminent changes.

The internal organization of record-keeping in the local offices is relatively simple, at least by comparison with that of the police. Their work is organized, usually both figuratively and literally, around two main files, one each for drivers and vehicles. The former is simply an array of index cards, arranged alphabetically by surname, one for every licensed driver resident in the juridisction of the local government body. The format of the cards differs slightly from one office to the next, but the content, under national regulations, is virtually constant. Basically, the pertinent information is the full name of the driver, his current address, date of issuance of the licence, dates of previous licences held, and limitation on eligibility to drive for medical or legal reasons.

The second main group of records, unlike the first, is bulky and voluminous. These are the records pertaining to the registration and licensing of vehicles themselves. They consist of heavy dossiers containing a variety of different documents, superficially resembling the 'criminal record files' in the police record-keeping system. These dossiers hold the original

---

* From 1 April 1971 the Secretary of State for the Environment assumed responsibility for vehicle and driver licensing functions throughout Britain. On that date, the Secretary of State became the licensing authority and the local authorities became his agents, though continuing to operate substantially as before. This arrangement is to continue for the transitional period until centralization is complete.

'declaration' of vehicle ownership filed when the vehicle is first put on the road. There the keeper gives identifying information on the vehicle itself, the period for which a licence is sought, and his own name and address. Similar information is submitted by the keeper of the vehicle and included in the file whenever he re-licenses and pays his tax on the vehicle. In addition, the file includes a standard document submitted by the keeper when the vehicle leaves his possession, and a similar form submitted on assuming control over the vehicle. A final form should attest to the point at which the vehicle is finally taken off the road for good. These various forms serve, or should serve if they are all present, to provide a comprehensive 'biography' of the vehicle: when it originally came into use, who has owned it and for what periods of time, where it has been kept, whether the tax owing on it has been paid, and where and when it finally 'died'. Rather than being filed by the names of the keepers, which frequently change, vehicle dossiers are arranged numerically, according to the registration mark of the vehicle.

Local licensing offices keep other files as well, though the content and organization of these may vary slightly from office to office. Many offices keep a separate file, which they may term the 'blacklist', of persons who have been refused a licence on medical grounds at that office during the last ten years, and persons who have been convicted by a court for a driving offence, whether or not the holder of a licence. In other offices, this same information will form part of the main index of licensed drivers. Local licensing offices also maintain files showing the movement of vehicle registration documents. These depict both the movement of vehicle files into the office from other jurisdictions, and the movement of such files from the local office to other licensing offices. Such recording makes it possible, for example, to trace vehicles whose keepers are sought by the police. Finally, some local licensing offices will retain records on persons prosecuted in the courts for failure to pay licence duty. As the following discussion will show, the use of all these subsidiary files depends very directly on the two master files of licensed drivers and vehicles.

As I have said, the business of taxation is an important part of the functioning of every licensing office. As all British readers will know, every vehicle actually used on public highways must display a circular paper badge showing that the keeper of the car has paid his current licence duty. While the pound required (in 1972) for the issuance of the driver's licence barely covers the administrative costs involved, the twenty-five pounds payable yearly for the licence of a passenger car represents a tax in its own right. Failure to display the badge leaves the keeper liable for a fine, and the information supplied by the keeper on the documents which must accompany payment of the tax in turn represent the main source of intelligence about the identity and whereabouts of the current keeper of the car. Nevertheless, the fact remains that compliance with these rules remains quite imperfect.

One of the main purposes of licensing activities, then, is the maintenance of compliance with the laws on taxation of vehicles, but these activities also accomplish another form of social control. Vehicle registration serves to link the vehicle itself with the person responsible for its use, and this linkage is important for a number of purposes. The police, as well as other public and private interests, have regular recourse to these files in order to associate specific vehicles with their keepers. For the police – much the most frequent outside users of the files – this recourse is often a matter of considerable urgency, as when they attempt to trace the driver of a vehicle reported involved in a motoring accident or otherwise suspected of involvement in a crime.

Law enforcement agencies are equally interested in who should and who should not be driving motor vehicles, and this, of course, is the reason for driver licensing. British motorists need not carry their driving licences as they drive, but are required to present them to the police within five days if asked to do so. Both the licence itself and the record of it kept in the licensing office are supposed to note any limitation on the use of the licence, mainly those imposed by the courts or as a result of failing a driving test. Given the temptation for persons so limited to evade the restrictions, the access by the police to information in local licensing offices represents a main check on the status of drivers.

Information Flow and Decision-making

The checks on eligibility of persons to drive are imperfect. I have already said as much for the controls inherent in vehicle registration. An understanding of these limitations, however, necessitates tracing the patterns of movement and use of information within these systems, and it is to this topic that discussion now turns.

Drivers

The requirements for the licensing of drivers are relatively strict in Britain in relation to the other Western countries, but the surveillance measures designed to enforce these requirements are distinctly vulnerable to circumvention. To obtain a 'full', as distinct from 'provisional', licence, the applicant must apply to his licensing office – not necessarily in person – present a certificate of competence to drive from the Ministry of Transport,* complete the necessary form, and pay one pound. The certificate of competence is issued only on passing a difficult driving examination whose failure rate is approximately fifty-four per cent. Moreover, the application form itself requires information on previous driver's licences held, the applicant's place of residence, any previous difficulties with the motoring law, and any diseases or conditions which might affect ability to drive. The application conspicuously threatens stiff penalties for evasion or falsification of any information sought, either on that form or with regard to the driving test. But there is no positive identification required in connection with the application procedure, and hence no certainty that the person who has passed the driving test is the same as the one whose name appears on the application form. Nor is there any foolproof way of knowing whether a denial of any relevant medical conditions is accurate or whether any other statement appearing on the application form is correct.

Thus, the applicant himself is the main, and often the

* The Ministry of Transport now functions as part of the Department of the Environment.

only, source of information for the driver's file. If someone declares on the application form that he has previously held a licence with another local licensing office, or has had his licence revoked, or has had 'endorsements' against his licence entered by the courts, the licensing office will go about verifying this information through checks with the relevant sources. Similar steps will follow if the applicant reports limitations of health of the sorts requested on the application form. But in the absence of special cues from the applicant, the system can avail itself of none of these sources.

Once the application is complete, however, other patterns of information flow may come into use. With the issuance of the licence, a card is entered in the driver's file in the licensing office, and one main purpose of this record is to facilitate communication with the courts. When a driver is convicted of any one of a wide range of motoring offences, the court must 'endorse' the licence. In addition, it may also suspend the licence for a period, and in some instances *must* do so unless it can find special mitigating circumstances. The accumulation of three endorsements within three years automatically results in the suspension of the licence for at least six months. The clerk of the court effects the endorsement by physically noting the conviction on the driving licence itself. At the same time, he will notify the authority which has issued the licence of the conviction. If the licence is suspended by the court, the clerk should also send the licence itself to the issuing office for the period of the suspension. Record of endorsements are entered on the appropriate card in the driver's file; suspension of the licence results in the removal of the card from the main file to the 'blacklist' category.

Probably the reader has already noted the difficulties inherent in these procedures. Knowing what is in store for him, a driver may simply refuse to produce his licence to the court, claiming that he has lost it in order to avoid the consequences of endorsement or suspension. One safeguard against such refractoriness, of course, is the notification of the court's action directly to the relevant licensing office. This will at least prevent the offender from obtaining a new licence without the authorities taking cognizance of the court's action. But it will not keep him from displaying the original licence, e.g., when stopped by the police at a later date.

But the vulnerability of the system is still greater to another related form of evasion. For in the absence of any fully centralized system of accounting, there is little to prevent a driver disqualified in one licensing jurisdiction from obtaining another licence elsewhere. True, he would have to submit himself once again to the routine of taking the driving test and applying for the licence, and he would have to swear falsely that he had not held a licence elsewhere. But for someone deeply determined to evade the law, these difficulties are far from insurmountable. Such a person might even obtain a second licence under a different name from the same office which issued the original. Here the only obstacle would be the possibility of face-to-face recognition by one of the licensing staff. For although drivers are supposed to obtain their licences from the licensing office of the local government area where they reside, it is only their own report which establishes their place of residence.

To put matters more formally, the capacity of the system suffers from difficulties inherent in *imperfect centralization* and the weakness of its system of *positive identification*. Information on drivers does circulate among licensing offices, specifically whenever a driver moves from one jurisdiction to another, or whenever he reports having previously held a licence in another jurisdiction. But the dispersion of information throughout the numerous centres in Britain, and the inability of the system to determine the whereabouts of relevant information on any one person, leaves it vulnerable to evasion. Indeed, with respect to reporting endorsements and disqualifications in the absence of a driver's licence, the courts may not ever know for certain where a driver is licensed, except in so far as he is apt to be licensed in the area where he currently resides.

There is one further, if also imperfect, check on driving by disqualified persons. In addition to the courts' reports of endorsements and disqualifications to the local licensing offices, the police routinely report the names of persons whose driving licences have been suspended to the criminal record offices in their regions. The CRO staffs file these names with the dates of the restriction from driving in a comprehensive file of persons so disqualified and consult this list whenever possible in answering 'stop checks' on motorists. Thus the stop check in such cases includes not only an inquiry to the wanted and missing index and possibly to the criminal records, but also a check to determine whether the person is disqualified from driving. The motorist may, like any other suspect, dissimulate concerning his identity, and the various criminal record offices must, of course, restrict themselves to listing drivers disqualified within their own areas. But some criminal record office staff nevertheless report that this practice results in a number of identifications of persons driving while disqualified.

Information from the courts concerning the legal standing of drivers is one of two main forms of input to drivers' records. The other is medical information bearing on a person's fitness to drive. Persons subject to any disease likely to impair their ability to drive safely are required to make a declaration to this effect on their application for a licence, and the application also includes a number of specific questions on epilepsy and mental disorders. Some diseases and conditions are *prima facie* grounds for denial of a licence; others, like milder forms of epilepsy, require further exploration before a licence can be granted.

If the applicant declares himself subject to certain of these conditions, he is apt to be disqualified outright. In this case, a card of the same sort as the one kept in the driver's file is prepared on behalf of the applicant with note of the condition and filed in what the licensing office personnel term the 'blacklist' of persons disqualified from driving. If there is any doubt as to whether the condition reported by the applicant requires denial of a licence, the applicant will be asked to agree to further inquiries concerning his health and perhaps to undergo an examination by the County Medical Officer. The latter is a physician employed by the local government who relays his judgement to the local licensing office as to whether the licence should be granted. Drivers afflicted with conditions warranting review before the renewal of their licence, but not disqualification, have this information noted on their file cards. These cards remain in the regular driver's file, rather than in the 'blacklist'. By checking the 'blacklist' every time they receive an application for a new licence, local office personnel aim to avoid issuing licences to persons already known to be ineligible. This check is obviously automatic in those offices whose 'blacklist' is part of the master file of drivers.

Nevertheless, it is apparent that the responsibility for bringing such medical information to the attention of the agency of control lies initially with those over whom control is to be exercised. And it is certain that many persons who might be judged medically unfit to drive choose to remain silent, withholding the required data from the local licensing authorities. The means of identifying these persons are limited indeed. In some cases the police may realize that an accident which they are investigating has resulted from the driver's loss of consciousness or other medical disability; here they will certainly report the matter to the licensing office. The courts also report such information to the licence authorities whenever it comes to their attention, whatever its source.

Then, too, licensing offices sometimes receive unsolicited communications, often anonymous ones, concerning the fitness of a given person to drive. The source may be an acquaintance or neighbour of the driver, a family member, or even, in one instance recounted to me, the driver's own physician. If the licensing office staff feel that the communication warrants exploration, they will then write to the person concerned asking for his comments and for authority for the County Medical Officer to communicate with his doctor. If permission is forthcoming, the resulting exchange of medical information should make it possible to reach a decision. If the driver declines to grant such permission, the licensing authority may decide on its own that there are sufficient grounds for revoking the licence. In this event the licence holder has the right to appeal to the courts.

My impression on talking to licensing officials is that these procedures are matters of some discomfort. One source of this discomfort, of course, is simply the fact that there is no means of knowing the extent of compliance with the medical regulations. The nature of the case makes it difficult to judge the amount of evasion, but one imagines that there are many drivers on the roads whose medical condition renders them potentially dangerous. Yet a more compelling reason for unhappiness at the law as it now stands is the fact that it does put licensing authority personnel, and implicitly the authority of the state, in the position of acting on highly personal information from possibly dubious sources. The licensing authority sees itself as called upon to investigate even those communications which are completely anonymous and which may, of course, be quite unfounded.

Information on medical disabilities is much the most volatile part of the personal data stored in local office files, especially in that it often tends to deal with socially stigmatized conditions like epilepsy or mental illness. Local office staff insist that all such information is held in strict confidence and that it is quite unavailable to the general public. I have found no reason to doubt that this is the case. Of necessity, however, the office staff themselves must deal with it in the course of their routine allocation of licences. As I have said, brief mention of the nature of the disability is listed on the file card kept in the drivers' file or in the 'blacklist' of disqualified drivers. More detailed notes on diseases and conditions are kept for reference in separate dossiers, but these are usually accessible only to senior licensing staff.

Vehicles

Like the patterns of information flow pertaining to drivers, those concerning vehicles are relatively simple. Here, too, most of the information used by the system is provided by its clients – in this case the registered keepers of vehicles. And, as in the drivers' case, the system of accounting on vehicles is weaker for its heavy dependence for information on those over whom it aims to exert control.

The first set of documents retained in the vehicle dossiers are those generated the very first time it goes on the road. The first owner, usually a dealer or agency, must present a sales slip or other document showing his ownership and the origins of the vehicle. Having inspected these documents, the licensing staff issue a registration book which is supposed to remain with the vehicle throughout its life and show the identity of each successive owner. By noting changes of ownership in the book and by requiring the presentation of the book whenever the vehicle is registered under a new owner, the system minimizes the chance of registration of stolen vehicles. Any attempt to register the vehicle in the name of a new owner without the presentation of this book results in a query from the licensing office to the previous owner to determine that it has changed hands legitimately.

At the first registration of a vehicle, the licensing office staff also assign it a registration mark, the number it bears on its number plates throughout its 'life'. Unlike other licensing systems, the British practice is to use the number to identify the vehicle, rather than the motorist. These numbers are assigned from blocks of numbers allocated to each local licensing office. Every office, as well as the police, also possess a comprehensive guide showing the originating office of every registration mark ever issued, so that the origins of any mark can be traced. Each local office, in turn, maintains a file of the present whereabouts of every vehicle which it originally registered.

Both the first and every subsequent licensing of most vehicles require the payment of the licence duty or tax mentioned above; valid safety and insurance documents; and an application form. The insurance and safety certificates are returned to the keeper after inspection. The applications for initial and subsequent licences are filed in the dossier. The application form requires, among other information, the name and address of the keeper of the vehicle, the date of expiry of the previous licence, the period for which the new licence is sought, and certain other identifying particulars of the vehicle itself. Since nearly all vehicles are relicensed either every four or every twelve months, these forms, added to the vehicle's file every time they are submitted, tend to mount *ad infinitum*. Licensing office staff are under instructions to cull redundant copies as they are encountered, but limitations of time frequently prevent more thorough weeding of redundant documents than this.

The accumulation of these standardized, highly repetitive licensing forms makes up the great bulk of all vehicle files. In addition, on acquiring a vehicle, and on surrendering one to a new owner, the keeper is supposed to notify the local licensing office by posting a simple form giving the details of the transaction, including the date of the sale and the names and addresses of the new and old owners. These, too, are retained in the file, as are occasional miscellaneous items of correspondence between the office and the vehicle's various keepers. Files may also include copies of correspondence, for example, with other licensing offices or insurance companies, concerning the status of ownership of the vehicle. The result is a motley and generally redundant collection of papers which may reach a thickness of nearly an inch for very old vehicles. Because of the desire to prevent registration of stolen vehicles, licensing offices never discard the whole vehicle dossier until they receive authoritative word that the vehicle in question has 'died' – usually in the form of a certificate from a scrap dealer to this effect. Even then, a brief record of the vehicle is kept in a small card file.

Like drivers, the keepers of vehicles are supposed to register with the licensing office in the local government area in which they reside. This means, of course, that the office where a given vehicle is registered is apt to change from time to time throughout the life of the vehicle, as it changes hands or as the keeper changes his place of residence. When the office of registration changes, the vehicle file itself is shipped from its former location to the new one. Many licensing offices consequently divide their files into two groups. One consists of files on vehicles originally licensed within its jurisdiction and hence all drawn from the same block of numbers. The other is made up of 'immigrant' vehicles, whose numbers will be drawn from those issued throughout the rest of Britain. No matter how frequently the vehicle changes hands, however, or how often it crosses jurisdictional boundaries, the licensing office which originally issued its registration must always retain a record of its whereabouts. Thus there is a highly developed routine, carefully adhered to by all licensing offices, of sending notification to the original office whenever a vehicle file from its collection is forwarded elsewhere.

One main purpose of this system of accounting on the movements of vehicles is to facilitate the activities of the police. As I noted above, the police rely heavily on local licensing offices for information on the names and addresses of keepers of vehicles, especially of vehicles suspected of involvement in crimes. Often these requests are urgent, and licensing office files are accessible to the police at all times, day and night, for emergency checks on the vehicle files. If the vehicle in question is registered locally, then the file will, of course, be on hand in the office itself. Otherwise, it will be necessary to contact the office which originally issued the registration to determine the record's current whereabouts. It is difficult to specify just how common these requests are, since the various local offices do not keep systematic records on the matter. An inquiry sponsored by the Ministry of Transport in 1965, however, estimated that there had been a total of one million such requests from the police in 1963, of which eight thousand were considered 'extremely urgent'. Projected figures for 1973 were four million and twenty thousand, respectively.

In some cases these searches can be extremely onerous for the police, and for the licensing office staff who must provide facilities for them. Witnesses to serious crimes can often identify vehicles involved only in terms of the most fragmentary information, for example that a car was a blue Rover with registration marks beginning ABC. If the crime is serious indeed, and if this is the only scrap of information available to the police, they may attempt to review every file in the local office whose vehicle answers to this description, and then to interview the registered keepers of such vehicles. These searches can involve weeks of work for whole teams of policemen, but they do occur.

Nor are the police the only users of vehicle files as a means of tracing the keepers of the cars. This information is actually quite widely available, though in some cases the local offices charge a fee for it. Ministry regulations provide a long list of agencies and persons to whom local offices are to make such information available. Included are the Department of Health and Social Security for purposes of tracing absconded husbands of recipients of welfare benefits; insurance companies, for use in tracing a vehicle responsible for damage against persons or property; persons to whom debts are due for repairs to the vehicle; solicitors in connection with legal proceedings; and others, including any 'person who wishes to trace the owner of a vehicle parked habitually on private property'. There are also a number of circumstances where, under Ministry regulations, disclosure is not allowed; these include legal proceedings concerned with paternity, bankruptcy, and hire purchase disputes. But, practically speaking, any well-informed and persistent inquirer can obtain the name and address of the keeper of a vehicle through presentation of its registration mark. It is impossible for the local offices to verify reasons presented for requiring such information, and they must therefore accept the explanations given by those who inquire. Thus, if a caller insists that a vehicle with a given registration number is habitually parked on his front lawn, there is little for the local office staff to do but to collect the twenty-five pence fee and provide the information requested.

Like the system of accounting on drivers, the system of surveillance over vehicles and their keepers is far from foolproof. For, like the first, the second depends very largely on the clients of the system themselves to provide the needed information. Thus, for example, there is no way of constraining the keeper of a vehicle to provide his correct address on the form he submits to register the vehicle. Yet a much more important shortcoming of the system has to do with the currency of information on the keeper's identity and address. For although it is probably rare for the keeper of a vehicle knowingly to enter an incorrect address on his registration form, it is extremely common for the keeper to change his address or to sell the vehicle without notifying the licensing office. When this happens the system will be without record of the current address of the keeper for perhaps a year, or even longer if the vehicle is not relicensed immediately after the lapse of the previous licence.

Nor is it necessarily easy to trace the identity of the current keeper of a car via the last registered keeper. The police, in attempting to locate such a person, may find that the vehicle has changed hands more than once, so that they must interview two or more previous owners before they can identify the party they are seeking. Then, too, it is by no means unheard-of to find that the last registered owner has sold the vehicle to someone whose name and address he does not know. In these cases the vehicle is 'lost' to the system at least until once again registered by the new owner. Theoretically, those who dispose of vehicles without informing the licensing authorities of the new owner are in violation of the law, but usually no action against them is taken.

The system faces similar difficulties, for similar reasons, in its efforts to enforce the payment of licence duty. Payment of this tax, of course, is an indispensable part of the original registration of the vehicle, but the inducements to regular subsequent payment are far from uniformly effective. The main check on the currency of licensing is through the display of the small paper badge on the window of the vehicle. These badges are available to the keeper of the vehicle on payment of the licence duty. Law enforcement officers, mainly police and traffic wardens, report sightings of vehicles without current badges to the local licensing office. These reports, which flow in great numbers to all licensing offices, form the basis for penalizing, and in some instances prosecuting, the violator.

One of the disadvantages of this system is the enormous amount of paper work which it involves. Once a vehicle is sighted, it must first be traced to the licensing office where its records are currently located. Then the local office staff must determine whether the registered keeper was in fact responsible for the vehicle at the time it was cited and, if so, whether there were any extenuating circumstances involved in the vehicle's being on roads. In many cases the registered owner refuses to respond to the inquiries from the licensing office, in which case an in-person visit is necessary. The larger licensing offices maintain staffs of inquiry officers, often retired policemen, whose sole function is to pursue these cases of tax delinquency. Needless to say, they often find their work hampered not only by the resistance of the tax defaulters themselves, but also by the fact that the vehicle in question may long since have passed out of the hands of the most recently registered keeper. The system works tolerably well when the level of delinquency remains relatively low, so that the system can devote its resources fully to a small number of cases. But it has been under considerable pressure in some areas of the Greater

London Council where very high levels of reported delinquency, combined with high residential mobility and shortage of enforcement personnel, pose a very resistant problem in social control.

Computerization and Centralization

In the terminology used in this book, these difficulties in administering the motoring law through the present organizational apparatus all represent deficiencies in the *capacity* of the licensing system. At the same time, they represent matters of intense practical concern to administrators in the local office and the Ministry of Transport. In 1965 a working group was formed under the auspices of the Ministry to review the over-all workings of the system, and particularly to recommend solutions to some of the problems just cited. One particular concern was the vulnerability of the system to various sorts of evasion made possible through its decentralization; another was the difficulties inherent in coping with the continually mounting paper work resulting from the transfer of vehicle files and the pursuit of tax delinquents. The result of their deliberations, offered in 1965, was a sweeping recommendation in favour of discontinuing altogether the involvement of local government in vehicle and driver licensing. In place of the old arrangement, the working party envisaged the wholly centralized and computerized system mentioned above, to be supplemented by approximately eighty local offices. At the time of this writing, the embryo of the new Centralized Licensing Office already exists in Swansea. Scheduled to begin record-keeping operations on a limited basis in 1973, it will clearly bring about decisive changes in the organization and capacity of licensing surveillance.

The Swansea installations will eliminate over-the-counter transactions for obtaining driving licences and will reduce the number of such transactions for vehicle licensing. Most of these transactions will take place by post, the relevant documents and payments being forwarded direct to Swansea. Certain post offices which at present renew vehicle licences will continue to give a counter service for the payment of vehicle tax. The approximately eighty outlying offices will store no vehicle or driver files. Their main purpose will be to handle certain transactions such as vehicle first registrations and to provide face-to-face advice on registration and licensing problems. But the equivalent of all drivers' records and all vehicle records will be stored, updated, and interrogated electronically at Swansea.

According to current plans, the new system will entail three computerized indices. The first to be activated will be the national file of drivers disqualified by reason of health or court action. There is obviously a special premium on the speedy operation of this file, since it will immediately be useful to law enforcement agencies in checking the eligibility of drivers. This file will contain the names and dates of birth of disqualified persons plus the reasons for the disqualification and the duration for which it applies. The second file to be activated will be the national drivers file, to contain the same data on each driver now kept in the manual files, plus his or her date of birth. The addition of the latter stems from the need for a further tool for positive identification; with all drivers in Britain in a single file, the duplication of names will be such as to necessitate some additional clue.

A highly significant feature of the computerized system will be its routine provision of information to the police. So extensive will be police access to the data held at Swansea that large parts of the latter might almost be seen as incorporated into the police surveillance system discussed in the previous chapter. The new Police National Computer will contain an extract of every vehicle record held in the Swansea files and a record of all drivers disqualified by the courts. It will daily receive updated information on changes in the status of vehicles and relevant drivers. This will mean that the police will have immediate access to the name and address of all keepers of vehicles. Such ready availability of information will greatly facilitate both the urgent and routine inquiries now made to local licensing files by the police in connection with crimes and suspected crimes involving vehicles. It will also make it easier for the police to maintain continuing surveillance over suspect persons and vehicles. But perhaps most important of all, it will considerably enhance the efficiency and effectiveness of the 'stop check' routine as applied to drivers. It will mean, for example, that any inquiry to the police National Computer should provide a definitive answer as to whether a given person is or is not eligible to drive. The police, in return, will routinely provide information on stolen vehicles to Swansea to help prevent their re-registration. Vehicles will be the third file to be computerized, again with the same basic information held in vehicle files at present: identifying data on the vehicle itself, and name and address of the keeper. The announced date for completion of the conversion process is the end of 1976.

Nor is this all. For the police are developing a system which will enable them to identify the registered keeper of a vehicle even from fragmentary information on the vehicle itself. Under the projected system, for example, the police computer would be able to provide the names and addresses of the keepers of all red Austin saloons with registration marks beginning with J – or, for that matter, a listing of vehicles answering to any description in terms of make, year, colour, and registration mark. Such searches of vehicles files are very occasionally done at present, manually, when the police are attempting to trace a vehicle involved in a particularly serious crime. Under the new system, such operations will be performed by computer, and the police will have at their disposal a new, highly discriminating and potent tool of surveillance.

Of course, the new system will also greatly increase the efficiency of many measures of social control now handled by the local licensing offices themselves. One significant anomaly of the present working of local licensing offices is their inability to use certain relevant information from vehicle files for purposes of social control. It would be theoretically possible, under the present localized scheme of things, to check all vehicle records, say, every month, to identify those on which registration is not current, and to contact all keepers of untaxed vehicles with the aim of obtaining the registration fee. This is never done, however, because it would involve an expenditure of staff time far in excess of the resources of any local office. One could hardly imagine a better illustration of the axiom that mere possession of pertinent information represents no help to a system of mass surveillance without efficient mechanisms for bringing it to bear on decision-making.

Under the new system, the computer will make these checks automatically, and automatically dispatch reminders to keepers of vehicles as their licences are about to lapse. These reminders are expected both to reduce delinquencies in renewing licences and paying duty, and to urge those former keepers of vehicles who have disposed of their vehicles to report the name and address of the new owner. In cases where the registered keeper obstinately refuses to communicate after several reminders, an investigator will be dispatched from the nearest outlying office to determine the status of the vehicle. The new scheme will not altogether do away with the necessity for law enforcement officers to report sightings of untaxed vehicles, since the possibility will remain that persons will use vehicles which they have declared not to be in use on the public roads. But it should greatly reduce the need for such vigilance and considerably curtail the amount of paper work involved in catching up with those whose licences are not current.

A final advantage of the new system, from the standpoint of social control, will be its tighter protection against those ruled medically or legally ineligible to drive. The centralization of files in Swansea will make it impossible for persons to take out licences in their own names after such rulings, thus closing one of the major loopholes in the present system. This feature, plus the increased speed and fullness of provision of data to the police, will represent the most important advances of the new system in terms of the capacity of surveillance and control.

The Capacity of Licensing Surveillance

The review of the organization and workings of licensing surveillance is now complete. It remains only to conclude this chapter with the same brief exercise carried out in each of the other case studies – an assessment of the capacity of the system in terms of the criteria developed in Chapter 1.

One of the four broad criteria of capacity is the *centralization* of a system, and it is in this aspect that the licensing system is undergoing its most sweeping change. The localized but intercommunicating system which exists at present is probably the weakest in this respect of any studied in this book, whereas the new, computerized arrangement will be as fully centralized as any. Probably none of the other case studies shows as clearly the difficulties which stem from decentralizing when an agency aims at enforcing a uniform and binding programme of social control throughout a large area. Having run foul of the system in one area of jurisdiction, the delinquent driver remains free to start over again elsewhere, or to take out a second licence under a different name at the original office. The new, centralized system will go a long way towards making the organization of social control commensurate with the uniform, nationally binding quality of the rules to be enforced.

Another important criterion of capacity is the sheer size of the system, both in terms of the *numbers of persons* subject to surveillance and the *amount of usable information* kept on each. In the first respect, this system is one of the larger studied here, dealing with nearly eighteen million drivers and almost fifteen million keepers of vehicles – the two categories, of course, largely overlapping. But in general the amount of information actually used on each member of these sizeable clienteles is small. For drivers it is generally little more than his name and address, the details of when the licence has effect, and note of any limitations on its validity. If special circumstances come to bear, like a medical disability relating to the person's fitness to drive, another, more voluminous file of correspondence between the licensing office, the driver, and the medical officer may come into being. But this is rare. Likewise, the vehicle files, though physically voluminous, generally contain little other than identifying information on the vehicle and its keeper, and no more than the name and address of the latter.

Of course, as the previous chapter showed, the most succinct and telegraphic data can often be the most potent in activating mechanisms of social control. The very terseness of information in the police wanted and missing index makes for quick decisions on whether to arrest someone encountered in a 'stop check'. But no one could argue that the brief information held in licensing office files affords decision-making of any special *subtlety*. The most important decisions made on the basis of these records are often binary ones, for example whether a given vehicle is currently licensed, or whether the licence of a given driver is current and unimpeded. Elsewhere the records serve mainly to make positive links between specific vehicles and their keepers, especially with respect to the place of residence of the latter. These simple 'yes-or-no' decisions, these basic linkages and identifications can be crucial for the workings of social control. But they hardly represent a sophisticated utilization of a rich array of data, nor do the decisions which result range through a wide variety of alternatives. This basic simplicity of the content of files and of the resulting decision-making will remain unaffected by the centralization and computerization of operations in Swansea.

Something that definitely will change with the inception of the Swansea centre is the *speed of information flow and decision-making*. In one respect, processes will slow down slightly since the new system, relying exclusively on the post, will require several days instead of a few minutes to complete licensing and registration transactions with the public. But in terms of surveillance and control, information will move much more swiftly. Exchange with the police, now often time-consuming and cumbersome, will occur daily at a national level. Moreover, the new system will make it possible to determine at Swansea within a few days – the time required to process a request for information through the computerized file – the status of any vehicle or individual. Similar periods of time will be necessary for the transmission of information from courts or medical sources to the central file, but in this respect the new system will differ little from the old.

The system is perhaps weakest, both in its present and future organization, with respect to what I have termed *the points of contact between the agency and its clientele*. Discussion has emphasized that the licensing system is largely dependent on clients themselves to provide the information needed for its surveillance activities. There are relatively few junctures at which the system can *induce or compel* the collection of information on its clients from sources other than the clients themselves. The courts are one such juncture, of course. The client has no control over the provision of information from the courts limiting his eligibility to drive, even though such information does sometimes fail to make its way to the correct licensing office. In the case of medical data, on the other hand, there is rather little the system can do to extract such information unless the client volunteers it. Anonymous communications or fortuitous intelligence forwarded by the police or the courts may provide the needed clue in some cases, but these are a very small minority.

One important exception to this limitation, however, is the provision of data on sightings of untaxed vehicles by policemen and traffic wardens. For this one purpose, these personnel represent an enormous array of points of contact between the system and its clients. The sighting of an untaxed vehicle in any part of Britain activates a response from the office where it is registered. Without the threat of this potential sanction, it seems certain that the rates of delinquency, which are already considerable, would soar.

Nor is the provision of information by keepers themselves in the course of vehicle licensing hardly fully voluntary. On the contrary, it is largely activated by the implicit sanction of fine or even prosecution in the event of the vehicle's being sighted. But the discussion has shown that sanctioning of this kind is uncertain and rarely swift. In some areas of Greater London, the system has been under considerable pressure. Part of the reason, in terms of the capacity of the system, is the relative difficulty of *apprehension* of delinquents. Neither in the case of drivers nor in that of the keepers of vehicles does the licensing system possess a highly effective means of locating and 'getting back' at delinquent clients. Like the police surveillance system, the licensing system is bedevilled by the fact that its records of clients' addresses are continually going out of date. But the licensing system has fewer investigative resources than do the police for determining that the original address is correct in the first place. For this reason, the system often finds difficulty in contacting drivers whose licences are to be reclaimed, and still more often finds it difficult to track down those who have failed to keep their registration current. The institution of the computerized system will wear away a bit at this second limitation, but the basic problem, in the absence of any more forceful inducement to the clientele to provide correct and current address data, will remain.

Finally, one important aspect of the contact between any agency of surveillance and its clients is its ability to obtain *positive identification* on them. Here, too, the licensing system is weak, especially by comparison to the police system. For purposes involving the use of 'criminal records', the police almost always can rely on fingerprinting to identify their clients. Elsewhere, for example in routine stop checks, they generally have at least a physical description plus name and date of birth. The licensing authorities, on the other hand, must virtually take the word of their clients as to the latter's identity. This seemingly causes few difficulties in the case of vehicles and their keepers. The problems entailed in the case of drivers, however, have already received considerable discussion. Some licensing systems in other countries require birth certificates, fingerprinting, and a photograph for the issuance of a driver's licence. Needless to say, this makes it vastly more difficult for disqualified persons to obtain licences, or for anyone to obtain a licence under a name other than his own. But British public opinion does not seem ready to accept any such measures. The new, centralized system will insist on the provision of dates of birth, but no further plans for tightening the identification system are involved in the changeover to centralized operations in Swansea.

Needless to say, the licensing system as a whole looks nothing like a system of total surveillance. Even more than the other cases studied here it touches on a very limited area of its clients' lives. Indeed, of the five systems under study, this is much the simplest in terms of the content of information stored, internal organization and the variety of sanctions and other responses of which the system is capable. Nevertheless, for its relative lack of complexity, it shows the same strains and actual movement towards increased capacity which seem inherent in the development of mass surveillance generally.

THE DEVELOPMENT OF THIS RESEARCH

Just as the organization and workings of this system proved less complex than those of the other four cases, the data-gathering efforts required to prepare this chapter were somewhat less demanding. Virtually all of the required material was collected in visits to just three sites. Two of these were local licensing offices, and the third was the Central Licensing Office in Swansea. The field research took place between May 1970 and September 1971. There were about ten visits to the two local offices, lasting between approximately half an hour and nearly five hours. I visited the Swansea facility three times, the conversations there lasting between approximately one and three hours. Useful corroborating information on various practices discussed in this chapter was also forthcoming from police sources contacted in the preparation of Chapter 2.

Local licensing personnel were exceptionally open and thorough in explaining their work to me. The Ministry of Transport Under-Secretary in charge of the Swansea facility, on the other hand, provided a peculiar mixture of helpfulness on some points with obstruction on others. He endeavoured, for example, to prevent me from communicating with other members of his staff and with local licensing personnel. Nevertheless, I did manage to speak independently with one other official at the Swansea installation, and the efforts from Swansea to discourage communication with local officials were generally quite unsuccessful. Moreover, the Under-Secretary himself provided much valuable and quite candid information in my face-to-face contacts with him. Comparing this information with that available from other sources, I found it entirely correct and to the point.

Both Swansea officials and certain local licensing officials reviewed with considerable care preliminary drafts of this chapter, and made valuable recommendations leading to its improvement. The Under-Secretary at Swansea has asked me to make it clear that this chapter does not represent an official account of any kind, however, and it should be clear that it indeed does not.

Notwithstanding the curious resistance from the Ministry of Transport to certain aspects of these inquiries, it is a pleasure to thank this body for the considerable help which it did in fact provide. I am also extremely grateful to the local licensing officials for all of their assistance, including especially the close commentary provided by one of them, on the preliminary draft of this chapter. To avoid possible repercussions from the Ministry, however, I regret that I cannot thank by name those who provided this help.

4

National Insurance in Britain

National Insurance is one of the main elements of Britain's Welfare State. Essentially, it is a programme of compulsory, government-administered insurance, binding on virtually all Britons, and providing financial protection against the stringencies associated with such common circumstances as sickness, unemployment, childbirth and retirement. National Insurance differs from other more 'welfare-like' programmes of assistance in that one's record of contributions to the system usually determines one's eligibility for benefits, and that contributions cover a large proportion of the costs of benefits paid out. The great majority of adult Britons must contribute to the system every week through payroll deductions or, for the self-employed and certain non-employed, through the purchase of National Insurance stamps. During 1970 there were over fifteen million claims for National Insurance benefits, of which 10.6 million were for Sickness Benefit.

The requirements of administering these benefits have given rise to a massive system of documentation and information exchange. This is most dramatically manifest in the National Insurance Central Office at Newcastle-upon-Tyne, which houses its main record repository. With a total staff of approximately 10,500 this is believed to be the largest clerical installation in Europe. Its main tasks are to register persons within the system, to reckon their contributions to it, and to direct the payment of benefits. For the purposes of this chapter, greatest interest lies in the activities of Records Branch at Newcastle. This branch alone employs some four thousand staff and specializes in recording contributions to the system and disseminating information on contributions and contributors to other elements of the system. Records Branch consists of one hundred 'ledger sections', each employing about twenty-four staff who perform highly standardized tasks of entering and extracting information by hand from a total of approximately thirty-seven million ledger sheets. The activities of Records Branch, and the patterns of information flow to and from it, link in turn to those of the nearly six hundred local National Insurance Offices whose total staff numbers over 29,000 throughout Great Britain. These local offices maintain considerable data on insured persons in their own right and act as small surveillance centres. The sheer human and geographical scale of these operations testifies to the crucial role of mass surveillance in maintaining the ties of social control between the institutions of the modern state and their numerous, scattered, and generally anonymous clienteles.

Some readers may find it strange to view a system like National Insurance in terms of surveillance and social control. Is it not true, after all, that the reason for this monumental record-keeping effort is to facilitate payment of benefits to those who need them? And if so, how can one characterize the relationship between such a system and its clientele as one of control?

The point is an important one. Certainly, provision of benefits is the ultimate purpose of the system. Certainly, too, the documentation generated and used in the process is designed for distributing these benefits correctly, according to the rules set down by the system. But any system for providing benefits to those eligible for them must also be one for withholding them from those who are not, and of providing no more than the 'proper' benefit to each claimant. At the same time, the obligation to contribute to the system is no negligible one for the contributor and, hence, hardly self-enforcing. Measures of social control are necessary, then, to constrain people to submit their contributions and to prevent people from claiming benefits to which they are not entitled. And this imperative of social control presupposes and requires a system of surveillance, a means of determining what action is appropriate to each client and, where necessary, of enabling the system to 'get back at' those clients whose cases require some form of corrective action. The benign ultimate purposes of the system do not in any way mitigate these requirements.

The clientele of National Insurance – between twenty and twenty-one million contributors during 1969 – is larger than either that of the police criminal records system or the vehicle and driver licensing system. But the tasks facing National Insurance are formidable in another way as well. For it must not only deal with very large numbers of persons, but also engage in a particularly wide variety of fine-grained, highly discriminating decision-making about them. The contrast is most striking in relation to vehicle and driver licensing. One might characterize that system as fitted to answer a limited number of binary, or at least relatively simple, questions about its clientele, and to enable the system to follow up these decisions with correspondingly simple actions. Such questions include, 'Is this person licensed to drive?', 'Is this vehicle insured and taxed?', 'Who is the keeper of this vehicle?' and so on. The options for actions are hardly more complex: to fine the keeper of a vehicle for driving without current registration, to penalize a driver for driving without a licence, and so forth. The most forceful response of that system is its use to apprehend persons guilty of serious crimes who have been identified through their vehicle registration numbers. While such decision-making may be important both to the agents of control and to their clientele, the *range* of factual information retained in the system, and the options for action based upon it, are comparatively narrow.

By contrast, the information kept in National Insurance files, and the decision-making based on these data, are extremely rich and complex. One must remember that contributions provide eligibility for more than six different benefits. Eligibility to each of these is determined by a multi-determinate calculus based on contribution history, marital and dependency status, date of birth and a number of other facts. Rules for the calculus differ for each of the benefits, and amount of benefit payable itself varies according to the number of contributions paid. At the same time, the system also uses the information which it compiles to identify and apprehend those contributors who have in one way or another broken its rules.

This complexity of information exchange and decision-making itself poses problems for the present chapter. The very extensiveness of the material requires a good deal of selection. The standing instructions to Records Branch alone form a volume of considerably greater bulk than this one. No normal reader could assimilate such a staggering load of material; nor, I imagine, would he forgive me if I presented it. But the purpose of this chapter is hardly to set out a comprehensive account of all the minute procedures which make up this system. Rather, it is to describe enough of its structures and processes to provide a basic idea of its capacity, its main strengths and shortcomings as a system of mass social control.

Besides limiting the sheer volume of factual information on the workings of the system, I have also applied several other forms of selection. Most importantly, I have limited discussions to the processes involved in administration of the so-called 'contributory benefits', those for which eligibility turns on one's record of contributions. This has meant, first of all, excluding the vast Supplementary Benefit programme also administered by the Department of Health and Social Security. Supplementary Benefits are payments made strictly on the basis of need, without reference to contribution history. This programme is more topical than National Insurance, since investigations of the lives of Supplementary Benefit claimants have come in for particularly bitter criticisms as invasions of privacy. But the very absence of central records for Supplementary Benefits disqualifies it as a system of mass surveillance, whatever other interest it may hold. For similar reasons, I have avoided discussion of Family Allowances and Industrial Injury Benefits, two additional programmes associated with National Insurance. These do involve some limited central record-keeping, but they are not tied to the same 'trunk line' of information exchange, nor do they seem to require such energetic measures of social control as do the contributory benefits. Thus the emphasis, here as elsewhere in this book, is on the use of centralized systems of information exchange in the service of social control.

Origins of National Insurance

National responsibility for social welfare and, hence, centralized national control over its administration is very much a thing of the present century, both in Britain and in most other countries. Before 1900 in Britain the only national legislation on the matter was the Poor Law Act of 1601, which placed responsibility for the care of the destitute on local parishes. During the Industrial Revolution and throughout the nineteenth century, the only other agencies of relief were charities and Friendly Societies. The latter were private organizations of working men, usually sponsored by trade unions, which provided both fraternal contact among their members and systems of private insurance against sickness, unemployment, and old age.

The first government-sponsored national pension scheme was enacted in 1908. This was a non-contributory scheme providing pensions for the aged. Following it, in 1911, was the first National Insurance Act to be financed by compulsory contributions, which provided relief for sickness and unemployment. The sickness scheme covered approximately three quarters of the working population. These persons paid their contributions, as many do under the present system, by purchasing and submitting special stamps. The associated system of employment insurance was by comparison limited in its application, restricted to certain industries and providing benefits for no more than fifteen weeks. The system of contributions, also relying on stamps, was different from that for sickness benefits.

In 1920, Lloyd George's coalition government extended contributory insurance to all manual workers except those in agriculture and domestic service, and to all non-manual employees earning less than £250, except those in teaching and public employment. Still another major contributory scheme was initiated in 1925: the Widows', Orphans' and Old Age Pensions Act. Employers and employees contributed equally to this scheme, and the government paid the difference between contributions and expenses. For most purposes, this third scheme was administratively quite unconnected to the other two. Finally, in 1937, still another scheme came into being, a voluntary, contributory scheme for both employed and self-employed non-manual workers earning between £250 and £400 per annum. This aimed at providing relief for widows, orphans, and the aged. This scheme again had a separate account at the treasury and was financed wholly by contributions varying according to the contributor's age.

This patchwork of measures obviously cried out for some scheme of rationalization. This was forthcoming in the Beveridge Report of 1942, which proposed an overhaul of the existing systems and their unification into a single comprehensive scheme. Beveridge's plan, which the Labour government made law in 1946, consolidated all previous contributory schemes, standardized benefits, and unified the system of administration, while also broadening coverage to the entire population. This meant inclusion for the first time of non-manual workers with incomes above previous limits, public servants, the self-employed, the non-employed and some other small groups previously excluded. The whole working-age population, except for married women, thenceforth paid a single flat-rate stamped contribution on one card, entitling them to a uniform schedule of benefits during loss of earnings for illness, incapacity, or unemployment. The only exception to the principle of universality was that the self-employed and non-employed were excluded from unemployment insurance. Non-employed were also excluded from Sickness Benefit. It was the implementation of this law in 1946 which gave rise to the organization and practices studied in this chapter and which, incidentally, necessitated the creation of Central Office at Newcastle.

The major outlines of National Insurance have not altered greatly since 1946. In 1959, the Conservative government instituted a scheme of graduated contributions over and above the flat-rate payment. These contributions, rising according to income, provide commensurately increased benefits during retirement. Still, as the following discussion will show, it is the flat-rate contribution scheme which still represents the main 'trunk line' of information flow within National Insurance.

Organization of the System

This section sketches the structure of the contributory benefits aspects of National Insurance. The 'structure' under discussion is actually of three kinds. The first concern is with the basic practices and obligations governing contributions to the system. Second is a description of the human and informational organization of the Central Office in Newcastle, mainly that of Records Branch. Finally, there is a discussion of the arrangement of tasks and of data in the local offices.

The Contribution Requirement

Every adult resident in Britain is required to register with National Insurance. Of those registered, the great majority are required to make weekly contributions to the system. The main exceptions are married women, who may elect to claim for benefits on their husband's contributions; widows; persons with very small incomes; and full-time students. Persons receiving National Insurance Sickness Benefit and Unemployment Benefit are also excused from contributing during receipt of benefit, but most other non-employed persons are required to contribute. For employed persons, the employer must accept responsibility for deducting contributions from wages or salary and must add a substantial contribution in his own right. Self-employed persons and the non-employed contribute at slightly different rates with corresponding differences in entitlement to benefits. Table 5 shows the size of the three contribution categories.

Local National Insurance offices supply every contributor with a contribution card bearing his National Insurance number and containing spaces for recording contributions. These are to be returned via local offices to Records Branch once per year with contributions for each week of liability. Employers retain National Insurance cards for their employees, enter the contributions, and forward the cards to the local office as they fall due. Contributions are often recorded by affixing National Insurance stamps to the cards for each week of liability; these stamps resemble postage stamps and are sold at post offices. Class II and III contributors generally pay by this

Table 5. *Average Number of Persons Paying or Officially Excused From Paying Flat-Rate Contributions During 1969 (in millions)*

	Men & Women	Men	Women
Class I Contributors* (Employed Persons)	18.81	14.68	4.13
Class II Contributors† (Self-Employed)	1.58	1.49	0.09
Class III Contributors‡ (Non-Employed)	0.22	0.12	0.10
All Persons	20.61	16.29	4.32

Source: Department of Health and Social Security, *Annual Report*, 1970.

method, as do the smaller employers. Larger employers generally prefer to avoid handling the stamps and enter contributions either with a special meter or simply by submitting regular cash payments accompanied by the appropriate supporting documents on behalf of all their employees.

Contributions entered on the National Insurance card are often termed 'flat-rate' contributions in that the rate of contribution does not differ according to the income of the insured. Since 1961, however, members of Class I earning in excess of a low minimum figure have also been required to pay 'graduated contributions', ranging from a few pence to £1.47 per week, at a rate geared to their income. These contributions count towards increased payments for Retirement Benefits – serving, incidentally, to preserve the income differential even in the administration of this Welfare State programme. The mechanisms through which graduated contributions are collected, however, are completely different from those for the flat-rate system. The Inland Revenue takes initial responsibility for graduated contributions, collecting them along

* Excluding persons not contributing in their own right for whom employers were required to submit contributions.

† Including persons excused contributions during unemployment or absence from work due to sickness, injury, or maternity.

‡ Excluding those persons under age eighteen and still under full-time education or training and widows who were credited with contributions as non-employed persons.

with income tax; records of the collection are then forwarded *en masse* once per year to Newcastle. Contributors in Class II and Class III do not pay graduated contributions.

These are the most important 'ground rules' governing contribution to National Insurance. Needless to say, the clientele do not comply automatically or universally, but these norms do receive sufficient compliance to form one of the main structures of the system. It should be apparent that the system places the burden of compliance in most cases – that is, the cases of Class I contributions – upon the employer, with respect to both flat-rate and graduated contributions. As the discussion will show, this practice considerably facilitates the task of social control, since employers in general are more amenable to compliance with the system than the private individuals who make up the Class II and Class III contributors. The result is a highly regular and predictable flow of information to Newcastle and an equally regular series of responses from Records Branch and local offices to the clientele.

The Central Office at Newcastle

Among record repositories, the Newcastle installation represents an extreme case in many respects. In human terms it is by far the largest encountered here. Physically, it sprawls over such a large area that the car provides the only practical means of transport over the longer distances within it. But perhaps more important than its size, for these purposes, is the extreme rationalization of its organization. It is fully centralized, holding contribution and benefit records for all persons throughout Britain: thus the movements of such persons within Britain pose little problem for its functioning. Further, the practices of this office are all closely and fully defined by highly formalized, written rules. It is but one portion of these, incidentally, which is embodied in the three-inch thick volume of Record Branch standing instructions. Finally, the whole of the Newcastle operation manifests an extreme division of labour which, along with the close definition of role, makes staff members highly interchangeable among jobs within the system. Table 6 shows the composition of the staff in terms of their formal positions within the Civil Service hierarchy.

Table 6. *Distribution of Staff at Newcastle Central Office*

Under-Secretary	1
Assistant Secretary	3
Senior Principal	8
Principal	25
Senior Executive Officer	79
Higher Executive Officer	237
Executive Officer	793
Clerical Officer	4,839
Clerical Assistant	2,972
Senior Machine Operator	106
Machine Operator	1,015
Total	10,078

Source: Department of Health and Social Security.

The physical and social scale of this office, however, stems more from the number of persons depicted in the files than from the amount of information held per capita. Like other advanced surveillance systems, this one bases its decision-making on limited amounts of highly succinct, telegraphic data, kept in uniform fashion and quickly accessible. What makes all of this remarkable is the fact that the predominant technology of the Newcastle office is anything but commensurate with its extreme bureaucratization. Most of the record-keeping activities rely on almost Dickensian, labour-intensive techniques, with armies of clerical staff laboriously entering data into ledger sheets and, later, extracting it for transmission to the local offices.

The largest division of the Central Office, and one of the greatest interests here, is Records Branch – a confusing name for the outsider, since all elements of the Office are engaged in record-keeping. Very generally, Records Branch is organized to accomplish two things: first, to maintain up-to-date documentation of persons' contributions to the system by receiving and recording National Insurance cards at the time of their yearly submission; second, to provide local offices with the information necessary to allow them to grant benefits. Every contribution to National Insurance is depicted in Records Branch on a single 'record sheet', a fictitious example of which

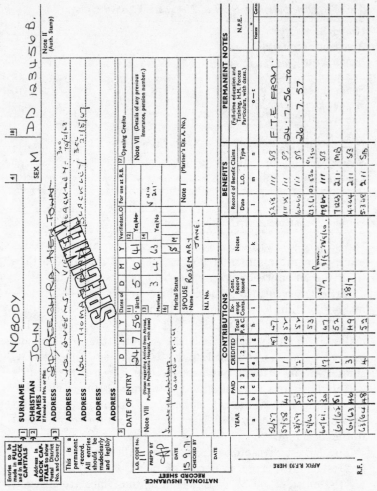

4. A representative but entirely fictitious record sheet of the kind prepared in local National Insurance Offices and held at Records Branch at Newcastle.

appears on page 132. Each record sheet is filed in a loose-leaf binder with approximately three hundred others, and these binders are in turn stored in approximately equal numbers in each of the one hundred 'ledger sections'. The ledger sections are large workrooms lined with ledger books and other files, including National Insurance cards in various states of processing. The organization of all one hundred ledger sections is virtually identical, with each staffed by four Clerical Assistants, nineteen Clerical Officers, and headed by an Executive Officer. It is no exaggeration to say that their functions are interchangeable. The close prescription of duties, the uniform staffing, and the random assignment of record sheets to ledger sections ensures this. The work is, however, subject to some seasonal variation. One quarter of all National Insurance cards are returned to Records Branch every three months, and their processing lasts until the next batch arrive. Moreover, requests for information from the files reach their highest level in winter, when claims for Sickness Benefit reach their peak. In other respects, however, the activities of the ledger sections are stunningly uniform from one week and one section to the next. Needless to say, staff morale can pose problems in this and other sections of the Central Office.

The records sheets contain virtually all that Records Branch 'knows' about every insured person. The ledgers themselves are organized serially according to National Insurance number, and this numerical organization facilitates the sorting of incoming contribution cards and inquiries from local offices. To cope with the problem of matching insured persons against their National Insurance numbers, however, there is a separate 'alphabetical index', much like the 'nominal index' kept in criminal records offices. Organized alphabetically by surname, this simple file contains the full name, date of birth and National Insurance number of every person currently registered with the system. With this index, compiled in volumes of small, loose-leafed sheets, the staff can usually determine a person's National Insurance number fairly readily.

Next to Records Branch the most important body within the Newcastle Office for these purposes is the Graduated Records Branch which stores and disseminates information on graduated contributions to the system. This is presently the only major repository of personal information at Newcastle stored electronically. The computer records on each person, however, are extremely elliptical, and this system consequently depends heavily on Records Branch, for example for the addresses of those depicted in its files. The data stored here consist mainly of the National Insurance number of the insured and the amount contributed during the years of eligibility. This information is updated once yearly, on receipt of the details of contributions collected from the Inland Revenue, and the system relies on this information for determination of the amount of Retirement Pension to which the insured is entitled.

There are two other repositories of centralized records on persons in Newcastle as well, in the Family Allowances Branch and Central Pensions Branch. Although these are outside the main sphere of interest here, they do at least bear mention. The Family Allowances Branch, with a staff of approximately 1,200, is responsible for payment of weekly grants to all families supporting two or more dependent children under the age of nineteen. These payments do not depend on any contribution record but do require considerable documentation for verification of the existence and age of the children involved. The Central Pensions Branch, likewise, files information on some 7.5 million persons currently receiving, or eligible to receive, retirement pensions. This Branch is also responsible for actually making payment of these pensions in most instances. But the record-keeping involved in pension payments is more a clerical exercise than a matter of surveillance.

The Local National Insurance Offices

For most purposes, Central Office remains quite insulated from direct contact with its clientele. The main point of communication between insured persons and the National Insurance is the local office. It is the staff of the local offices who engage in most of the actual decision-making on benefit claims and who act as the immediate agents of surveillance and social control. The latter functions include both the collection of information and the enforcement of compliance with the system's rules. In the course of these activities the local offices develop and maintain systems of records of their own which, on a *per capita* basis, may be more extensive and up-to-date than those kept centrally at Records Branch.

Every local office has jurisdiction over a closely delineated geographical area, and its records invariably refer to persons who are, or have been, resident in that area. The main repository of records found in every local office are the General Benefit Units, or GBUs. With minor exceptions, one of these exists for every living person who has ever claimed a contributory benefit. These files consist of a manila pouch, the exterior of which contains basic identifying information on the insured, and a variable array of sheets inside dealing with the insured person's history of contribution and benefits. Examples of some of these, made out on behalf of an imaginary but typical contributor, appear as Figs. 5 and 6 on pages 136 and 137.

The contents of the GBU differ according to the benefit history of the insured and hence, vary considerably. Some entries, however, are highly predictable. Name, National Insurance number, and date of birth are standard. Marital status, numbers of dependants and address will also be present but no more current than the most recent claim for some benefit. Also included on the BF4 form kept in every GBU will be a comprehensive listing of all the contributory benefits ever claimed, giving the nature of the benefit sought, the date, and the period during which the benefit was paid. In most cases other forms will also show the amounts paid in benefit, and will list documents presented by way of verification of vital information like birth, marriage, and death. Beyond this, however, variability is quite great. GBUs also generally contain recent correspondence received from the insured, for example, along with recent information from Newcastle concerning his entitlement to benefits. But these entries are by no means universal.

Nor is the GBU the only file held by the local office, though it is certainly the most important and the one held in greatest numbers. Claims for Industrial Disablement Benefits, for example, result in the opening of a special file to contain the

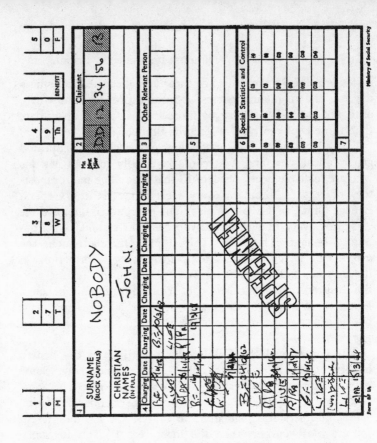

5. (*right*) The manila envelope referred to as the 'GBU'.

6. (*below*) The two sides of the 'Benefit History Sheet' which represents one of the basic contents of the GBU. The documents are in the name of a representative but entirely fictitious person.

BENEFIT HISTORY SHEET

1 Verified dates	Intls & Date	2	
Ex'd	Ch'd	MF 15	

SURNAME: **NOBODY**

CHRISTIAN NAMES: **JOHN**

Marital Status: **S.** M. | D. | 2 | 3 | 6 | 15 |

Birth 5.6.41 / ૨.

Marriage 3.4.63 AM La 9/1.9.2

3 Notes:—

wife
Rosegory Jam
(my. Jooro.)

4 Registered Papers

5 OVERPAYMENTS

Index Card No.	Date Cleared

Sick Visits or References to R.M.O.

S.V. or R.M.O. (6)	Date (7)	Result (8)
	Am 1.3.68	Final.

OTHER BENEFITS

Type (9)	Rate (10)	From (11)	To (12)

Marriage V—Box 1

Wife's full maiden name

Rosemary Jam
s. Scolors.

Form BF4

SHORT TERM BENEFITS—Periods of interruption of employment—See overleaf

---

SHORT TERM BENEFITS—Periods of interruption of employment

Type (13)	Period From (14)	Period To (15)	Nature of Incapacity (16)	Remarks (17)	Class (18)	No. (19)	CF 20f (20)	Stats. (21)	Initials (22)
SB	3.2.58	12.2.58	Influenza		1	1		C	
SS.	8.10.59	2.10.59	gastro-ulcers		1	2		C	
SB.	1.10.60	20.1.61	Medicalcus		15	C			
SB	19.9.62	24.9.62	Cold.		1	1		C	
SB	13.2.64	21.3.64	Broch Strain.		1	4		C	

(980463) Dd. 036847 1,000m 12/67 St.S.

details of the claim and the medical information brought to light in connection with it. Cases of fraud and non-compliance with the contribution condition also result in the creation of special files detailing the evidence of the infraction and the actions taken by the local office; needless to say, these files grow larger almost without limit as the cases become pro-tracted. Then, too, the local Employment Exchanges, which are part of the Department of Employment but which must cooperate closely with Records Branch in the payment of Unemployment Benefits, keep their own equivalent of the GBUs containing the details of payment for this benefit. All of these extra files are significant at various points. But the GBUs in the local National Insurance offices represent the main trunk line of information exchange and the form of documentation impinging most widely on the public.

As for the social organization of local offices, most patterns of activity directly or indirectly have to do with the allocation of benefits. Claims for benefits arrive in a never-ending stream, mainly by post, and most of the office staff devote most of their time to assembling the relevant information for action on the claims. This means requesting further information from the claimants, from Newcastle and various other sources, collating it, deciding whether or not the benefit should be granted, and reviewing the claim after a given period. Another major task of the local offices is the actual preparation of the Giro order, or order book, through which payments are made. In all of these activities the local office must take responsibility for its own decisions. The decision-making proceeds according to rules quite as formally and fully elaborated as those guiding the procedures of Records Branch in Newcastle, and the local office staff act largely on the basis of information received from Newcastle. But the actual decision-making responsibility remains with the local office.

The need to assemble relevant information on claims and claimants and to take authoritative decisions on the basis of this information implies a corresponding need to maintain surveillance over the claimants. As a result, one important element of the staff of every local office is the inspectors who specialize in ensuring compliance on the part of the insured with the rules of the scheme. The inspectorate, composed of Executive Officers, represents about six per cent of the local office staff engaged in contributory benefits work. In the discussion of information flow through the local offices, the activities of the inspectors will receive the most detailed attention since they represent the active 'front line' of surveillance *vis-à-vis* the public at large.

Information Flow and Decision-making

The above describes the basic patterns and structures of National Insurance as they concern this study. The next task is to chart the movement of information within these structures and the uses made of it for purposes of social control.

For all the systems studied here the endemic problem is not so much simply to *compile* relevant information, but to marshall the right information on the right persons at the right time to combat disobedience. In relation to any one of its clients, the surveillance capabilities of National Insurance are awe-inspiring. Its enormous capacity for acquiring and storing documentary information, its large and well-dispersed force of investigators, and its legal right to seek the information which it deems necessary for its tasks – these things make it easy for the system to turn a powerful spotlight on any case which it chooses. And yet, resources are meaningful only in relationship to the size of the task, and much of the task in this case lies in determining where the system should deploy its attentions. Arrayed against any single client, its surveillance capability is insuperable. But, in relation to a clientele amounting virtually to the whole of the adult British public, the matter is by no means so simple. Here, as elsewhere, the problem is one of applying available resources to those persons and cases which most seem to warrant it – and, therefore, one of making the most of all possible clues which might suggest where such application is best applied.

National Insurance surveillance relies on two broad media of information flow. First there is documentation, provided routinely and moving constantly through its various structures. Such documentary information takes many forms. Much of it is generated outside the system; for example, certificates of birth, death, and marriage, requests from insured persons for benefits, forms from physicians authenticating Sickness Benefit claims, and the contributions themselves. Other documentation is created within the system for its own purposes, including the various forms noted in the previous section. The second main avenue through which information enters the system is through the work of its inspectors. Here the system is less passive in the acquisition of information, deciding where to dispatch the investigator, and allowing him to select the data which he deems necessary to fulfilling his task. The means available to the investigator include unannounced visits to the premises of employers, visits to the homes of persons who have failed to meet their contribution obligations, and spot checks on persons tendering questionable benefit claims.

But while documentation is relatively cheap, so cheap that the system can rely on it very widely, the resources of the inspectorate are expensive and limited in relation to the magnitude of their task. The cost of dispatching an investigator to check on the validity of any single claim or to encourage a delinquent contributor to make good his arrears is apt to exceed any short-run savings which result. And by directing the attentions of the inspectorate at any given case, the system automatically forgoes applying its attentions elsewhere, thus running the risk of failing to spot some other instance of disobedience. Thus, again, the problem of choosing where the resources are best invested. The standard solution is to allow documentation to suffice for the bulk of everyday cases where non-compliance with the various rules of the system seems least likely, and to rely on the inspectors to pursue those cases where there is reason to believe that compliance is problematic.

Enforcing the Contribution Condition

The first step in ensuring payment of contributions is the registration of those liable to pay; this means, essentially, no more than the creation of a record sheet and the allocation of a National Insurance number. The great majority of new registrants, of course, are young Britons leaving school and entering the labour force for the first time. The Department of Employment, through its Careers Offices, act as agents of the Department of Health and Social Security in carrying out these registrations. This activity is, of course, related to the function of the Careers Offices in helping school leavers to find work. The Careers Offices allocate National Insurance numbers and complete the record sheets, which they then forward to Newcastle for inclusion in the appropriate ledger section.

Persons coming from abroad to reside in Britain who are required to contribute to National Insurance on the same basis as British citizens are somewhat more difficult to register. In most cases their employers will insist that they register and contribute so that the employers themselves will comply with National Insurance regulations. But there are some non-citizens, either self-employed or non-employed, who find the contribution condition irksome, especially if they do not plan to remain in Britain long enough to claim benefits. One example often cited by National Insurance officials is that many itinerant labourers are believed to be more interested in maximizing their weekly pay than in complying with contribution conditions. Persons in this position may go to considerable lengths to define themselves as self-employed so as to avoid the deduction of contributions from their pay. They may also take steps to remain unregistered. These cases pose a more resistant problem for social control.

Class II and Class III contributors in fact pose the most serious problems in contribution compliance, whether registered or not. The great majority of persons, of course, belong to Class I, and this means that their employers take responsibility for deducting their contributions and forwarding them to the local National Insurance Office. Employers are generally much more susceptible than private individuals to the constraints applied by the system, and so these contributors pose comparatively few problems. But for the self-employed or non-employed the contribution is not an automatic payroll deduction but an out-of-pocket expense. This makes it easier to slip into arrears, to avoid purchasing National Insurance stamps regularly at the post office, until perhaps the year's contributions are due and no stamps have been purchased.

To understand the system's response to non-contribution,

it is necessary to trace the flow of information in connection with National Insurance cards. The cards are issued randomly in four categories, each due for return to Newcastle at the beginning of a different three-month period. When the card falls due, its holder forwards it with all the contributions which have been recorded for the year to the local National Insurance Office. The latter then issues the contributor a new card for stamping during the next contribution year. After checking the card for certain gross irregularities, the local office staff sort all cards into ledger section order and forward them to Newcastle for recording.

Records Branch also collect at the end of every contribution year notice of 'credits' to insured persons as issued by National Insurance Offices during receipt of Sickness Benefit. Similarly, Employment Exchanges 'frank' persons' cards for periods during which they registered as unemployed. The ledger section staff at Newcastle in turn record both franks and credits on the record sheets in lieu of contributions during periods of sickness or unemployment. They then reckon the total of contributions, credit and franks for the contribution year, and at this point failure to meet the full contribution requirements is immediately evident.

Some measure of such failure is quite common. Every contributor is legally liable to submit one contribution every week, however, and contributions totalling less than fifty for the entire contribution year result in reduced entitlement to benefits. To maximize the ultimate rates of compliance, Records Branch have adopted a highly routinized series of responses to contribution deficiencies. These entail first sending written reminders to all those registering even one week's deficiency, noting the requirement to contribute and warning that failure to make good the deficiency can result in reduced entitlement. Frequently, the contributor responds either by paying the arrears or by supplying information to the effect that the deficiency corresponds to a period when he was not liable to contribute, for example because he was abroad. As Table 7 shows, however, compliance is not perfect even after routine reminders from Newcastle.

When the initial communications from Records Branch meet

Table 7. *Summary of Initial and Final Contribution Deficiencies,*
1965–6 Contribution Year

Number of Weeks Deficient	Persons Showing Apparent Deficiency* in Contributions After Recording at Records Branch	Persons Still Showing Apparent Deficiencies* After Normal Action Taken on Deficiency Notice
1 and 2	1,957,800	613,276
3–13	1,026,800	1,251,610
14–26	199,400	818,114
27–52†	1,748,000	34,200
Total	4,932,000	2,717,200

These figures show that the efforts of the system to recover contribution deficiencies meet with considerable, but not total, success. The number of those showing the largest initial deficiencies is substantially reduced by corrective action. But since some measure of deficiency is still common after such action, those in the 27–52 category help swell the figures in the other categories of the right-hand column.

Source: Records Branch, Newcastle.

with no response from the insured, the system obviously faces a problem. The results of allowing substantial non-compliance to go unchecked are obviously serious, both for National Insurance and for the insured, who after all must suffer loss of entitlement to benefits. On the other hand, there would be little wisdom in applying major efforts to make good small deficiencies. For costs of such correctives could far exceed the value of the contributions, and very small deficiencies of only one or two contributions do not even jeopardize entitlement to benefits. The solution adopted is generally to take no action beyond a written warning to the insured in cases where the deficiency does not fall below a fixed level. Those cases which

* Records Branch officials believe that many of these persons were not in fact liable to contribute during all or part of the period of apparent deficiency. They estimate that contributions actually owing to the system amount to about 48 per cent of those apparently owing.

† Includes cases where the insured submitted no contribution card whatsoever.

fall on the other side of this cut-off point, however, are referred to the nearest local office for action.

For the inspectorate at local offices ensuring compliance with the contribution conditions both from insured persons and employers is the most time-consuming of responsibilities. In instances of deficiencies on the part of Class II and Class III contributors, the inspector will first write to the contributor inviting him to make good the deficiency and then, if necessary, call on him at his home. Sometimes the visit reveals that the apparent deficiency has stemmed from a clerical error, for example the failure of the local office to enter credits during receipt of Sickness Benefit. More often, however, the inspector simply encounters someone who has failed to contribute. Here his response is to ask for payment. Sometimes this is forthcoming, sometimes not. A large proportion of persons in these two categories are chronically in difficult financial circumstances, and inspectors must continually form judgements on the ability of specific persons to pay. Depending on this assessment and upon the judgement of his superiors, the inspector will attempt to reach an agreement with the insured for gradual payment of the arrears. If this appears impossible, the inspector may be authorized to suspend provisionally the liability for missing contributions on the promise of regular payment in the future. Finally, if the delinquent contributor appears able to pay but continues to disregard warnings to do so, the system will initiate prosecution with the likely result of a court order for payment of the arrears and a fine as well. In 1970 the Department authorized criminal proceedings in 6,601 instances and civil proceedings in 5,330 instances.

In relation to the rate of initial default on Class II and Class III contributions, this rate of prosecutions is not great. One reason, of course, is that many delinquent contributors make good their arrears once confronted by an inspector. But many cases are also written off simply because of the inability of the insured either to pay his arrears or to meet future contribution obligations as they fall due. An experienced inspector should have no difficulty, for example, in assessing the situation of a father of a large family whose low income obviously scarcely covers the weekly essentials. People in such straitened circumstances have little hope of meeting contribution obligations and may even at the same time be drawing Supplementary Benefits from the Department of Health and Social Security. Here prosecution would be self-defeating. Under these circumstances, the local office generally issues the delinquent party with a notice advising that payment of contributions will not be pressed but that failure to pay will result in a loss of entitlement to benefits. The local office will review the case after the specified period but otherwise take no further action.

In these instances, then, the mechanisms of social control fail to achieve compliance despite ready access to the delinquent parties. But another limitation lies in the system's doubtful ability to apprehend those delinquent contributors who systematically conceal their whereabouts. For the system depends primarily on its clients to provide information on their addresses, and thus finds difficulty in locating those who wish to avoid contact. Persons do list their addresses on registration with the system; these addresses are probably accurate in most cases but quickly out of date. People are also required to note changes of address on their National Insurance cards before submitting these at the end of the contribution year, but most people ignore this requirement, if indeed they are aware of it. Inspectors seeking to contact delinquent contributors can, of course, avail themselves of other sources to determine their addresses – known personal associates, telephone directories, lists of voters, and so on. But those responsible for most contribution delinquencies are Class II and Class III contributors prone to itinerant work patterns and straitened finances. These factors militate against the maintenance of a stable address. Thus, the system is continually 'out of touch' with a substantial minority of its clients. The exact statistics are unavailable but some idea of the gaps is apparent, in fact the Graduated Contributions Branch, who use contributors' addresses as listed with Records Branch, find that approximately one twelfth of their yearly communications to contributors are undeliverable. Since these statements go to the relatively more stable and prosperous Class I contributors, the corresponding figures for the other two classes are probably distinctly higher.

Yet all of this may make the matter of evasion sound more

attractive than it actually is. For once delinquency occurs, the Newcastle office retains the record of it and remains prepared to act on it as soon as the whereabouts of the client comes to light. As soon as the delinquent takes up regular employment on a Class I basis, or as soon as he applies for a benefit, he will automatically alert the system to his whereabouts. Even if he takes up employment or seeks a benefit far away from his last known residence, Newcastle will direct the local National Insurance Office holding his records to forward them to the office nearest his new location. The inspectorate in that district will immediately go into action. The price which the insured pays for remaining outside the net of social control – movement, anonymity, and renunciation of benefits – is thus considerable. Here again the crucial importance of centralization of information is apparent – as is the premium on the ability to use information generated for one purpose for apprehension and control anywhere.

There is one further technique for apprehending delinquent contributors, though its main use is as a check against employers' non-compliance. This is the unannounced 'survey' by inspectors of an employer's National Insurance records with an eye to determining that all National Insurance regulations are being obeyed. The goal of the Department is to survey every employer every five years, and it appears that practice very nearly keeps up with this figure. Under the law, inspectors maintain the right to inspect the records of the employer with regard to National Insurance at any time, and also to inspect the premises themselves and to interview employees. Occasionally this procedure will reveal the presence of an employee working without paying contributions – perhaps by colluding with the employer so that both avoid the contribution requirement, perhaps by working as a self-employed contractor. But informants seem to agree that the process is not highly fruitful of such apprehensions, despite its agreed importance in assuring correct procedure from the employers themselves. In most surveys there is also an effort to check the registration status of the employees themselves. But in these instances, the majority of non-compliance is from persons in Class II who may well be enrolled in the system but who, nevertheless, fail to contribute. These persons represent the most serious problem in contributions compliance, and the survey is not necessarily a very effective weapon against them.

Allocation of Benefits

Except for the apparently rare instances where people completely avoid registration, failure to meet the contribution condition is at least evident to the agents of social control through the monitoring activities of Records Branch. But the system is much less fortunate in its efforts to control the allocation of benefits and, specifically, to prevent the payment of fraudulent claims. For entitlement to every National Insurance Benefit turns on an often complicated series of conditions involving contribution history, marital and dependency status, and often medical and employment status as well. These things can be very difficult to verify, not to say sensitive in the volatile personal information which they involve. Because of the difficulty of maintaining surveillance over such matters, the system is vulnerable to fraudulent claims in a way not true of failure to comply with the contribution conditions.

Table 8 portrays the main contributory benefits payable by National Insurance in terms of some of the conditions bearing on the payment of the awards. The array of detailed conditions for eligibility all represent facts which should, at least in theory, be verified before payment of the relevant benefit. This in itself suggests the magnitude of the implicit surveillance tasks which the system faces.

The differences in the contribution conditions for the various awards are intricate, and it is well to give them a brief explication here. In general, awards of longer duration are contingent upon longer periods of contribution history. Thus, eligibility for Retirement Pensions and Widow's Benefit is contingent upon the average of contributions and credits throughout the years of the contributor's eligibility to participate in the scheme. Sickness Benefits, Maternity Grant, and Unemployment Benefits, on the other hand, depend on the number of contributions submitted during the last 'contribution year' on record at Newcastle. These are basically short-term benefits, although Sickness Benefit can continue indefinitely. Perhaps the most

Table 8. *Major Contributory Benefits Paid Through National Insurance*

Benefit	Period of Contributions Determining Eligibility	Supporting Documents Usually Required for Payment of Benefit	Is Benefit Increased for Dependants	Duration of Award	No. of New Claims Made for Benefit During 1970
Sickness Benefit	Last recorded contribution year*	Physician's statement certifying incapacity	Yes	Duration of incapacity; can be indefinite	10,632,000
Unemployment Benefit	Last recorded contribution year	Statement from former employer†	Yes	Duration of unemployment up to 312 days	3,159,000
Maternity Allowance	52-week period ending 14 weeks before expected date of confinement	Physician's or midwife's certification of birth; employer's statement or National Insurance card to verify contributions	Yes	18 weeks	901,000 claims to both forms of benefit
Maternity Grant	Claimant's last recorded contribution year or that of her husband	Physician's or midwife's certification of birth	No	Lump sum per live birth	
Retirement Pension	Lifetime contribution average; wives may claim on husbands' lifetime contribution average	Birth certificate; marriage certificate for wife claiming on husband's record	Yes	Lifetime	780,000
Widow's Benefit	Lifetime contribution average of husband	Marriage and death certificates	Yes	Until retirement age or remarriage	70,000
Death Grant	Varies considerably according to age of the deceased	Death certificate	No	Lump sum	537,000

* The 'last recorded contribution year' refers to the most recent year of contributions recorded at Records Branch.
† The employer's statement attests that the claimant did not leave his job voluntarily and that he was not dismissed from his work for reasons of misconduct, or in connection with a labour dispute.

complicated contribution condition is that for Maternity Allowance, as distinct from the Maternity Grant. Eligibility for this benefit turns on contributions for the year up to three months before the expected date of confinement. Hence it requires either the presentation of the claimant's National Insurance card or a direct inquiry from the local office to the employer. Rates of benefit also depend on the number of the claimant's dependants, a matter which the local office also must theoretically substantiate before the paying at the increased rate. And all benefits are payable at reduced rates if the record for the relevant period shows deficiencies in contributions. This obviously further complicates the discrimination task of the local office staff, who must decide not only whether to make an award but also at what rate to do so.

The process of awarding a benefit begins when the insured submits a claim to the local office or, in the case of Unemployment Benefits, with his appearance at the local Employment Exchange. In most cases, the claimant posts the form to the local National Insurance Office although a minority of claims take place over the counter. If the claimant seeks an increase in his benefit because of his dependants, he must submit further forms to this effect. The local office, whether a National Insurance Office or Employment Exchange, then goes about assembling the necessary information for the payment of the claim.

The first step is the preparation of an inquiry on contribution status for Records Branch at Newcastle. The means of making these inquiries is the 'shuttle card', a small slip used for transmitting information on a single insured person back and forth between local offices and Newcastle. The local office staff enter on the shuttle card the name, sex, date of birth, and National Insurance number of the claimant, punch the two digits of the National Insurance number which represent the number of the ledger section holding the record sheet, and dispatch it to Newcastle. In some cases they may also add in longhand a request for further information from the record sheet. Records Branch received and dispatched during 1970 a total of slightly more than thirteen million shuttle cards. Of these, seventy-four per cent were dealt with and returned to the local office on the day of receipt, so that most local offices would have had the needed information on the third day after the request. Shuttle card requests lacking the National Insurance number generally take another day for processing at Records Branch, since they must proceed through the alphabetical index. Once in the correct ledger section, the shuttle card is completed with the number of contributions and credits from the most recent contribution year and latest information on marital status and date of birth, then returned to the local office.

At the same time as it forwards the shuttle card to Records Branch, the local office also sets about establishing any further facts necessary for the award of the benefit. It requests, where necessary, copies of birth, marriage and death certificates. If the claimant does not possess the required document, the local office obtain the information directly from the Registry of Births, Deaths and Marriages in London. Further information, for example a statement on dependency status, may also be requested from the claimant by letter. Once all the relevant data are on hand, the Clerical Officer handling the award will calculate the amount of award payable based on contribution record, dependency status, and all other pertinent considerations, and set the rate of benefit and the period for which it is payable.

The local office will hold no records on any insured person – save possibly record of failure to meet the contribution requirement – until he claims for a benefit. The initial claim for benefit is what first generates the detailed information held in the General Benefit Unit. Besides the information already cited, the GBU will also contain, where appropriate, record of confinement in prisons and hospitals; note of periods spent in the armed forces; current address; record of marriage, divorce, maternity and dependency status, and a number of other sensitive or potentially sensitive topics. None of this information is gathered for gratuitous reasons; all of it can be necessary for the determination of amount of benefit payable or of the contribution obligations of the insured. The goal of the local office staff in maintaining the GBU is to develop a file of information giving a comprehensive account of past claims and benefits and thus providing a basis for decision-making on further claims. Shuttle cards containing contribution and other data from Records Branch and letters from claimants also remain in the GBU for some time in case they should prove useful in processing further claims. It occasionally happens, for example, that a second claim based on the same contribution year is payable without recourse to Newcastle on information already held in the GBU, and the information found there on marital status, date of birth, and current address can always be useful.

Naturally, most GBUs do not spend their entire 'lives' within a single office. As the insured moves from the jurisdiction of one National Insurance Office to another, his GBU should move as well. The same applies to the records held in Employment Exchanges relating to Unemployment Benefit. This is so that benefits cannot be claimed at two different locations. Thus, when someone makes a claim for benefits at a new location and the resulting shuttle card request goes to Records Branch, the ledger section staff will note on the ledger sheet the location of the old GBU and will notify that office to send the GBU to the new office. The latter is not supposed to make any payment until it receives the records from the former office, thus making it impossible to obtain benefits without having the full weight of one's record come to bear. In this way the system preserves the advantages of centralized record-keeping while still maintaining the convenience of locally compiled and, hence, speedily accessible files.

Control over Access to Benefits

These simple routines creating and checking documentary information of claimants represent the system's 'front line' of control over unwarranted claims. One essential reason for the existence of Records Branch, after all, is to ensure that the system expends no more of its resources in meeting claims than it is required to do. Likewise, the recourse to documentation on claimants' family status and other relevant circumstances is the simplest way of ensuring that benefits are paid according to the prescribed formula for entitlement. But these checks are partial and preliminary at best. They leave open other matters, such as whether the claimant for Sickness Benefit is really sick, or whether the woman drawing Widow's Benefit is really a widow. These matters may be crucial to eligibility for benefit, and they are matters over which it is much more difficult to maintain effective surveillance. How, if at all, the system can maintain such surveillance now deserves attention.

In discussing these more subtle surveillance problems with officials engaged in the day-to-day efforts to solve them, one encounters what is at first an uncanny discrepancy of view. A number of my interlocutors were quick to praise the 'basic honesty' of 'ninety-nine per cent of the British public', and to insist that their own work would be impossible were it not for the integrity of the system's clientele. On the other hand, one often heard, frequently from the same informant, that 'fraud is rife' and that 'no one really knows how much cheating goes on'. After initial bafflement at what appeared to be total inconsistency, I have come to believe that both sets of beliefs, in their way, are correct. It is literally true that no one can be certain of the extent of frauds in benefit claims. The means of surveillance available are simply not sufficient to inquire fully into the great bulk of claims, not by a considerable margin. The system works in such a way as to exercise close surveillance over a distinct minority of claims where some special clue or circumstance suggests that such a check is advisable. But there is often no way of knowing how much fraud goes undetected elsewhere. And, in light of this inability to know about unchecked cases, there is little choice but to assume honesty in the absence of direct and compelling evidence to the contrary.

Discussion has already touched on the importance of cost considerations in limiting the scope of social control. For such reasons, I have suggested, the less expensive recourse to documentation takes on the role of routine check while the more costly reliance on the inspectorate serves more for special cases. But it is significant that the volume of cases is so great and the costs of checking so daunting that the system often cannot afford to avail itself even of large amounts of readily accessible and highly pertinent documentation which might serve to check fraud. One instance of this occurs in the processing of requests by claimants for increased rates of benefit in consideration of dependent wives and children. The form for this highly routine request requires the claimant to list the names of such dependants and to provide relevant supporting information such as whether they live with the claimant. It also requires, in the case of children, the entry of the order book number for Family Allowance payments and a statement of the exact weekly amount of such payments. Much of this information is subject to authoritative verification through records kept at Family Allowance Branch at Newcastle. But it is nevertheless common to process the requests for increased benefits at local offices without recourse to this information. If a *prima facie* check there shows the information provided to be plausible and internally consistent, the local office staff will likely make the award strictly on the word of the claimant as to his own circumstances.

Nor is this by any means the only juncture where cost considerations discourage the use of available documentary information. It would also be possible to determine whether wives claimed as dependants do in fact accept employment in violation of their claimed status, though such a check could not take place until months after the fact; for the record of contributions submitted to Newcastle under the name of the wife would clearly establish any such infraction. But it has been shown that checking returned contribution cards against possible claims would exceed the amount of overpayment, let alone fraud, by several million pounds annually. These decisions *not* to check then are hardly capricious. They stem from assessment, and sometimes actual statistical determination, of the losses sustained by not checking against the costs of doing so.

Still, there are a number of cross-checks against fraud, checks built into the system and hence relatively cheap, yet still effective as means of curtailing violations. Such controls are especially important in checking cases of persons working while drawing Sickness Benefit, probably the most common form of benefit fraud. During receipt of this benefit, the reader will recall, the local National Insurance Office enter 'credits' on behalf of the insured in lieu of National Insurance contributions. At the end of the contribution year, notification of these credits goes to Records Branch for entry on the relevant record sheets. For Class I contributors who remain employed while drawing this benefit, credits forwarded to Newcastle overlap with contributions submitted in the normal way by employers. This provides a signal, much in the same way as a contribution deficiency, that wrongdoing may have occurred. Very limited periods of overlap may not lead to any response from the system, since it has been established that pursuing such cases is inordinately costly in relation to the relatively small amount of fraud actually uncovered. But, in many instances of small amounts of overlap, and in all cases of what the system regards as major discrepancies, Records Branch refers the matter to the local office for investigation and, where appropriate, prosecution. Table 9 shows the rates of such referrals for a three-month period in 1969.

Table 9. *Cases of Overlapping Contributions and Credits Referred from Records Branch to Local Offices for Investigation, 17 March–13 June 1969*

Weeks of Overlap	Number of Cases
7 or fewer	2,669
8	571
9	420
10 or more	1,550
Total	5,210

Source: Records Branch, Newcastle.

Nor is this the only such check. The claim for a Death Grant, for example, acts as a signal that payments of all benefits on behalf of the deceased must stop, although survivors may still make some claims on the contribution record. Not only do the Records Branch staff make it a point to mark the contribution record to indicate death, but they notify Central Pensions Branch to cease issuing pension books. This is important. Retirement Pensions are awarded for the lifetime of the insured so that the losses stemming from failure to cross-check would be considerable.

In most cases, however, more active measures of intervention are necessary to maintain surveillance over the access to benefits. The largest amount of detected fraud concerns

Sickness Benefit, and the system invokes some special routines to contravene such fraud. The form for claiming this benefit is ordinarily available only from one's physician and requires the physician to state that he has examined the claimant, to cite the expected duration of his incapacity, and affix his signature. Continuation of Sickness Benefit beyond the period of incapacity stipulated by the physician requires the submission of another form. But experience has shown that some physicians provide these estimates rather uncritically, or at least less critically than National Insurance officials might like. And, in any case, some special check is considered necessary if the claim for Sickness Benefit becomes prolonged.

This check takes two forms. First, for many forms of incapacity the local office dispatches a Clerical Officer to pay an unannounced call on the claimant after the illness has lasted a specified period of time. This period depends on the form of incapacity and is set down explicitly in the regulations governing local office practice. The visitor is hardly qualified to arrive at any medical judgement of the claimant's condition, but he can suggest that a second medical opinion be obtained. If the caller finds the 'incapacitated' person occupied in a way inconsistent with his incapacity, for example in repairing his roof, a second medical opinion is obviously required. If he is working in any employment or in profitable self-employment, the benefit would be stopped and prosecution might result. For other forms of incapacity, the claimant will be referred, without a preliminary visit, for an examination by a physician in the Regional Medical Service run by the Department of Health and Social Security. In about eight to nine per cent of cases referred, the opinion of the examining physician is that the claimant is well enough to return to work. About the same proportion get a physician's note to show they are fit for work before the time of the examination. This last fact is, perhaps, not remarkable when one remembers that the check is made at a time when, in the normal way, the claimant could be expected to have recovered from his illness.

The system also makes certain other less forceful checks on the employment status of dependent wives of those receiving Sickness Benefit, Unemployment Benefit, and Retirement

Pension. Extra benefit is paid on behalf of the wives of such persons, but only so long as the wife herself does not earn above a certain amount. The local office, on initiating the benefit, obtains the name of the wife's employer and makes inquiries to the employer at intervals thereafter to verify the amount of work actually undertaken. For the claimant who initially reports that his wife is not employed there are routine queries as to whether she has subsequently taken up employment. These checks probably uncover a good deal of negligent non-compliance with the rules, but it is doubtful that they prevent really cynical, energetic attempts at evasion. For they depend directly or indirectly on the initial candour of the insured person.

A relatively infrequent but nevertheless thorny aspect of National Insurance surveillance is connected with Widows' Benefit. These benefits are awarded for the duration of widowhood and are based on the contributions paid by the late husband. The National Insurance Acts stipulate that this benefit is not payable after the widow's remarriage, or for any period during which the widow is cohabiting with a man as his wife. The instructions in the order book containing weekly payment vouchers for this benefit include a notice that the recipient must not cash orders if living with a man on this basis. Identification of the occasional instance of widow's cohabitation is both difficult and awkward, for most, if not all, of the normal relationship between man and wife must be determined to be present. In about half the instances some action by the widow, or more rarely by the man in the case, raises suspicion: a claim for Maternity Benefit – although pregnancy does not necessarily indicate cohabitation – the adoption of the man's name and its accidental use on a document, or his claim for her as a dependant. In the balance of cases, suspicion usually arises from communications, usually anonymous, from private individuals who may be disgruntled neighbours objecting to the receipt by an unmarried couple of payments which would be unavailable if they were married. Whatever the origin of the suspicion, it is followed up by routine investigation by local inspectors.

The investigation aims at forming a judgement of whether cohabitation has taken place, a judgement based on such criteria as residence in the same house, the woman's performance of household duties usually performed by a wife, support of one partner by the other or pooling of financial resources, the woman's adoption of the man's name or its common attribution to her, sharing a common bed, and the question of children stemming from the union. The inspector is told to consult official sources such as the voters' list and local office record for corroborative information. More rarely, he may consult vehicle registration records at the local licensing office. He will interview the widow in her home but is instructed not to harry her. He will interview the man after his interview with the widow, but his instructions forbid him from seeking confirmation from neighbours and tradesmen. The title to benefit will be reviewed by the statutory authority and the inspector's report, and the corroborative evidence he can produce in support will form the basis for the decision.* This will either disqualify the widow from receipt of further benefit or confirm her title.

The incidence of such investigations is not high, at least by comparison to the much more numerous cases of Sickness Benefit fraud. National Insurance officials estimate that suspicion of widows' cohabitation arises in about twelve hundred cases per year and that facts sufficiently firm to lead to disqualification from benefit come to light in about half these instances. Criminal proceedings against those responsible are

---

* Claims for benefit (as distinct from questions concerning contributions, insurability and classification) are determined by insurance officers appointed by the Secretary of State. In exercising their powers of adjudication they act independently of the Secretary of State. Their decisions are based on the evidence in the claim papers. They may call for such further evidence as they require to determine the questions before them, but they arrive at their decisions without a hearing. If there has been a change of circumstances or the decision was based on a mistake as to material facts the insurance officer may himself review the decision. Otherwise, a claimant has a right of appeal to a National Insurance Local Tribunal composed of a legally qualified Chairman and two members drawn from panels of employers' and self-employed and other insured persons' representatives on the one hand and employees' representatives on the other. There is a further unrestricted right of appeal from the local tribunal's decision to the National Insurance Commissioner.

still more rare. Two hundred and ninety-eight cases were considered for such proceedings in 1970 and prosecutions completed in only seven. While evidence of cohabitation is sufficient to disqualify, for criminal proceedings it must be shown to the satisfaction of the court that the widow knowingly made false statements, that is that she committed some fraudulent act in order to obtain benefit. This, added to the problems of satisfying the courts that an unmarried couple are in fact cohabiting as man and wife, limits prosecutions.

Like local authority officials charged with investigating anonymous communications concerning the health of drivers, those National Insurance officials to whom I spoke who were engaged in these investigations seemed to regard them with discomfort. This feeling appeared partly to stem from the difficulties of obtaining firm evidence on such delicate and difficult questions. Partly, too, it seemed to arise from the unpleasant associations involved in using anonymous, unfriendly information as an occasion for a state-sponsored inquiry into persons' private lives. The Departmental requirement here, incidentally, is that the source of the information leading to the inquiry must not be disclosed to persons under investigation. Department officials emphasize that the intent of the law on widows' cohabitation is not to legislate morality, but merely to establish equity between those widows who freely relinquish their claim to this benefit on 'remarriage' and those who do not. There is no reason to doubt this, and some of the officials to whom I spoke who were charged with carrying out such investigations would obviously have preferred to avoid the whole issue if they could. But the conclusion is plain. When any agency sets out to discriminate in its treatment of individual clients in terms of intimate subtleties of personal relationships, it must arrive at some means of surveillance over those subtleties or else lose control over the discrimination process. It is difficult to imagine any form of surveillance which could accomplish such a task without taking steps which at least some would regard as objectionable.

Quite apart from the issues of privacy involved in these investigations, a number of my interlocutors expressed dissatisfaction with them as means of curtailing the full extent of the problem. For the true extent of fraud over Widows' Benefit, like that of any other form of fraud, inevitably remains problematic. And for all anyone knows, the costs of investigating and prosecuting suspected frauds may well exceed the resulting savings in benefit payments. But why, then, should the system bother to carry out such measures at all, either in the case of widows' cohabitation or of any other fraud? Part of the answer certainly lies in the pressure of public opinion upon the Department to do everything possible to prevent 'parasitism'. But there is a more subtle point involved as well. For the costs of laxness in enforcement activity must be reckoned not only in terms of failure to correct current violations of the rules, but also in terms of new disobedience which might spring up in response to the loosening of controls. In other words, if the great majority of any system's clientele come to believe that it no longer enforces its rules energetically, the rates of disobedience might rise from the level of an endemic nuisance to that of epidemic disaster. Such second- and third-order consequences of cutting the costs of control could well be much more serious than the immediate ones. In any case, such considerations are not lost on those in this system and elsewhere who must actually proceed with the enforcement of rules *vis-à-vis* mass clienteles.

On the other hand, different constraints limit the number of prosecutions. For one thing, the Department of Health and Social Security endeavours to take into account what it terms 'compassionate' reasons for moderating its response to certain instances of fraud. These may include the amount of the benefit overpaid, the nature of the false statements made, the mental health of the person, and the possibility of over-all adverse effects on the family of the person who would be subject to prosecution. The image of an enormous government department pursuing an impecunious benefit recipient, however guilty the latter may be, is as repugnant to one sector of public opinion as the suspected 'parasitism' of some recipients is to another. Thus the policy is to prosecute less readily in cases where there are mitigating circumstances. When prosecutions do occur, local officials may inform the press of the date and place of the court action, and it is hoped that action against fraud will thus receive sufficient publicity to develop a deterrent effect.

Although no statistics exist on the matter, many of those engaged in enforcement activities believe the deterrent value of such measures to be greater, the less urban the setting. Prosecutions are believed to result in a noticeable increase in compliance, for example, in localities where the press is apt to carry accounts of the events and where the parties involved are apt to be widely known among neighbours and fellow townspeople. Informants recount instances of sharp increases, immediately after such actions, of voluntary renunciations of benefits by claimants previously unsuspected of fraud. In London and other large cities, however, where social life is more anonymous and newspapers less likely to publicize such prosecutions, their salutory effects are believed to be much smaller.

In the final analysis, the crucial question is not how much fraud the system can detect so much as what members of the clientele *believe* it can detect. One must remember that to receive any of the benefits discussed here the claimant must affix his signature to his statement of circumstances, below a warning reading 'TO GIVE FALSE INFORMATION MAY RESULT IN PROSECUTION.' In the face of general ignorance about the true surveillance capabilities of the system, vague uneasiness about the likelihood of detection must certainly act as a prop to honesty in very many cases.

Certainly it is clear, however, how great is the sociological distance which separates this system from 'total surveillance'. As I have already noted, its surveillance capabilities are mammoth in relation to any single case, but far less formidable in relation to the clientele as a whole. As things are now, the system manages by singling out those cases where intense surveillance seems particularly warranted, ignoring the matter of undetected deviance, and trusting to the honesty of 'ninety-nine per cent of the British public'. This works so long as whatever non-compliance occurs remains quietly endemic rather than rampantly epidemic. For, given the subtlety of the behaviours under surveillance, and the massive clientele, really widespread disobedience could only be curtailed by a massive increase in the resources invested in maintaining control.

Communication with Other Agencies and Disclosure of Information

For most purposes, the movement of personal data associated with National Insurance surveillance represents a 'closed system'. National Insurance has created a pattern of information flow to serve its own needs, and the structures and processes described above reflect these needs above all else. The result is that, for the great majority of insured persons, information is generated, stored, transmitted and used strictly within the organizational boundaries of National Insurance itself. Nevertheless, there are points where, either accidentally or purposely, personal information makes its way into the other surveillance systems, or into the hands of private persons. These points hold considerable interest here, for they tell much about the place of this and other surveillance systems in their broader social contexts, and about the social forces impinging on any system which efficiently gathers information on, and maintains contact with, a mass clientele.

Inevitably, this is one of the most sensitive areas of record-keeping practice. The Department of Health and Social Security is subject to a variety of frequently conflicting pressures in this connection – pressures to disclose personal data for certain purposes, pressures to guard the confidentiality of all information at all costs. In recent years, as issues of privacy and disclosure have become more topical, these pressures have grown. Summing up his Department's policy, Sir Keith Joseph stated in the House of Commons on 4 November 1970:

... instructions, which embody the Department's long-standing policy, provide that information in any of its records concerning individuals is to be regarded as strictly confidential and is not to be disclosed to third parties without the consent of the persons concerned. Exceptionally, information, but not files, may be disclosed in the departmental and public interest to other Departments or public bodies to prevent the duplication of payments from public funds, to meet statutory or welfare requirements and to assist the police in the prosecution of cases other than trivial crime.

This statement touches briefly on a number of difficult and complicated points, points which deserve more detailed attention here.

Perhaps the commonest form of interchange of information is that with the Area Offices of the Department of Health and Social Security. As the reader will recall, these offices are responsible for the allocation of Supplementary Benefits to needy persons without regard to any contribution record. One of the main responsibilities of these offices lies in making the discrimination between those who are and are not needy enough to be eligible to receive benefits, something which they do with virtually no central record-keeping system of their own. The desire to adjust Supplementary Benefits so that they really do supplement National Insurance benefits gives rise to regular cooperation between the two types of offices. Thus, Area Office staff may have recourse to files in the nearest National Insurance office to verify whether a claimant has been drawing Sickness Benefit, or whether a woman claimant is in fact unmarried. Such data obviously bear on eligibility for Supplementary Benefits. Elsewhere, the Area Office may rely on National Insurance, either through the local office or through Newcastle, to locate an absconded husband, so as to constrain him to accept liability to share in his wife's support. These are only a few of the more common occasions when recourse to National Insurance information is useful to the Area Office.

Even before these two categories of local offices were part of the same Department, information concerning National Insurance payments and addresses of missing husbands, where known, were generally available to the predecessors of the Area Offices. Under the new arrangement, however, Area Office officials maintain virtually the same access to National Insurance files as the National Insurance staffs themselves. The official reasoning behind this close cooperation is that the two kinds of offices deal with many of the same people, with many of the same ends in view.

There are other points of interchange, as well. I have already mentioned the occasional use of information from vehicle licensing files, by both National Insurance staff and those concerned with the administration of Supplementary Benefits. Another point at which a limited amount of information flows both ways is between National Insurance and the police. Here the nature of the surveillance tasks faced by local police and local National Insurance inspectors sometimes makes it advantageous for each to cooperate with the other. The impulse to such cooperation lies in the position of each organization *vis-à-vis* its clientele. The police often find themselves urgently desiring to contact persons whose whereabouts are unknown – either criminals, suspects, or persons whose safety is felt to be in danger. National Insurance records, probably the most comprehensive centrally accessible listing of persons and their addresses in Britain, represent a good bet as a possible source of such information. Conversely, National Insurance inspectors frequently find themselves hard pressed to locate persons delinquent in their contributions, or to form an opinion of someone whom they suspect of benefit fraud. In some of these cases, the local police may be able to provide useful information.

The official position of the Department of Health and Social Security on these matters is very firm. Along the lines of the Parliamentary statement cited above, instructions from Headquarters to local offices set down very detailed limitations on the circumstances in which National Insurance data can be provided to the police. Such provision is to occur in connection with 'serious' crimes, but not 'trivial' ones. The written instructions detail certain offences falling into each of these categories and specify that communications of this kind must remain oral and confidential. Ambiguous cases in these and other matters of disclosure are to be referred to the appropriate branch of the Department for advice. Further, official spokesmen for the Department particularly emphasize in their communication with the writer that any such provision of information must occur according to the letter of official policy rather than in response to any *quid pro quo* with the police or other outside agencies.

Having said this much, I am bound to state that my research

has convinced me that certain departures from official policy do occur at the level of the local inspectorate. Specifically, conversations with National Insurance staff directly engaged in this kind of work make it plain that the needs of local police and local inspectors as described above do, in a significant number of cases, give rise to reciprocal sharing of information which goes beyond the letter of official policy.* Local inspectors do rely on the police for advice on the whereabouts and character of persons of interest to the former. And National Insurance inspectors do sometimes provide information to the police in instances not specified by Departmental Instructions, for example where the police are pursuing a matter in which no crime has occurred. The degree of such cooperation is bound to vary from locality to locality as a function of the personalities of officials on both sides and of the opportunities for communication between the two. One has reason to believe that this unofficial sharing does not occur in the provision of data from Records Branch at Newcastle, which sometimes uses its alphabetical index to trace persons whose whereabouts in Britain is otherwise quite unknown. Because of the insulation of Records Branch from local affairs, there is little possibility for pressure to deviate from official policy. But at the local level, such pressures do exist, with the result that, as one well-informed figure pointed out to me, 'Every good inspector will want to maintain good relations with the police.'

The Department of Health and Social Security also authorizes under closely specified circumstances the release of

* The preceding paragraph should make it clear that this is by no means the official view, and spokesmen for the Department of Health and Social Security have therefore asked me to explain the sources on which I have based my judgement in this matter. As the note at the end of this chapter explains, all the information in this chapter derives from interviews with officials in six different locations: two local National Insurance offices, one regional office, one area office, Headquarters in London, and Central Office at Newcastle-upon-Tyne. In the course of these interviews, I spoke with two officials on independent occasions who had become familiar with the work of local inspectors through direct acquaintance and experience with people in this role. It was their reports relating to a variety of instances which led me to develop the views cited in this paragraph.

information to other government agencies. Among the most frequent recipients here are government bodies whose pension or welfare schemes supplement National Insurance. Local government relies on such information in the case of persons to whom it provides welfare services of various kinds, as do the police and fire services in maintaining their own pension schemes. Elsewhere, the Ministry of Defence seek and receive from National Insurance the current addresses of deserters, in so far as they are known. Likewise, information on the whereabouts of absconding husbands may be provided to the courts, or more rarely to the wife or her solicitor, for purposes of instituting or enforcing a maintenance order. The courts, as one might expect, are able to obtain information from National Insurance records quite readily, as are solicitors of insured persons, when such information pertains to matters under adjudication.

Apart from the police and other government agencies, there are many other persons and agencies with a deep interest in the content of National Insurance files. In general, however, the system is quite unfriendly towards requests from private interests – in both official policy and everyday practice. Probably the commonest of these are private investigating services and credit bureaus, which, like the police, often find it useful to consult a comprehensive listing of persons' current whereabouts. As a result, both Records Branch and the local offices are subject to attempts to obtain information of this kind. Standing instructions to local offices explain in considerable detail efforts made by such organizations to obtain information, and stress that all such overtures must be denied. Instructions also set down a series of procedures for identifying illicit requests, procedures mainly involving positive identification of those who make such requests. This is important, because a common ruse in making unauthorized requests is for a caller to claim that he himself is a National Insurance official.

In May 1971 a major story appeared in one of the national newspapers asserting that a journalist for that publication had managed, by retaining the services of a private investigator, to obtain personal information from, among other sources, National Insurance files. The story gave rise to a controversy lasting several weeks, including further accounts in the press, questions in Parliament, and assurances from the Prime Minister of renewed efforts to safeguard the confidentiality of information. National Insurance Headquarters officials, however, insist that they 'do not accept' that a leak had taken place, and the whole matter remains as I write *sub judice*.

One wonders how common such dishonest acquisition of information can be, given the earnest efforts of the National Insurance system to prevent it. Local offices do occasionally receive urgent requests from other local offices for details from insured persons' GBUs. Such requests most commonly occur when the insured makes a pressing request for assistance at an office other than where his records are stored. Under these circumstances, standing instructions to staff insist that the office receiving the request must return the call to the one purporting to place it after having verified the telephone number. In most cases it appears that local office staff adhere closely to this rule. But some of my interlocutors within National Insurance have suggested that the press of urgent business may occasionally lead the staff to omit checks, and that such omissions may permit some cases of unauthorized access. In any case, the 'call back' rule seems to work well in the great majority of instances, and it is difficult to believe that National Insurance information is nearly so readily available as, say, that held in police files.

The Capacity of National Insurance Surveillance

The review of the structure and workings of National Insurance is now virtually complete. All that remains is to summarize these observations in terms of the capacity of National Insurance as a system of surveillance and control.

First, consider the size of this system. In terms of sheer numbers of clients and frequency of decision-making about them, National Insurance is certainly impressive. With ledger section records on some thirty-seven million persons, approximately twenty million contributors during 1970, and probably at least ten million claimants during that year, this system can be said to have a clientele consisting of most of the adult populace of Britain. The clientele is still larger if one includes the numerous recipients of continuing benefits like Retirement Pension or Family Allowances; but here, of course, less active surveillance is involved in the tie between system and client.

At the same time, National Insurance files store an impressive amount of usable, pertinent data on each client. Comparisons are difficult here because of the great variations in amount of data held per file, and because of the absence of any statistics on the matter. But the typical pair of National Insurance files – central and local – certainly hold more relevant data than either the typical vehicle or driver file in the licensing system or indeed than these two files combined, where they refer to the same person. Probably the police criminal records files hold slightly more on the average than National Insurance files, but the comparison is a fine one. In general, too, data kept in National Insurance files is condensed and highly pertinent to the decision-making job at hand. There is rather little discursive prose; crucial information is stored in code or abbreviated statements of various kinds, mostly in such a way as to be maximally accessible and useful for further decision-making. Some local office files do accumulate backlogs of correspondence with clients and other dated entries, but departmental policy dictates that most such materials, where clearly useless, must be regularly weeded, and generally this is what happens. Much of the data actually kept serves a number of uses, often helping to make ingenious cross-checks against possible fraud. This is especially true with respect to contribution data which both establish entitlement to benefits and represent a check, for example against drawing Sickness Benefit while employed. Other data such as that on date of birth or marital status, once verified, recorded in local or central files, is considered authoritative and held in readiness for use later on.

One further significant but subtle aspect of the size of any system is the comprehensiveness of its view of its clients' lives. To what extent do National Insurance files depict the whole of the person to whom they pertain? Of course, these files never provide the sort of comprehensive portrait one would expect in a situation of total surveillance. And for clients who never happen to have extensive dealings with the system the files may be slender indeed. But it is fair to say that the file of a typical, middle-aged insured person, with a typical history of contributions and claims, does yield a sort of mental picture of the client. Family status, health, frequency of various forms of claims, employment, place of residence – the brief, telegraphic data on these matters does in the end create a comprehensive picture of the sort not provided, say, by the files described in the preceding chapter.

Finally, the data held in these files makes possible decision-making of considerable subtlety. This subtlety does not lie in the exercise of imagination or discretion on the part of National Insurance staff, for there is little scope for either. Rather, it lies in the ability of the system's closely-specified, written rules to take account of small graduations of difference in individual clients' affairs. This is evident in the wide array of circumstances which may bear on the amount of benefit payable for any particular claim. The discussion has not been long enough to cite all of these conditions, but it is clear that dependency status, age, and above all the fine details of contribution history all figure in the decision-making on benefits as they are awarded by local office staff. Such subtlety is none the less significant for being prescribed by well-developed, written rules, and perhaps even the more impressive for being virtually uniform in application throughout such a massive organization.

Before leaving the matter of extensiveness of information held, however, it is important to recall the points at which available information is not extensive enough for certain purposes. For the discussion has emphasized a number of purposes, such as the contravention of benefit fraud, where more data would clearly be useful. But National Insurance files generally do not contain the kind of material which can show definitively, for example, whether a widow is really a widow in the sense intended by Department regulations. Likewise, none of the information held in local office files provides grounds for certainty that dependency claims are valid as presented. So, although National Insurance files may be extensive by comparison to those of other systems, they would considerably facilitate the task of social control if they held more.

The second broad criterion of capacity is *centralization* of information, and here National Insurance is also strong. The location of the crucial core of information in Newcastle and the necessity of consulting this information whenever it can possibly bear on a decision, makes it virtually impossible for persons to evade the effects of social control by fleeing from their records. Action on past delinquencies can and does come to bear whenever someone previously out of touch with the system again makes his whereabouts known. Very rarely, some of my interlocutors have told me, a claimant will manage to take advantage of the system by making an urgent but fraudulent claim for benefits at a local office other than the one where his records are stored. But the prescribed practice of contacting Newcastle and awaiting the transmission of such records before allowing benefits generally prevents this. Over-all, the division of responsibility between central and local record-keeping operations seems to combine the advantages of centralization with many of those of ready local access to pertinent data.

With respect to the *speed of information flow and decision-making*, National Insurance presents a highly mixed picture. In one sense the flow of information on contributions *into* the system is slow, in that more than a year may elapse between the purchase of a contribution and the point where it becomes useful as a basis for decision-making. On the other hand, the system assimilates other information quite rapidly. It obtains data directly from the central registry of births, deaths and marriages, for example, within three or four days of the time of request. And clients themselves may very quickly provide necessary supporting information for the payment of claims. Then, too, the movement of information within the system can be quite rapid. Shuttle card inquiries to Newcastle usually yield a response to the local office within three or four working days. Once at Records Branch, the shuttle card is most often completed with the relevant information on the day of receipt. In urgent cases, Records Branch responds to local office inquiries by telephone and telex; although such urgency is exceptional, Records Branch did transmit some 38,500 such messages in 1970. Over-all, in so far as such judgements are possible, the speed of information flow and decision-making within National

Insurance appears at least comparable to that in the police criminal records system, and generally more rapid than that in the locally organized form of the vehicle and driver licensing system.

In terms of the *points of contact* between system and clientele, National Insurance again presents a mixture of strengths and weaknesses. The system certainly has a very strong hold over its clients through the contribution system. Very few manage to avoid registration altogether, and registration provides an efficient means of monitoring compliance with the contribution condition. Perhaps more important, the registration of the great majority of the clientele in Class I effectively places these people's employers in the role of agents of social control on behalf of the system. This means that the employer not only provides information to the system about its clients but also enforces compliance with the rules themselves, by requiring the purchase of stamps. Discussion has shown the enormous advantages which this yields to the system by comparison to the difficulties entailed in enforcement of contribution compliance on the part of Class II and Class III contributors.

But there are few other points where the staging of social control is so favourable to the system as in the case of Class I contributors. Elsewhere, unless the individual voluntarily places himself in contact with the system, the means of locating and sanctioning him are generally weak. Sometimes the police may provide information on the whereabouts of those sought by local office inspectors, and sometimes National Insurance files themselves may provide current addresses which suffice. But those who energetically attempt to remain out of contact with the system generally stand a good chance of doing so. Still, the discussion has stressed that anyone who attempts such evasion pays a considerable price – including the avoidance of any employment in the Class I category and the renunciation of all National Insurance benefits. For any contact with the system for any purpose activates the mechanisms of social control and brings the full weight of the client's record to bear in the system's actions towards him.

Finally, how strong are the means of *positive identification* of clients? In this connection, as elsewhere, the system profits from exercising a measure of deliberation over its decisions; benefits need not be paid until decision-makers can be certain of the identity of the claimant. Presentation of the National Insurance number speeds recourse to the relevant record sheet, but the same end can be accomplished in most cases through a day's extra work by the staff of the alphabetical index at Records Branch. In about one seventh of all cases, the staff of the alphabetical index must refer back to the local office for further identifying information on the client, such as the place of initial registration within the system. Usually this is the most energetic measure necessary to establish identity. Occasionally, it is discovered that a single contributor has been registered more than once, something probably most likely to happen in the case of women who, on divorce, change their names and re-enter the labour force. Then, too, it may theoretically be possible to defraud the system by claiming benefit on someone else's record. But the checks against such fraud, in terms of the necessity of presenting supporting documents for most benefits, and the likelihood of contradictory claims or contributions from the authentic holder of the record, make this possibility quite remote. Thus, though the system of identification here may not be foolproof in quite the sense of the police criminal record system, the wealth of identifying information in its files makes it fairly strong. No statistics exist, but it is difficult to believe that losses to the system through mistaken identity are at all significant.

Again, the enormous disparities between the capacity of this system and that of a system of total surveillance are obvious. But the main usefulness of that abstract *absolute* standard is to provide a handy reckoning of the *relative* strengths and weaknesses of concrete, existing organizations. By comparisons to other systems of surveillance and control, National Insurance is notably strong in a number of respects. Specifically, its ability to remain in relatively close touch with such an immense clientele, and at the same time to carry out finely-nuanced decision-making geared to small details of their circumstances, has no equivalent in the systems studied in the preceding two chapters. These accomplishments are all the more remarkable when one realizes that participation in National Insurance is not voluntary, but must itself be enforced. On the other hand, the discussion has detailed a number of points where the ability of National Insurance to carry out tasks set for it remains uncertain. For the most part, these are points at which the *staging* of social control is particularly problematic, where the behaviours or facts under surveillance are especially subject to concealment or where the system lacks means of contacting delinquent clients.

This citation of the relative strengths and weaknesses of National Insurance surveillance could continue at some length. The most significant point to be drawn from this discussion, however, and from that of the other cases presented here is not just what these systems can and cannot accomplish in terms of social control. Even more important is an understanding of the causes of such strengths and weaknesses. What aspects of the organization of the system, what problems in the staging of control help or hinder the system in accomplishing its goals? In this light, I hope that the present discussion has provided some insights not only into what National Insurance can and can not accomplish, but also into the sociological roots of these capabilities.

THE DEVELOPMENT OF THIS RESEARCH

Unlike any of the other case studies, this one derives its material exclusively from a single organization. This fact made the cooperation of the Department of Health and Social Security essential. One of the first steps in initiating the study was a series of meetings with Department officials, in which I explained my objectives and sought permission to make the inquiries which I desired. The Department in turn provided not only permission to go ahead, but also extensive assistance and advice, on the basis of an agreement that the final version of the chapter would be subject to official review and comment before going to press. This understanding stopped short of granting veto power over the content of the chapter, but assumed a willingness on both sides to discuss the final text in detail before publication.

Once this agreement was complete, I enjoyed considerable freedom in my work; with very few exceptions, neither persons nor topics seemed 'off limits' to my inquiries. As in the other case studies, interviews and observations represented much the most important sources of information, but documents and statistics from the Department were also indispensable. In all, I visited six different locations: Headquarters in London; two local National Insurance offices; one Area Office, dealing with Supplementary Benefits; one regional office, and the Central Office at Newcastle-upon-Tyne. Some of these places I visited only once, whereas I returned to others time after time. Interviews began in April 1970, and the exchange of information continued until January 1972, when the manuscript was finally completed. During some of this period National Insurance research represented my main preoccupation; at other times months went by without much contact with the Department. It is impossible to cite any meaningful total number of interviews, since my visits to Department offices ranged between quick meetings of only ten or fifteen minutes and marathon sessions lasting two working days and involving conversations with dozens of persons. It might be useful to note, however, that my card-file of names and addresses of contacts within the system finally came to include thirty entries. These persons tended to be ones with whom I had worked especially closely, and I am sure that the total number of persons with whom I spoke during the period of the research was at least twice that figure. Again, these encounters included everything from brief conversations to lengthy interviews with persons to whom I returned again and again. As for other communications, my file of correspondence with Department officials came to number about seventy letters sent and received during the course of the research.

In August 1971 I forwarded to Headquarters in London a working draft of the present chapter. Reactions ran from criticism of certain factual errors to chagrin that certain information not intended for public consumption had found its way into the text. Even the basic friendliness of the Department officials to this research did not override their deep instincts of candour in clarifying the official position on these matters, and a lively exchange of views ensued. Through a process of give-and-take, the final version of the chapter evolved in a form acceptable both to the Department and to me. In some instances I agreed to modify statements considered to give an excessively detailed view of the workings of National Insurance, in cases where these modifications did not vitiate presentation of the main ideas of the chapter. More importantly, to me, discussion of the draft chapter made it possible to correct certain factual errors which otherwise would have flawed the final version. In this version, then, factual statements have received review, and, where necessary, correction by Department officials, while responsibility for statements of opinion or interpretation rests with me. A few points of discrepancy between official view and my own are noted as such in the text.

For any agency whose activities are controversial or sensitive, the presence of an outside investigator working within the boundaries of the organization is bound to be trying. So far as I am concerned, it is morally and politically imperative that any organization financed by public monies or dealing with personal information on members of the public remain open to careful and competent research. Nevertheless, the strains involved in allowing such research are obvious and inevitable. Therefore I should like to extend my warmest and most sincere thanks to the Department and all of its members who provided such extensive help under demanding circumstances. I have in mind both the officials at all levels who spent hours and days explaining their work to me, and those who provided such careful and painstaking attention to the drafts of this chapter. The number of persons involved makes it impossible to mention them all by name. But Mr Douglas Whiting of Headquarters deserves some special recognition for seeing the research through from start to finish with impeccable conscientiousness and diplomacy.

5

Consumer Credit Reporting in America

This chapter and Chapter 6 mark a departure from the pre-
ceeding three case studies, in that they deal with organizations
which are neither British nor agencies of the state. The present
chapter concerns itself with surveillance over private persons'
use of consumer credit in the United States. Specifically, it
deals with the activities of credit bureaus, organizations which
specialize in collecting, storing and selling information on
persons' willingness and ability to honour consumer debts.
Although credit bureaus are now extending their operations to
Britain and other consumer-oriented industrial societies, their
activities are nowhere so extensive and their techniques nowhere so sophisticated as in the United States.

This change in national context and in the relationship
between surveillance systems and the state should not disturb
the momentum of the study. The subject here, after all, is
neither any specific state, nor the activities of the state agencies
in general. Rather it is the *genre* of social processes designated
as mass surveillance and control, and their place in advanced
industrial societies. All such societies seem to nurture the conditions giving rise to systems of mass surveillance – the need
for large, bureaucratic agencies to collect information on mass
clienteles, in order to make discriminating, forceful decisions
about individual clients. And these needs are by no means only
felt by the state, although the state is probably bound to be the
largest agent of surveillance.

The systems studied in this and the following chapter have
been chosen not because they are American, nor because they
are 'private' institutions, but because they represent well-
developed, authentic instances of the phenomenon under

study. Nevertheless, the use of material on a second society, and from private organizations within that society, will emphasize the similarities in the processes and structures of surveillance systems, regardless of differences in context. Indeed, looking beyond the more superficial differences, it will be clear that the organization and working of the consumer credit reporting industry bears more similarities to that of the British driver and vehicle licensing system, in its old form, than the latter does to the two other British systems. And at the same time, the study of the American systems should underscore the similarities in the social forces conducing to the growth of surveillance systems in general. For the growth of these two systems, as surely as that of the British systems, stems from broader changes in the *scale* of social relations in modern industrial societies.

Chapters 5 and 6, then, actually represent a pair. Both deal with aspects of consumer credit surveillance in America. This chapter deals with the industry itself, with the system of reporting information on private consumers' credit status to merchants and lenders for use in extending credit. The following chapter, on the BankAmericard system, deals with the use of information in a much more highly focused setting of a single organization. Together, these two studies should provide a portrait of some broad patterns of change from the relatively loose and inefficient practices of the conventional credit bureau industry to the development – in the more modern aspects of this industry and in the BankAmericard system – of some of the most sophisticated surveillance practices encountered in this study.

The Industry and the Firm: Organization

As with the other case studies, the concern here is the whole of a single system of surveillance and control. In this case, that system entails somewhat more than the credit reporting industry alone. For, as in the relations between the British police and the courts, the 'consumers' of the information generated by this industry stand outside the organizations which 'produce' it. Just as the courts represent the final destination, for many purposes, of criminal record information, it is credit *grantors* who finally use credit reports for authoritative decision-making. Therefore, though the organization and workings of the credit reporting industry will claim most attention here, it will also be indispensable to note the ultimate use of credit reports once they have crossed the organizational boundaries of that industry.

Following the pattern of previous chapters, this section deals with questions of organization. A complicating factor here is that the credit reporting industry itself is not a single organization, but a congeries of organizations under autonomous direction, which nevertheless cooperate to form an interlocking system of information flow. The first portion of this section, then, will deal with the structure of the industry as a whole, whereas the following portions will take up the organization of individual credit bureaus and of their files.

The Industry

The *clientele* of the consumer credit reporting industry are, of course, the general public of consumers – indeed virtually everyone in America who borrows money for personal purposes or who buys 'on credit'. But the *customers* of the industry are mainly credit-granting firms. It is these firms – lending institutions, credit card companies, department stores, auto agencies, and so on – who purchase information on individual consumers from their local credit bureaus. Credit bureaus, in nearly every case, are profit-making firms in their own right, whose revenue derives from the sale of such information to other businesses. When credit grantors must decide whether to extend credit to a new customer, they almost always purchase a report on the latter. A favourable credit report will always be a necessary, and sometimes even a sufficient, condition for granting credit.

The growth of the credit reporting industry to its unique state of development in America has been a direct result of the unprecedented growth of consumer debt itself. Consumer debt, as the term is generally used, refers to debts contracted by the purchase of goods and services 'in credit', and to those stemming from consumer loans. The reliance on consumer credit is not so much a luxury as a necessity for many North

American families. Whereas the business of contracting a debt for consumer expenditures was once marked with an unfavourable moral taint, reliance on credit is now nearly universal among all but the poorest American consumers. Lacking cash-in-hand for the purchase of a car, television set or new home, many American families would find the expenditures necessary to obtain these 'essential' items beyond their reach, were it not for consumer credit.

The American business community have not failed to benefit from the growth of credit buying, although many firms were remarkably slow to realize the potential profits which it represented. For most firms extend consumer credit at considerable rates of interest, either identified as such or as a 'service charge' on credit accounts. It is not unusual for a grantor of consumer credit to charge a rate of two and a half per cent per month on the unpaid balance of account, which of course amounts to thirty per cent per annum. Among all retail firms, one and a half per cent per month is probably closer to the mean rate, however. For most firms extending consumer credit on merchandise, the interest charged merely covers the costs of extending credit, and the purpose of the credit programme itself is the stimulation of sales. But some very large retail merchants are said to realize more profits from extending credit on their merchandise than from the sale of merchandise itself.

The extension of credit, however, does not yield these high profits automatically. An element of risk – risk that the buyer or borrower will not, in the end, make good by paying his debt – is inherent, and any consumer credit system rapidly becomes unprofitable when the rates of default become great. For very many consumer credit transactions, the costs of taking punitive action against a delinquent account holder, either through legal constraints upon him to pay or through repossession of merchandise, are too great to warrant such steps. This is not the case with very large purchases like cars or houses, but even there the costs of default generally wipe out any profits from the transaction. Thus the art and science of credit management lie in determining, in advance, who will pay and who will not, and in screening credit applicants accordingly. This is of course a problem of social control.

Perhaps even more than the systems studied in the preceding chapters, this one works through *prevention* of default rather than through *coercion* of those who misbehave. Credit reporting serves partly to punish those who fail to pay their debts, but more to prevent this sort of 'misbehaviour' in the first place, that is, to exclude would-be delinquents from the opportunity to disobey the rules. As in other systems, the decision as to whether a person is to be accorded the privilege in question turns on his past record of credit information. But the consumer credit system is different from many other systems in that it more often involves highly interpretive decision-making not only about what the person has done in the past, but also about what he is *liable* to do in the future.

All credit grantors – whether merchants, lending institutions, credit card firms or whoever – maintain some more or less consistent policy over deciding to whom they grant credit privileges. In the largest, most bureaucratic firms these policies may be the subject of highly detailed written rules; in tiny firms, they more likely represent nothing more than *ad hoc* practices observed as the occasion arises. Although virtually all such procedures involve the purchase of credit reports, the use made of these reports, and especially the weight attached to various items of information found there, varies enormously from firm to firm.

The source of these reports is the local credit bureau. North America is blanketed with bureaus, with one in virtually every community or metropolitan area with sufficient credit business to generate demand for the reports. It is very difficult to give a figure representing more than an educated guess on the matter, but it is probably reasonable to say that a population of approximately ten thousand is the minimum necessary to generate this much business. No precise statistics are kept on the number of bureaus in the United States, but the Associated Credit Bureaus, Inc., the trade association representing the great majority of firms, reports a membership of 2,053 in 1971. Probably there are not more than two hundred unaffiliated operations. Bureaus range from tiny one-man offices to giant operations employing more than five hundred. The size of the firm is almost precisely correlated to the size of the communities which they serve; the largest bureaus are those centred in the largest metropolitan areas, and the smallest those in more sparsely populated regions.

The origins of the credit reporting industry are even less well documented than the present number and activity of its members. According to the Associated Credit Bureaus, the first known consumer credit reporting agency in the United States started in New York in 1869. The number of bureaus grew slowly until early in the present century. After that, in the words of an Association spokesman, 'As communities grew in population, mobility increased, and dealings with customers became less personal, the pressure of bad debts resulting from poor credit forced merchants [to rely more and more on the services of bureaus].' Table 10 shows the growth in the number of member bureaus of the Associated Credit Bureaus and its predecessor organizations; it may be taken as an indication of the rate of growth of the industry as a whole.

Table 10. *Membership of ACB and Predecessor Organizations*

Year	Number of Member Bureaus
1924	267
1927	800
1948	1,453
1958	1,893
1965	2,038
1971	2,053

Source: Associated Credit Bureaus, Inc.

The first bureaus, as far as one can determine, were little more than central listings of persons who had defaulted in credit accounts with retail stores. Various firms within a single city would develop and refer to such lists in screening applications for credit, in hopes of avoiding the replication of another firm's mistake. Soon these informal blacklisting systems coalesced into separate organizations, usually owned by the large retail merchants who had initiated them. The pattern of ownership of credit bureaus by the larger merchants who make up their most important customers, incidentally, has continued down to the present in many large cities. As the industry developed, the forms of information collected became more varied, and the services offered by bureaus came to be used by a wider and wider circle of credit grantors. Originally characteristic only of large cities, credit bureaus gradually extended their presence to less and less urban settings. In 1966, the Associated Credit Bureaus reported that seventy-seven per cent of its member bureaus were in localities of 25,000 or less; most of these bureaus, of course, are bound to be quite small in number of staff and of reports issued.

All but a small handful of all credit bureaus are local in their operations. That is, they collect information on persons from a single, well-defined area, and disseminate it primarily within that area. In the case of the newest firm in the business, an insurgent company relying on computer methods for storage and retrieval of information, these areas of coverage make up large regions of the country, but the principle remains the same. Until very recently the consumer credit reporting industry has generally been distributed in fairly small local monopolies, with each bureau serving its local area and avoiding encroachment on the reporting jurisdictions of other bureaus.

Perhaps the most important statistics on the over-all impact of credit bureaus have to do with the total numbers of files maintained and credit reports issued. Because of the lack of centralized accounting, resulting from the highly dispersed structure of the industry, this information, too, is unavailable in precise form. TRW Credit Data Corporation, the computerized newcomer to the business, reports that it maintains files on some thirty million Americans, and issued eleven million reports during 1971. On a more conjectural level, experienced officials of the Associated Credit Bureaus estimate that their member bureaus, among which TRW Credit Data is not included, maintain perhaps one hundred millions of files, and issue approximately that number of reports yearly. These latter figures are more problematic, in that, besides representing educated guesswork, many of the total of files will be inactive or duplicated among bureaus.

Still, the point is clear: probably the majority of American adults have credit information recorded about them, either in their own names or under those of their spouses. The likelihood of one's being covered is by no means random, however, but is associated with one's place in the social structure. Young persons, for example, who have never made any credit purchases in their own right are unlikely to have a file, although their names may be listed in their parents' dossier. The poor – as distinct from the stable working classes – are less likely to be depicted in credit files, as they are less likely to be in a position to make credit transactions – although some firms, often quite disreputable ones, specialize in instalment selling to the poor. On the other hand, it is difficult to see how a married couple of moderate means, a growing family and a 'normal' American life-style could avoid accumulating a credit file, or how they could manage to go for as long as a year without causing a report to be drawn from that file.

Besides issuing reports relating to private consumers' credit standing, many credit bureaus also engage in one or more related activities. Many bureaus, for example, also specialize in the collection of bad debts. Some bureaus, too, engage in investigative reporting, the preparation of reports on persons being screened for employment, for an insurance policy or for rental occupancy of a house or apartment. These latter forms of reporting are much more detailed and wide-ranging in their concerns than are credit reports; investigative reports tend to centre on the subject's consumption habits, morals, style of life and other especially sensitive areas. Such information is solicited from friends, neighbours and work associates of the applicant. There are two firms which specialize in this form of reporting, Hooper-Holmes of New Jersey and Retail Credit Company of Georgia, and these two do relatively little in the way of credit reporting in the sense described in this chapter. But some other credit bureaus also offer this service, even though most of their volume is in reports on credit. This chapter will have rather little to say about investigative reporting, which takes place outside the main patterns of information flow concerning credit. It is worth noting, however, that information generated in these reports does sometimes make its way into credit files, and that information on character, health or life-style may be included in some bureaus' credit report if the issuing bureau, or the buyer of the report, deems it relevant to the decision involved.

The Firm

The task of providing a composite portrait of the 'typical' credit bureau is not an easy one. Twenty-two hundred separate organizations, varying widely in size, technology and regional context, represent a difficult subject-matter for generalization. Still there is no way of making sense of the whole without offering some summary statements, and common objectives and working constraints have brought about a considerable degree of similarity in internal operations of even the most outwardly different bureaus.

For example, with the two exceptions mentioned above, every bureau will confine itself to a well-delineated geographical area of reporting. This means, first, that those depicted in the bureau's files will be overwhelmingly persons who reside or carry out their trade or litigation within the area covered by the bureau. Secondly, it will mean that the main customers of the bureau are credit-granting firms located primarily within the same area. Bureaus in fact sell their reports to any firm with a 'legitimate' interest in someone's credit standing, which means in practice virtually any firm willing to profess such an interest. But the firms who require reports on a regular basis from any bureau always tend to be local firms. And as a sub-category of bureau customers, there will be a group of 'members' of the bureau, all but certain to be located within the area of reportage. The members will be credit grantors who use the services of the bureau especially regularly, paying an annual membership fee to the bureau in exchange for pre-ferential service, including lower prices for reports. The members of the bureau, besides being 'consumers' of its infor-mation, also enter into an agreement with the bureau to provide information on their own credit accounts for inclusion in bureau files.

The visitor to virtually any credit bureau, moreover, encoun-ters much the same spatial organization of work. Nearly every bureau organizes its work, both literally and figuratively, around one comprehensive file of credit information. The main focus of activity will be a single large room, and the most prominent feature of the room the files themselves. These will consist of drawerful after drawerful of cards, folders or large envelopes, arranged alphabetically according to the surname of the person depicted in them. These files represent the bureau's major capital investment, accumulated not only at considerable expense, but also over considerable time. The files are in a sense the 'raw materials' from which credit reports are 'manufactured' for sale. The manufacture of such reports, however, does not deplete the files, but actually enriches them.

Bureaus differ considerably with respect to the amount and kind of information maintained in the files. There is, however, a core of data which nearly all bureaus *seek* to file whenever they can. The subject's name and date of birth will be listed as fully as possible, for example, in an effort to secure positive identification. Most bureaus also desire to include: the subject's occupation; place of employment and duration of time at that employment; in many cases, there will be similar information for previous employments, as well. Likewise, current address will almost always be listed, often with the length of time at this address, and perhaps former addresses and durations of residence there. Subject's salary, perhaps that of his spouse, and their previous salaries are also apt to be found.* It is also very common for bureaus to seek information on family status, including the spouse's name, date of marriage, number of children, and record of any previous marriages of either. In general, credit bureaus compile information on families as single consumption units, so that data on husband and wife will be filed together. Finally, all bureaus seek to list certain information on litigation involving the subject: records of lax liens, lawsuits, and, above all, bankruptcy.

It may have struck the reader that none of the information just cited is 'credit' information, that none of it represents record of credit transactions as such. Nevertheless, the data

---

* An important exception in some of these respects is TRW Credit Data, a leading computerized firm, which declines to record certain information on matters other than credit accounts including that on salaries and employment.

just cited are indispensable, and sometimes more important to the ultimate credit decision than record of credit accounts. But credit account information is of course also present. The bureau will list records of accounts which the subject has held, both loans and purchases, showing how much credit was outstanding, over what period it was repaid, and noting how promptly and how fully the payment took place.

It would be highly misleading to leave the reader with the impression that every file in every bureau contains all of this information. The opposite is the case; only a small minority of all credit bureau files will comprise elements of all the varieties of information just mentioned. Many files, in fact, are opened with only a single scrap of information, though they usually accumulate more data with the passage of time. The preceding list, however, represents a core of information that nearly all bureaus would probably regard as desirable and relevant for inclusion in files, information which all bureaus would file if it came to their attention, and which most credit grantors would regard as pertinent to their decision-making. Indeed, data of these kinds probably represent the great majority of entries in all credit files. But bureaus are free to enter additional materials in their files at will, and many do also include a variety of other information. An example of a credit file, referring to a fictitious consumer, appears on pages 186–7.

From these files, the bureau draws up reports of a number of different kinds. In a minority of instances, these reports relate to the subject's search for a job or a place to live, or his application for an insurance policy; but mainly they have to do with credit-worthiness. Even here, however, there are differences, in that reports are drawn up in many gradations of detail, according to the nature of the pending credit transaction and the quality of the data already contained in bureau files at the time of the request.

The simplest, and probably also the commonest form of credit report is the 'in-file' report consisting, as one might imagine, only of data already held by the bureau in its files. Most bureaus at this writing probably charge their members about $1 to $1.50 for these reports. Credit grantors normally

NAME AND ADDRESS OF CREDIT BUREAU MAKING REPORT

☐ SUMMARY REPORT ☐ SINGLE REFERENCE ☐ TRADE REPORT
☐ SHORT REPORT ☒ FULL REPORT ☐ PREV. RES. REPORT

Gainesville Credit Bureau
117½ Distand Street P.O. Box 708
Gainesville, Idaho

DATE RECEIVED	DATE MAILED	CBR REPORT NO.
1-2-72	1-4-72	#1

DATE TRADE CLEARED	DATE EMPLOY VERIFIED	INCOME VERIFIED
1-4-72	1-4-72	☒ YES ☐ NO

CONFIDENTIAL *Factbilt®* REPORT FOR Ampex Department Store

IN FILE SINCE: 1962

This information is furnished in response to an inquiry for the purpose of evaluating credit risks. It has been obtained from sources deemed reliable, the accuracy of which this organization does not guarantee. The inquirer has agreed to indemnify the reporting bureau for any damage arising from misuse of this information, and this report is furnished in reliance upon that indemnity. It must be held in strict confidence, and must not be revealed to the subject reported on.

REPORT ON (SURNAME):	MR., MRS., MISS:	GIVEN NAME:	SOCIAL SECURITY NUMBER:	SPOUSE'S NAME:
DOE:	Mr.	John Andy	254-52-6271	Susie P Jones

ADDRESS:	CITY:	STATE:	ZIP CODE:	SPOUSE'S SOCIAL SECURITY NO.:
1144 Riverside Terrace, N. W.	Gainesville, Idaho		30504	254-54-5454

COMPLETE TO HERE FOR TRADE REPORT AND SKIP TO CREDIT HISTORY

PRESENT EMPLOYER AND KIND OF BUSINESS:	POSITION HELD:	SINCE:	MONTHLY INCOME:
Sloan Paper Company	Salesman	8-7-62	$1,000. salary

COMPLETE TO HERE FOR SHORT REPORT AND SUMMARY REPORT AND SKIP TO CREDIT HISTORY

DATE OF BIRTH:	NUMBER OF DEPENDENTS INCLUDING SPOUSE		
4-3-40	→ Wife & 2	☒ OWNS OR BUYING HOME	☐ RENTS HOME

FORMER ADDRESS:	CITY:	STATE:	FROM:	TO:
982 Maple Drive,	Athens,	Georgia	1958	1962

FORMER EMPLOYER AND KIND OF BUSINESS:	POSITION HELD:	FROM:	TO:	MONTHLY INCOME:
Student in School at Alps University	Student	1958	1962	$

SPOUSE'S EMPLOYER AND KIND OF BUSINESS:	POSITION HELD:	SINCE:	MONTHLY INCOME:
Coggins Department Store	Secretary	1963	$ 650.month

CREDIT HISTORY (Complete this section for all reports)

KIND OF BUSINESS	DATE ACCOUNT OPENED	DATE OF LAST SALE	HIGHEST CREDIT	AMOUNT OWING	AMOUNT PAST DUE	TERMS OF SALE AND USUAL MANNER OF PAYMENT
B 101	1958	1-71	$3285.	1586.	0	I-100.-1
	Subject maintains 4 figure checking account .					
C 92	1-71	12-71	105.	92.	0	R-45.-1
H 11	12-71	12-71	18.	18.	0	I-5. -0
A 13	1965	4-71	116.	45.	0	R-10.-2
B 158	1-9-69	1-9-69	11,000.	5,462.	0	I-118.-1

INDICATE IF FILE CONTAINS

☒ Items of Public Record   ☒ Any record of accounts placed for collection   ☒ Any reports received from other Credit Bureaus

IF ANY OF THE ABOVE ARE CHECKED, GIVE DETAILS

Details on page #2.

John Andy Doe, is a native of Gainesville, Idaho. Since 8-7-62 subject has been employed with Sloan Paper Company as salesman. Prior to his present position he was student at Alps College, Athens, Georgia where he graduated with degree in Business. Administration. Wife supplements income employed with Coggins Department Store as secretary.

AFFILIATED WITH   PRINTED IN U.S.A.

 Form 100 Associated Credit Bureaus, Inc. *CREDIT BUREAU REPORTS* inc

GAINESVILLE CREDIT EXCHANGE
CREDIT BUREAU OF GAINESVILLE
117½ N. Bradford St., P. O. Box 376
Gainesville, Georgia 30501
Telephone: 534-5361 (404)

**SPECIAL NARRATIVE
OR SUPPLEMENTAL
REPORT**

DATE RECEIVED	DATE MAILED	IN FILE SINCE:
1-2-72	1-4-72	1962

CONFIDENTIAL *Factbilt*® REPORT   FOR

Ampex Department Store

This information is furnished in response to an inquiry for the purpose of evaluating credit risks. It has been obtained from sources deemed reliable, the accuracy of which this organization does not guarantee. The inquirer has agreed to indemnify the reporting bureau for any damage arising from misuse of this information, and this report is furnished in reliance upon that indemnity. It must be held in strict confidence, and must not be revealed to the subject reported on.

REPORT ON (SURNAME):	MR., MRS., MISS: GIVEN NAME:	SOCIAL SECURITY NUMBER:	SPOUSE'S NAME:
DOE:	Mr. John Andy	254-52-6271	Susie P. Jones

ADDRESS:	CITY:	STATE:	ZIP CODE:	SPOUSE'S SOCIAL SECURITY NO.:
1144 Riverside Terrace, N. W.	Gainesville,	Idaho	30504	254-54-5454

COLLECTION ACCOUNTS:

For'd 5-6-68 by Dr. Alp Anderson $115. unpaid.
For'd 8-9-69 by Jones Phcy. $82. paid 9-69.

COURT RECORD:

8-6-69 Bankruptcy Petition Case # 8645 filed by John A. Doe 1144 Riverside Terrace, N. W. Gainesville, Idaho; Assets 835. Liabilities 11,845. Discharged 4-71.

8-7-69 Tom's Bait Shop vs John Andy Doe suit on account 85.00 still outstanding.
8-1-69 June Dress Shop vs Mrs. John Andy Doe, garnishment 25.00 paid 8-69.

MORTGAGE RECORD:

1-8-71 Doe, John Andy to First National Bank , 1971 Buick, $3285.
1-9-69 Doe, John Andy to Anderson Bank and Trust , 11,000. Tract Glade District , security deed.
1-9-69 Tippett, Mary conveyed to John Andy Doe , Tract Glade District.

7. These two sheets are a credit report on a plausible but thoroughly fictitious American consumer. This report contains somewhat more information than most credit reports, but the kinds of data which it contains are entirely representative. The entries on the first sheet under 'kinds of business' and 'terms of sale and usual manner of payment' are in a code standard to the industry.

request these reports over the telephone in connection with relatively small purchases. In these cases the buyer of the report usually seeks to make the sale immediately, before the customer has a chance to leave the store and possibly reconsider the transaction. If the contemplated transaction is more substantial, or if the information in the bureau's files proves too sparse or dated, the credit grantor may request an 'up-dated' report, for which the bureau carries out additional research. These reports may take several days to prepare, and they cost commensurately more than in-file reports. The credit grantor usually sends the credit application itself, as completed by the applicant, to the bureau as a basis for its inquiries. Usually, the bureau issues these reports in writing. These 'up-dated' reports themselves vary considerably according to the detail of information and the thoroughness of the search desired, and according to the purposes for which the report is being drawn. Reports in connection with mortgages, the largest consumer credit transactions, may run to several pages of closely-spaced typescript, require a week to prepare, and cost up to thirty dollars.

Information Flow and Decision-making

So much for matters of organization. The effectiveness of any surveillance system rests on its ability to make the appropriate data available in the right place at the right time. How, then, does the consumer credit reporting industry manage to collect, store and disseminate information so as to allow for discriminating decision-making on the people depicted in its files?

Intake of Information and Creation of Files

In reviewing the passage of information through the credit reporting system, it is perhaps best to begin at the point where credit files first come into existence. In so doing, however, it will also be necessary to introduce the entire range of information flow into credit files. For the intakes of information which give rise to the creation of new files are in most cases the routine points of addition of information to existing files, as well.

Perhaps the most frequent occasion for the creation of a credit file is the bureau's receipt of a request for information on someone not already depicted in its records. If the request is simply for an 'in file' report, the bureau will merely reply that the particular name has no file, and the matter may end there. If, however, the customer persists or wants a written report, the bureau will take the opportunity to open and develop a new file. It will usually obtain information from the credit application completed by the consumer, and use this as the basis for an investigation. An important by-product of this investigation, of course, will be the opening of a file in the bureau on the person in question.

Credit applications vary in the amount of information which they seek, according to the importance of the credit sought and the other requirements of the credit grantor. Most, however, seek at least the following information: name; date of birth; address, and length of time at the address; occupation, place of work, and length of time at the job; income; family status; and the names of other firms with whom credit accounts are or have been held. These data, of course, represent much of the same basic information which credit bureaus wish routinely to maintain in their files, and so the bureau makes its task first to verify the information, insofar as necessary, and then to commit it to its files. Many bureaus would probably take the information on address, age, and marital status as read, and avoid verifying it unless there were some special reason for doubt. Some bureaus, however, would routinely check even this information. Other information will be checked more predictably. The bureau will first of all telephone the employer listed on the application, identify itself, and ask whether the applicant is indeed employed in the position he has listed. The bureau will then ask whether the salary figure is correct. Most employers are accustomed to answering such inquiries, and some in fact provide salary and other information on request, without even determining the identity of the caller. The bureau will also be at pains to verify time on the job, and may even request that the employer verify the applicant's previous employer, as well. Practices vary among credit bureaus, of course, and employers vary in terms of their willingness to disclose information – which their employees generally do not realize is being released, anyway. But most employers are accustomed to inquiries of this kind, and those who decline categorically to provide these data are few.

The second broad category of checks made by bureaus in preparing 'up-dated' reports have to do with the subject's financial and credit standing *per se*. The most important of these checks will be with the firms with which the applicant currently holds or has in the past held credit accounts, as listed on the credit application. The bureau will contact these firms by telephone, wanting to know whether the account did in fact exist, the period during which it was open, the 'high balance' or largest amount ever owed, and above all, the fullness and promptness of payment. All this information will be recorded, both in the bureau's files and subsequently in the credit report. In some cases, the bureau will note verbal descriptions of the way in which the account was paid, for example, 'slow but good', meaning that payments were late but ultimately forthcoming, or 'paid as agreed'. Elsewhere, this information will be entered in terse code.

Depending on the thoroughness of the bureau and the intensiveness of investigation demanded by the credit grantor, the inquiries may go considerably farther than this. In some instances, the bureau will ask the creditors listed on the credit application for the names of other creditors as provided to them by the consumer at the time of his previous application. The bureau, in turn, will contact these firms and obtain the relevant account information from them. Elsewhere, if the applicant appears to have no credit history at all, the bureau may attempt to contact his landlord, or the billing departments of the public utilities which serve his home, to determine how well he has paid his debts there.

It is also common for credit bureaus, in the process of developing detail on a given credit applicant, to telephone their member businesses to inquire whether they have had credit experience with him; if so, information is collected in much the same way as from creditors listed on the credit application. Many bureaus also contact the applicant's bank, as listed in the credit application, to determine the approximate range of his current and recent balances and to inquire whether his checking account has shown overdrafts. All of this information, too, goes both to bureau files and to the report in preparation. Some bureaus carry their inquiries even farther and telephone or visit the applicant's neighbours, to ask about life-style, consumption habits and financial stability. These latter practices, however, serve mainly not for reports on consumer credit status, but for those in connection with screening for employment or insurance.

How, the reader may wonder, does the bureau manage to obtain all these data? The answer is that the persons and institutions possessing it give it freely, and free of charge. I have already pointed out that most employers have no reservations about the provision of data required from them, even when it includes the applicant's salary. They assume, usually correctly, that the applicant has filled out a credit application which lists certain personal data and authorized verification of their authenticity. Similarly, firms holding information on credit accounts generally feel little reluctance in providing these data to callers who identify themselves as representing a credit bureau. For one thing, these firms realize that they, themselves, may need the bureau's services in the course of their work; for another, they assume – again, often justly – that the inquiry stems from the applicant's own request. Banks are more likely than employers to demur about requests for information without written authorization from the individual. But here the picture is mixed, and many banks in America are no less open than employers or credit-granting firms. Part of the technique of credit bureau operation involves the cultivation of an 'authentic', authoritative way of making these inquiries, and my own acquaintance with credit bureau personnel has left me with the impression that the discretion of others does not represent much of an obstacle to their research.

It is very common, of course, for bureaus to receive requests for reports on persons whose names already appear in files. If the request calls for 'up-dating' of information already in file, the bureau will use this as an opportunity to enrich its store of information. Obtaining the credit application, the bureau will check the information in it against what it already has in file, bringing the latter up to date with respect to employment, family status, residence, and credit and financial standing. Most of this information, however, will be verified with the relevant firms and organizations before being added to the data already held in file. One must remember that a major asset of any credit bureau is its record of inquiries concerning the persons depicted in its files. By recording the identity of every firm requesting information on a given consumer, the bureau develops a backlog of 'leads' for future inquiries – so that these firms can be tapped later on for information on their experience with the customer. The amount of further information accumulated will, as always in credit reporting, depend on the amount of detail required by the buyer of the report and on the thoroughness of the bureau itself. What is certain is that all information garnered in the process of writing any credit report will find its way into the bureau's files, either as new entries or as addenda to old ones. It is rare for a bureau systematically to weed out dated information from its files, nor do bureaus discard any file until the subject is known to be deceased.*

Of course, the receipt of a request for information on someone unknown to the bureau is hardly the only point at which new files are opened – any more than the amplification of such inquiries is the only way additional information can enter existing files. Credit bureaus also routinely collect information from their member businesses without the impetus of having specific reports to write, information deemed relevant to the long-term purposes of enriching their files. Here, again, practices vary considerably among bureaus. The commonest practice of all is a standing arrangement between the bureau and its members through which the latter forward details of seriously delinquent accounts for listing among the files. In some cases, members do this as part of their income tax reporting procedures, so information on credit accounts written off as bad debts for income tax purposes can be used at the same time by the bureau. Elsewhere, the provision of this derogatory information, as it is called, occurs monthly, as

---

* Recent legislation, discussed below, does limit the age of information which bureaus may report.

part of the member's billing procedure. In either case, the bureau records the information in the relevant file or, if no file already exists, opens a new file containing for the time being only this one datum.

As the reader may have gathered, most credit bureaus place a special emphasis on seeking unfavourable or 'derogatory' information. Information on failure to pay, or to pay on time, is nearly always more valuable to the bureau than record of credit accounts 'paid as agreed'. The same applies, *mutatis mutandis*, to other forms of information provided in credit reports. This bias to negative information may appear gratuitously unfair to the consumer, but although it may be unfair it is by no means gratuitous. It is a fact that most credit customers *want* to pay their debts. Although people differ greatly in the pains which they are willing to take to meet credit payments and in their ability to do so, those who undertake credit obligations without at least a vague intention of paying are a very small minority. As a result, most people, even those regarded in the credit industry as bad credit risks, have some 'good' items in their credit histories, some instances in which they have paid their obligations as agreed. The great majority of credit customers, in fact, probably possess credit records which are largely composed of 'good' accounts, and it is of course their 'good' accounts which people cite in applying for further credit. Nevertheless, most credit grantors are not satisfied to extend credit to persons who pay only most of the time, but want instead to reduce their credit losses to an absolute minimum. Thus it is much more efficient to aim at excluding bad risks than at including good ones, and derogatory information is to this extent at a premium.

A further intake of information to credit files is from what are termed the 'public record' sources. These are court records and periodicals listing information deemed relevant to persons' creditworthiness, and available to the general public. Information received in this way may either be added to existing credit records, or it may form the impetus for opening new files.

Some of the most important public record data are records of litigation involving clients or potential clients of the bureau.

Bureaus take a special interest in lawsuits involving credit, especially suits brought by creditors against customers; equally important are tax liens, divorce actions and petitions for bankruptcy. Most credit grantors take a dim view of applicants with records of disputes with former creditors, fearing that the same may happen to them. Tax liens may also represent a danger signal, in that they indicate either contentiousness over debts or insolvency, neither of which is welcome to a credit grantor. Divorce actions, especially recent ones, can be troublesome to creditors, in that they often result in disputes between estranged partners over responsibility for bills. At the same time, the process of estrangement itself is widely believed, in the credit industry, to result in irresponsibility in the payment of debts. Worst of all, in the eyes of credit grantors, are bankruptcy petitions, since they indicate a desire to shirk all debts, which is the most serious sin of all in an industry which profits only from willingness to pay. Sensitive to the concern of their members over all of these matters, most credit bureaus regularly send staff members to court houses and record offices in their regions of coverage to cull information of this kind and record it in bureau files.

Periodicals provide the other main source of public record information. In some parts of North America, in fact, there are specialized publications serving local legal and commercial interests which publish the sorts of public record information cited above, thus saving the bureau the trouble of dispatching a staff member especially to obtain it. Whether or not this is the case, the credit bureau staff will regularly read and clip items relevant to their concerns from the local newspapers. Notices of marriages and births, for example, are regularly filed, since they are seen to pertain to persons' financial status and 'stability', the latter a matter of considerable concern to credit grantors. Notices of divorce, separation, and disclaimers of responsibility for the debts of spouses are also highly likely to be culled and entered in bureau files. Some bureaus, probably a minority, routinely cull and file stories from the local press relating to criminal charges against local persons, on the assumption that this sort of information is bound, in some way, to pertain to his creditworthiness.

To summarize, then. The discussion has noted six main sources of information to credit files: first, the subject of the file himself, who provides the bureau with the first indispensable tools for its investigations in the data in his credit application; second, the applicant's employer, who verifies the basic information about duration of employment and salary; third, the firms with whom the individual has held or currently holds credit accounts, who provide data on what he has purchased, how much he has owed, and how well he has paid; fourth, the applicant's bank, which will usually disclose at least approximately how much money the individual has and how carefully he manages it; fifth, the member businesses of the credit bureau, who contribute data on credit dealings with the individual, especially if their experience with him has been adverse; finally, there are the courts and the local press, whose contributions have just been discussed. Information drawn from any of these sources, depending on the practice of the individual bureau, can be either added to existing files, or can be the occasion for opening a new file.

Variability among bureaus is enormous with respect to how and how much each uses each of these sources. True, it would be unusual to find any bureau which does not avail itself of all of them at one time or another, for the necessity of using all these forms of information seems virtually built into credit reporting. But statements about how often and under which circumstances the various forms of information figure are much more problematic. Virtually every credit bureau will open a file on a local person on whom they have furnished a report; failure to do so, after all, would amount to throwing away costly information which stands to be re-saleable later on. Then too, most bureaus maintain arrangements for regular intake of derogatory information from their member businesses, and most would probably open a file on a local person cited in such information and not already depicted in the files. Nearly all bureaus regularly consult employers and former creditors of persons on whom they are writing reports; it is difficult to imagine how they could produce their 'product' without doing so. But in matters like the extent of collection and use of public record information, and the extent and amount of information sought and filed from member businesses, bureaus differ very widely indeed.

I wish it were possible to provide more precise descriptions of the rates of these various practices among bureaus. Given the dispersion of the industry and the consequent absence of systematic statistics on bureau practices, however, such generalization would only be rash. To some extent, these differences in basic practice among bureaus stem from authentic differences of opinion as to what information is most relevant to the purposes of the bureau and its customers. For the most part, however, they result from nothing more complex than discrepancies in the ambitiousness and thoroughness of credit bureau management. The quality of the 'product' sold by credit bureaus, the report itself, is often quite difficult for the buyer of the report to evaluate immediately, since he is apt to lack any means of determining whether the information in the report is as full as it should be. A sketchy report, in other words, can mean either that the individual in question has accumulated rather little in the way of relevant data, or that the bureau simply has not taken the necessary pains to check all the relevant sources. In many cases, it is very difficult for the buyer of the report to determine which is the case – or at least not until it is too late, and the credit account has 'gone bad' in a way which should have been predictable in the first place. Thus consumer credit reporting is not only relatively dispersed and decentralized, but very uneven in its capacity as a surveillance system.

Dissemination of Information and Decision-making

I have already noted the various different ways in which credit information is 'packaged' for dissemination to the customers of the credit bureau – the different varieties of reports, their differing content of information, and the commensurate scale of prices. These reports go to a considerable variety of credit grantors, ranging from small retail businesses to enormous lending institutions. According to figures collected for 1965 by the ACB, sales to retailers accounted for 40.7 per cent of the revenues of association members. Also accounting for major shares of bureaus' income were finance companies, with

18.3 per cent, and banks, with 8.6 per cent. Other credit bureaus, through fees charged for inter-bureau reporting, also generated 8.6 per cent of the typical bureau's business.

For each of these categories of users, and indeed for each individual firm within each category, there are distinctive decision-making criteria which govern the extension of credit. Many Americans believe that credit bureaus maintain single 'credit ratings' on each consumer – a belief fostered by an industry which has been notably energetic in shielding itself from public awareness of its activities. But this practice is actually quite rare; and so it is bound to be, given the structure of the credit reporting industry and the requirements of the businesses which it serves. For the fact that every user of credit information employs his own standards in evaluating credit reports means that no one rating can serve every purpose.

Any viable credit-granting policy must deal with an endemic dilemma: stringent standards in the screening of applications can cut losses from bad debts to virtually nil, but result in very low sales volume; indiscriminate acceptance of credit applications, on the other hand, will generate high volume but also unacceptably great credit losses. An equally important consideration in setting policy is the size of credit transactions, and hence of the potential losses from bad debts. A firm selling small household appliances, other things being equal, will be much more likely to extend credit for the purchase of a vacuum cleaner to a person with a slightly dubious record than will a bank in making a personal loan of, say, five thousand dollars. Then, too, prevailing economic conditions have much to do with the standards employed by different firms. In times of boom, standards are apt to be less stringent at all levels, given the expectation that most people will have the money necessary to meet their obligations. In times of recession, however, this will not be the case, and credit-granting firms will carefully screen every application in order to minimize their own losses to bad debts. All of these considerations conduce to great variation in credit-granting policy.

Nevertheless, quite despite differences in standards and criteria of decision-making, there is considerable consensus about the *significance* of the various items of credit information cited in the preceding section. Virtually all credit grantors, for example, regard conscientious and prompt payment of previous credit obligations as a good sign, and past delinquencies as undesirable. Then there is the importance of the elusive set of virtues which people in the credit industry tend to call 'stability'. In general, length of tenure of one's job and length of residence at one's address are positively correlated with creditworthiness; this may not apply, however, for many upper-middle-class persons for whom occupational and geographic mobility is a concomitant of success. Divorce for many of the same reasons is generally regarded as slightly suspect, bachelorhood or spinsterhood somewhat preferable, and the steady support of a moderate-sized family most auspicious of all. Then, too, as one might expect, high income and accumulated assets, whether liquid or capital, are good signs in nearly all circumstances – though, as the following chapter will show, many credit grantors prefer a 'stable' applicant of moderate means to a wealthy man whose past fortunes have been chequered. Finally, a record of litigation between applicant and other creditors is almost always a bad sign, no matter what the circumstances. Every creditor fears the customer who would rather go to court than settle his debts 'amicably'. Worst of all, of course, is bankruptcy, one item of information likely to be disastrous to any credit application.

The significance of these basic forms of information, then, is fairly predictable. The enormous variation in credit-granting procedures stems not from the significance attached to the information, so much as the *amounts* of information required, the *stringency* of judgement applied to the various items of information, and the *weights* ascribed to different kinds of data. For firms with highly selective credit policies, no application may be acceptable unless the applicant proves to have good records with a considerable number of former creditors. By contrast, a firm intent in building up its volume of business may be happy to open accounts with applicants having little in the way of past credit accounts, provided that other information given in the credit report appears acceptable. For some firms, a record of slightly dilatory payments on one or two previous accounts may be acceptable; elsewhere – say, in the case of a bank contemplating a sizeable personal loan – any past shortcomings of this kind will be fatal to the credit application. Some firms may place greater weight on 'stability' than on past credit accounts; others may regard the size of the applicant's income and assets as the most important consideration of all. In preparing up-dated reports, bureaus may tailor the information they gather to the needs of the purchasing firm. In gathering data primarily for their own files, however, most simply collect information of the sort apt to interest most customers most of the time, and leave it to the users of the reports to interpret them in whatever way they choose.

It would be wrong to leave the reader with the impression that credit-granting firms represent the only destination of credit reports, although they certainly represent the most important customers of credit bureaus. Any institution or individual with an interest in the financial standing and consumption habits of a private person will find credit reports useful. Law-enforcement agencies, including both local police forces and the FBI, occasionally purchase reports in the course of their investigations. So, one would imagine, do private detective agencies, although this matter is difficult to verify. Until very recently credit bureaus have been free to sell their reports to virtually any person or agency willing to pay the price. Recent legislation curtails this freedom in theory, but the practical mechanisms preventing non-credit-grantors from obtaining reports remain weak. The difficulties of any bureau in assessing the purposes of an unknown firm in purchasing a credit report, or indeed in knowing whether such a firm is more than a façade, are enormous. Furthermore, if any one credit bureau proves resistant to selling a report to an 'illegitimate' purchaser, that purchaser need only approach other bureaus or other credit grantors until he finds one willing to order the report in question. For although the bureau possessing the desired information may refuse to deal with one buyer, it will certainly not refuse to deal with any of its regular customers, and no credit bureau refuses to sell reports to other bureaus.

Areas of Coverage and 'Foreign' Reporting

The preceding discussion briefly raised, but did not much

dwell upon, two important and related matters: first that credit bureaus restrict themselves to defined local areas of coverage; second, that bureaus have until recently tended to remain small local monopolies within these areas. These facts have important implications for the surveillance capacity of the system, and they deserve further attention.

Consider the constraints facing credit bureaus as profit-making businesses. One of the main initial investments, and continuing costs, which every bureau must meet are those involved in developing and maintaining the files themselves. Before it can realize profits from the sale of reports, a bureau must accumulate a considerable backlog of data in file. And, if the reports are to be of any quality, the bureau must continue even after it is well established to invest in the accumulation of information, for example from public record sources, without direct and immediate return. To a large extent, the expense involved in this accumulation grows as a function of the distance of the sources. It is relatively easy to cover the relevant sources within the immediate community served by the bureau, more difficult to do so far afield. These considerations are part of the reason why consumer credit reporting has been and remains weak to non-existent in sparsely populated, rural areas. The costs of accumulating information in these places has simply been excessive in relation to the demand for credit reports on persons living there.

At the same time, there is a considerable premium, from the standpoint of the purchasers of credit reports, in having all available information on persons in a given area accessible from a single place. It would be useless, for example, for any bureau to maintain files on a small number of randomly selected American consumers, since no would-be purchaser of a report could be certain of finding the particular file there which he needed. No, the selling appeal of any bureau lies in its ability to convince customers that the relevant data from a given area are in its files. And once a bureau has invested the time and money necessary to gather together a 'critical mass' of credit data from an identifiable region, its competitive position is difficult to assail. Without a backlog of files, no insurgent bureau will have much to offer an established bureau's customers. And, without customers of its own, the new bureau will have little opportunity to develop the needed information, since the data for these files derives largely from member businesses. These circumstances help to explain why there has traditionally been an almost unbroken pattern of local monopolies within the credit industry.

The tendency is for these areas of coverage to correspond to 'natural areas' of people's lives, especially with respect to their jobs, their credit buying, and their litigation. By 'natural area' I mean any locality in which an identifiable group of people concentrate their activities. The simplest example is a relatively self-sufficient city, surrounded by countryside. One could take it for granted that most persons who reside there would also be employed there, do most of their buying and borrowing there, and probably engage in any necessary litigation there. So long as these things are true, a credit bureau operating in that community will find it worth its while to collect and file information in the way described above. For a person coming to the attention of the bureau in one context is likely to do so again and again. Thus it will pay the bureau to cull all relevant public record information from the local court house, since the persons depicted there are apt subsequently to be the subjects of requests for credit reports. By the same token, it will pay any would-be user of credit reports on persons in that area to seek them from the local bureau, since the information will be there if it exists anywhere. All but a very few credit bureaus organize their coverage so that it corresponds with some kind of 'natural area', although the size of these areas may differ. The area involved may be as small as a rural community or a minor suburb, but without observing this basic principle, any bureau will be hard pressed to gather a coherent set of files and to make its services saleable to customers. To put the matter more formally, various forces conduce to shaping the area of coverage of a credit bureau to the *scale* of the community it serves.

The system as presently constituted, one imagines, would work best if every consumer did indeed restrict his credit buying and litigation wholly to the area of coverage of his local bureau, and if he never changed his place of residence, at least not across boundaries of credit bureau coverage. Obviously, these things are not the case. People do certainly *concentrate* their lives in such limited areas for limited periods of time, but it would be difficult for any normal consumer to restrict himself completely and indefinitely to this local orbit. Even the most parochial consumers are apt to open a credit account with a national organization, like a mail order house or petrol company, or take out a loan with a bank in a neighbouring town. One must further remember that American families change their place of residence more and more frequently. People, and the information which people generate, do cross the lines of coverage of credit bureaus, and this creates considerable difficulties for the maintenance of effective credit surveillance. For, as in any other surveillance system, information misplaced is ultimately information lost.

Under its present organization, the system can meet these difficulties only imperfectly. It is fairly common for a credit grantor to receive applications from persons either residing outside the area of coverage of the local bureau, or only recently resident there. When this happens, the application will commonly be forwarded to the local bureau, upon whom the task will fall to obtain the relevant information from the applicant's previous place of residence. To this end, the Associated Credit Bureaus publish a comprehensive listing of the areas of coverage of their member bureaus. This loose-leaf volume, kept current with changes in bureaus' coverage, lists the bureaus which cover every town and city in America. Member bureaus order reports from one another, called 'foreign reports', by means of this book. Non-members of the national association can also purchase reports from member bureaus. But they cannot avail themselves of the directory, and they pay slightly higher prices for reports than do members.

The recourse to 'foreign' reports works well enough when the credit applicant willingly calls attention to the fact that he has lived or does live elsewhere, and where he provides a previous address which corresponds unambiguously to the listings in the national directory. But these conditions are not always met. Often, either through negligence or through conscious attempt to evade the consequences of his previous record, the applicant will fail to list previous addresses. Bureau records can sometimes detect such misrepresentation, but not without meticulous attention, and not with certainty even then. The system is especially lax if the credit grantor pursues liberal policies with respect to the screening of applications. If he demands only an absence of 'bad' information, rather than a positive record of good data, he may interpret such evasion as a signal to go ahead. And the bureau itself, if the applicant is a young person, is likely to attribute the lack of information about him to his youth, rather than to brief residence in the area. Even if the applicant is not young, it takes a thorough credit bureau, and an alert credit department in the credit-granting firm, to note the possibility that there may be another record elsewhere. Patient checking by the bureau of details of the applicant's employment and residential history can often reveal such data, but bureaus vary greatly in their willingness to take such pains.

Even more problematic are the means of dispatching information generated by local persons outside their local areas back to the local bureau. When someone is involved in legal action outside his local area, when he opens a credit account with a firm outside this area, or when he is married or divorced outside that area, there are considerable difficulties in seeing to it that the relevant information finds its way back to the bureau. The institutions with which the information is generated have little vested interest in bringing it to the attention of the local bureau, and the subject of the information may have considerable interest in their not doing so. Credit bureaus, in collecting public record information, can only feasibly check with those sources – court records, periodicals, and so on – within the local area. Thus they are virtually helpless when it comes to obtaining even highly pertinent data from distant public record sources. Likewise, if the consumer defaults on a credit account with a national firm, like a petrol credit card company or a mail-order firm, it is uncertain whether this information will be forwarded to the local bureau. The Associated Credit Bureaus, Inc., does maintain a service specializing in collating account information from national firms and forwarding these data to local bureaus, and this service appears to have grown more efficient in recent years. Then, too, some such data may come to the attention of the local bureau if and when bad accounts are forwarded to the local community for collection. But neither of these possibilities comes into play universally, nor is it certain that, when attempted, these techniques will lead to the information's 'finding' the consumer's main credit file.

Collection of Bad Accounts

It would be wrong to leave the reader with the impression that delinquency on credit accounts leaves consumer credit institutions with no recourse other than a negative listing in credit records. True, most credit-granting businesses themselves have no mechanisms for actively accosting and apprehending delinquent account holders. Their response, in such instances, is to send progressively more threatening letters to the party over a period of several months and, if this fails, to turn the account to a collection agency. This is a separate firm specializing in obtaining payment of bills which the credit grantor himself has found unrecoverable. In some cases collection agencies purchase outstanding bills for a percentage of their face value; more commonly, they work directly for the credit grantor, taking a fixed percentage of what they collect.

The methods used to obtain collection vary extremely widely. Firms regarded within the credit industry as the most reputable confine themselves to increasingly forceful letters to the debtor, threats of grave consequences to his credit standing, and persuasive visits to his home. In some instances these measures include the threat, and indeed the actual enforcement, of legal proceedings to recover the debt. At the other extreme, some of the more heavy-handed methods of debt collectors can run to physical intimidation. Legislation limiting the techniques available for debt collection does exist, but is uneven from state to state within the United States.

Two aspects of collection agency work hold special interest here. One is the significance of these institutions as 'points of contact' between consumer credit organizations and their clienteles. Collection agencies must constantly concern themselves with bringing the forces of social control to bear on those who would prefer to evade their pasts in this context. 'Skip tracers', collection agents who specialize in tracing absconded debtors, become experts at following the trails of such persons and, not incidentally, knowledgeable 'folk sociologists' in predicting the paths which they take. The existence of these techniques considerably enhances the grip of consumer credit surveillance on its clientele. And the possibility of sending representatives, *in extremis*, personally to accost the delinquent client represents a further parallel between this system and the others studied here.

The second aspect of collection agency techniques holding special interest here is the symbiosis which these organizations form with credit reporting agencies. The listings of bad accounts received for action by collection agencies represent precisely the highly pertinent, derogatory information which most credit bureaus particularly seek. Moreover, by working closely with the credit bureau, a collection agency enhances the believability of its threats to impair the credit standing of those who refuse to pay. At the same time, credit bureau files represent a valuable source of information to collection agencies in their efforts to trace and to assess the resources of debtors. For all of these reasons, it is extremely common for credit bureaus and collection agencies to operate jointly, under the same ownership and management. Membership in the Associated Credit Bureaus, in fact, is composed of both credit reporting agencies and collection agencies.

Future Trends: Computerization

If I were writing in 1965 instead of 1971, all this would represent a relatively full and balanced portrayal of consumer credit surveillance. Events since the mid-sixties, however, have added considerably to this picture, and have done so in ways of special significance to the concerns of this book. The most noteworthy change has involved the introduction of computer methods for storage and retrieval of consumer credit files. But the technological change in itself is not the most important aspect of this development. More significant are its implications in terms of the *capacity* of credit surveillance and its relation to changes in social structure. For the impact of the change has been to increase the scale and hence the capacity of consumer credit surveillance to match the increased scale of American life.

TRW Credit Data Corporation, the first credit reporting firm to rely on computers, began computerized operations in Los Angeles in 1965. Its objectives were to deal with much larger volumes of data than had previously been possible, and to centralize these data on consumers living over much wider regions than has been the case with previous, locally-based credit reporting organizations. TRW now maintains a single, massive file of credit information on consumers in eight of the main metropolitan areas of the country, and their environs. Access to this central file is through eleven TRW Credit Data offices, distributed around the regions served by the files.

Considerations of technology and centralization apart, TRW Credit Data operations are in some ways very similar to those of conventional bureaus, though elsewhere quite distinct. Like conventional bureaus, the new firm organizes its work on a membership basis – it calls its members 'subscribers'. But unlike the others, it sells reports only to these subscribers. Most credit bureaus do the great bulk of their business in 'in-file' and 'up-dated' reports on credit applicants; TRW engages only in these forms of reporting and declines altogether to issue reports for purposes of employment or tenancy. Like other bureaus, TRW devotes considerable resources to culling relevant information from public record sources, and, again like the others, it requires its subscribers to provide information for inclusion in its files. In a sharp and significant departure from the practice of conventional bureaus, however, TRW routinely incorporates the whole of subscribers' back account information – full records of both good and bad accounts – as a basis for reporting. This gesture towards 'total recall' of persons' credit histories is obviously possible only with the use of the massive retentive power of computerized storage, and with the application of the considerable capital investments which TRW has poured into its operations.

A visit to any of this firm's offices immediately drives home the differences between its operations and those of conventional bureaus. The large work-room filled with a female clerical staff is the same, but the absence of the voluminous stores of manual files is conspicuous. Instead, the staff are all equipped with telephone earphones, and seated in front of telephone hookups which link them directly to the single computerized information store located near Los Angeles. Each operator faces a cathode-ray screen, on which information appears from the computers. A central switchboard constantly funnels incoming telephone inquiries to the various operators, and they in turn transmit the requests through the keyboard consoles to the computer. Information fed into the machines includes the name, age, social security number, address and former addresses of the person on whom reports are desired – data which the machines use to identify the individual. Within about ten seconds, the entire contents of the individual's credit file flash back to the operator on her screen, and she orally relays the information to the waiting inquirer. Such requests for in-file information generally can be answered within three minutes, at least as fast as the most rapid service available from any conventional bureau. Like conventional bureaus, however, TRW Credit Data is vulnerable to overloading of its services during rush periods.

TRW also supplies computer-printed versions of the in-file information, and up-dated reports created by adding to the information in the files further data obtained through additional research. The latter are also submitted in writing. The printed in-file reports reach the credit-grantor within twenty-four hours of the time of request, while the up-dated reports, depending on the amount of additional information sought, take perhaps a day longer. As with conventional bureaus, the different kinds of reports answer to different needs on the part of credit grantors. The in-file reports go largely to those members who want to make an immediate decision on an applicant's creditworthiness, preferably before the latter leaves the place of business. Most of these firms are department stores and other retailers. Banks, however, who generally contemplate larger transactions than do department stores, typically require written reports, often amplified by further research.

TRW began as a conventional credit bureau, with operations

in Detroit and San Francisco. Since 1965, however, the firm
has moved purposefully away both from manual operations
and from localized reporting areas. In that year it initiated in
Los Angeles the first fully computerized credit reporting
operation. The following year it computerized the contents of
its San Francisco files, and added them to the pool of information already held in Los Angeles. In 1967 the company began
computerized operations in New York City, and the following
year these files also came to cover certain upstate metropolitan
areas. In 1969 the Detroit credit bureau went over to computerized operations, and since then a number of other metropolitan areas of the United States, including San Diego and
Chicago, have come under the coverage of TRW files. In 1971,
the computerized files were merged into a single master file
held near Los Angeles. This file is interrogated directly from
TRW offices throughout its areas of coverage, which now
include eight of the largest metropolitan areas of the country.
One of the advantages of the central file, of course, is that
information entered in the pool at any point in the country can
be retrieved in answer to a request from anywhere else.

Like conventional credit bureaus, TRW has had to come to
terms with the forces working to limit the amount of territory
covered by any single bureau. Much of its competitive appeal
lies in its ability to offer its customers access to a single comprehensive file of information drawn from a series of major
metropolitan areas. At the same time, the process of building
up this comprehensive file has been a struggle, and an expensive
struggle at that. The management have had to invest very considerably in the accumulation of filed information, in communications and computing systems before the proceeds from
sales of reports began to rise to profitable levels. Certainly it
has not been able to develop full coverage of any one area
overnight, and, in fact, the TRW file as it exists now is
obviously not exactly a national one. Although it contains
information on persons from various parts of the United
States, these are all major metropolitan areas. The TRW file
is thus a series of regional files, rather than a comprehensive
national one.

Necessarily, TRW has developed these files gradually, first

in the urban centres where it is located, then extending out-
ward to the surrounding metropolitan regions. The policy has
been first to make the original central operation economically
viable, then to expand operations to serve larger and larger
areas. This has required the firm to confront the forces governing
placement of bureaus and the allocation of territory mentioned
above for the conventional industry – forces limiting the area
which a single bureau has to date been able to serve. TRW
spokesmen suggest that even in the long term, they cannot
envisage carrying their operations to the more sparsely populated
parts of the country. For in these rural regions the high operating expenses are simply not justified in terms of the numbers of
credit reports which are to be sold. What TRW definitely does
envisage, however, is the development of a single pool of data
on persons residing in all of the metropolitan areas of America.

In its highly aggressive efforts to extend its area of coverage,
and to form a comprehensive surveillance 'net' for credit
information, TRW have sought business primarily from the
biggest possible credit-granting organizations. As a means of
establishing a very high volume operation, this is quite a
shrewd move. TRW depends heavily on the massive infusions
of data which it receives from its member businesses to provide
the 'raw materials' for further reports, and it depends likewise
on making the intake of this information as cheap and efficient
as possible. At the same time, the system needs to do business
on a very large scale in order to justify the enormous investments which it requires. Under these circumstances, doing
business with those firms in a position to purchase the largest
numbers of reports and to generate in turn the greatest amounts
of data for the files is the only rational step. Thus the most
important customers of TRW Credit Data are major banks
and loan companies, department stores, credit card firms,
and so on. Smaller firms are free to become TRW subscribers
if they are willing to comply with the membership requirements. But it is the giant credit-grantor on whom the firm
depends for the success of its operations.

To say that the advent of TRW Credit Data has jolted the
rest of the industry would be to put things mildly. All conventional bureaus in areas served by TRW have felt the pinch

of its competition, and the success of the insurgent firm has been especially great in recruiting as subscribers the very largest credit-granting firms, which probably represent the fastest-growing element of any bureau's business. In a way it is strange that the credit bureau industry had not taken steps towards computerization before the advent of TRW. Certainly such a conversion has been technically feasible since at least 1960. But in the absence of the spur of competition, the dispersed, capital-poor and generally conservative credit reporting industry was unable to muster the considerable resources necessary for such a change.

In responding to the challenge of TRW, the conventional firms still faced considerable problems. Perhaps the most serious has been the same dispersion which had always represented an obstacle before. The Associated Credit Bureaus, Inc., is in fact a trade association representing more than two thousand different credit bureaus, most of them quite small. Some plan of computerization was necessary which would at least appear to provide a role for all existing bureaus, and yet at the same time comprise a suitable competitive response to the centralized, concerted policies of TRW.

The response adopted by the ACB bureaus has aimed at meeting these requirements. With the advice and encouragement of the national Association, a number of the larger bureaus, those located in major metropolitan areas, have computerized their files. In so doing they have to some extent shared know-how and techniques instead of developing these independently. To accommodate smaller bureaus, and to maximize the areas of coverage, many of the larger bureaus have arranged for the participation of other bureaus in surrounding areas, so that all credit files for a given area are stored in the same repository. Under this system, each participating bureau continues to collect its own data and to derive revenue from the sale of 'its' information. A special advantage lies in the fact that all information is accessible through a single point, thus approximating to what TRW offers. In a variant of this arrangement, also sponsored by the national Association, several bureaus more distant from one another may share the same computer facilities without a central system of access to their files. A number of the major metropolitan areas of the United States are now covered by cooperative computerized systems with single points of access; these include greater San Francisco, Los Angeles, Dallas, Oklahoma City, New Orleans, Houston, Chicago, Detroit, Boston, Kansas City, Indianapolis and Denver – a number of these directly in competition with TRW Credit Data operations covering the same areas.

The competitive struggle is now wholly in earnest, and any prediction as to its ultimate results would be rash. TRW Credit Data have the advantages of an early start, a single pool of data from eight of the major metropolitan areas of the country, and a single policy-making centre. The more recent ACB entries are perhaps stronger in that they can rely on files compiled conventionally as a basis for their computerized operations instead of starting entirely from scratch. In any case, the long-term results of the competition are not a main concern here. The important point is clear: the growth in scale of consumer credit surveillance, through centralization and computerization, is certainly the pattern which will dominate the system for the foreseeable future.

One further form of change has to do with the size of organizations providing information for credit bureau files. TRW, as I have said, does the great bulk of its business with very large firms. One of its competitive advantages in dealing with these firms is that account information from their files can be entered *en masse* to the Credit Data computer, without the intermediary steps involved in funnelling it back to a large number of local bureaus. By the same token, of course, information filed by TRW is immediately available to users without having to be sought among an array of possible sources. Probably these facts help considerably to account for the notable success of the new firm in gaining the participation of these large credit-grantors. On the other hand, as the rest of the industry grows more centralized, it will also be able to exchange data more swiftly and efficiently with the giant credit-grantors. To cater to these firms is obviously very important, since there seems to be no question but that their proportion of all credit business is continually increasing. As these changes continue, it seems likely that credit files will consist more and more of information from regional or national credit grantors, for example large banking and loan agency chains, regionally or nationally organized retailers, and credit card companies. At the same time, the proportion of information from small, local businesses, like jewellery and department stores, without regional or national affiliation, will necessarily decrease. If these changes come about – and the patterns are only just discernible at present – then they will represent not only a growth in the scale of credit reporting, but also a parallel development in the scale of *sources* of credit information.

The Public Response: The Politics of Credit Surveillance

Like the other systems studied here, consumer credit surveillance represents an elaborate mechanism for compiling and communicating highly pertinent facts about people. Like the others, it sometimes does its job much too well, at least from the standpoint of its clients. During the period since the mid-1960s, the activities of credit bureaus have come in for increasingly broad and critical public interest.

Indeed, this critical public response would certainly have come earlier had it not been for general ignorance of credit bureau practices. Credit bureaus and their customers in the past have often left consumers in the dark about the role of credit reporting in the granting of credit. Indeed, the standard reporting supplied by the Associated Credit Bureaus for use by its members, still stipulates that information contained in credit reports 'must not be revealed to the subject reported on'. And even where the customer did become aware of the effects of credit reports drawn on him, he remained very much at the sufferance of the bureau in the matter. For the law exerted no constraint whatsoever over the activities of credit bureaus. Bureaus were not even legally obliged to report accurately, remaining outside the purview of legislation on libel and slander. Many bureaus were willing, if approached by a private consumer, to review his record with him, and to amend it if they were convinced that their data were erroneous. But most bureaus avoided such encounters as far as they could, and even the amendment of blatantly inaccurate information remained wholly at their discretion.

At length, as consumer credit and hence credit reporting came to assume greater and greater importance in American life, these practices received more attention, and considerable criticism. In general the critics have been clustered at the liberal side of the political spectrum, but not invariably. Much of the criticism has centred on the invasion of privacy attributed to credit reporting. Here the most strenuous objections have had to do with reporting on persons' character and life-style, especially that of the sort associated with reports for purposes of employment, insurance and tenancy. But nearly as great has been the more general indignation that information on essentially personal matters was being bought, stored, collated and sold wholly as a business proposition, without the knowledge or control of the persons to whom it referred.

Distinct from these issues was the question of justice and accuracy in credit reporting. Particularly galling was the fact that inaccuracies in credit files – and the system suffers from inherent tendencies to generate such mistakes – could, in the ignorance of the consumer, continue indefinitely to affect his credit status adversely. Many of these errors are virtually endemic in the system, for example in the case of lawsuits filed against the consumer by creditors, and subsequently thrown out of court. Bureaus often recorded these suits along with other public record information, continuing to report them indefinitely, never noting the ultimate disposition. The effects of such mistakes are virtually always damaging to the consumer, even if the suit is finally dismissed. And, beyond even the matter of mistakes and inaccuracies in filed information, there were emotional questions of what kinds of information bureaus should be allowed to report, and under what circumstances various kinds of data should be allowed to bear on this or that credit decision.

For years the industry resisted efforts aimed at enacting legislation which would regulate credit reporting practices. Finally, the year 1970 saw the passage of national legislation – the first affecting credit bureaus at this level.

The Fair Credit Reporting Act in its entirety is a complex

and detailed document; let it suffice here to cite a few of its more important provisions. First, it limits the purposes for which credit reports can be drawn – though it still allows reporting for credit, employment, tenancy, insurances and any other 'legitimate' business purpose, as well as to government agencies. It limits the length of time which derogatory information can be retained in files, so that records of bankruptcies may remain no more than fourteen years, and other derogatory information only seven. It requires firms rejecting credit applications on account of credit reports to refer the consumer to the issuing bureau. The bureau, in turn, is required to review with the consumer all information in its files, to reveal the sources, and to disclose to whom reports have been sent within six months previous to the inquiry. If the consumer disputes the accuracy of filed information the bureau is to 'reinvestigate and record the current status of that information unless it has reasonable grounds to believe that the dispute by the consumer is frivolous or irrelevant'. Information thus found inaccurate is to be deleted. If the dispute remains unsolved, the consumer may file a statement giving his position concerning the data, to be reported along with subsequent credit reports on the consumer. However, bureaus are under no obligation to include such a statement if 'there is reasonable grounds to believe that it is frivolous or irrelevant'.

It is the genius of American liberalism that, when faced with a particularly unconscionable practice by some powerful interest, it regulates that interest in such a way as both to mitigate the sting of the abuse and at the same time to consolidate the position of the perpetrators. The Fair Credit Reporting Act stands in this tradition. Although the new law is just going into effect in the United States as I write, many of its effects are immediately apparent. Certainly it will curtail some of the more flagrant injustices of credit reporting, particularly by making mistakes in credit files more conspicuous and hence more susceptible to correction. It seems very likely that bureaus will correct these mistakes, once they come to their attention, even though, *in extremis*, the burden of constraining the bureau to do so remains with the consumer. It will enable the consumer to note who has purchased reports on him – provided that he takes the initiative to consult the bureau. Thus it does involve the consumer more in the processing and selling of information about himself, and to this extent gives him at least a say in how all of this is to be done.

At the same time, it virtually ratifies the position of credit bureaus with respect to the main patterns of their operations. Except for the statute of limitations on derogatory information, it does not constrain the ability of credit bureaus to collect any information which they deem useful. It does not constrain them against selling reports to any of the main customers who now comprise the bulk of their business. True, the Act does require bureaus to maintain 'reasonable procedures' to identify buyers of reports and to determine that the sale conforms to the provisions of the Act. But it forbids their selling reports only if they have 'reasonable grounds' for believing that the report will *not* be used for such purposes. Thus, although the provisions for consultation with consumers will result in certain extra demands on the time of credit for bureau staff, and entail extra expense because of the need to verify the accuracy of filed information, the new law should curtail none of the basic credit reporting activities described in the preceding pages.

Thus there is every reason to think that the pattern of growth of consumer credit reporting will continue to increase in scale and efficiency. According to one of the opening statements of the Act, 'Inaccurate credit reports directly impair the efficiency of the banking system, and unfair credit reporting methods undermine the public confidence which is essential to the continued functioning of the banking system . . . Consumer reporting agencies have assumed a vital role in assembling and evaluating consumer credit and other information on consumers . . . It is the purpose of this title to require that consumer reporting agencies adopt reasonable procedures for meeting the needs of commerce for consumer credit, personnel, insurance and other information . . .' There are other homilies on the importance of privacy and accuracy in credit reporting as well, but the intent of the Act is clear: to remove some of the popular objections to credit reporting in the interests of making it work as efficiently as possible.

The Capacity of Credit Surveillance

At this point, discussion of consumer credit surveillance is almost complete. It has not been the exhaustive treatment that one might have preferred, given unlimited space. But it has served, I hope, to portray the more important features of the organization and workings of the system, at least as they pertain to the concerns of this book. If I have succeeded, these pages should have made possible direct comparisons between this surveillance system and the others studied here. All that remains, at this point, is to formalize the information presented above in terms of the criteria of surveillance capacity.

First, consider the *amount* of useful information maintained in this system. In terms of numbers of persons depicted, certainly it is formidable. Though the consumer credit reporting system does not hold data on quite such a large proportion of the adult population in America as does National Insurance in Britain, it is probably larger in this respect than the other two British systems. This is the more remarkable when one notes that there exists no legally binding means of constraining people and institutions to provide information for credit bureau files. One must remember, however, that information in credit bureau files varies considerably in accuracy and currency. The industry has traditionally operated on the principle that collecting and reporting a certain amount of inaccurate or dated information is acceptable, so long as the over-all operation remains profitable. The new legislation should provide some impetus to reducing this looseness in bureau practices, but the system remains at present distinctly less accurate in the factual content of its files than the three British systems considered.

If the exact number of files kept is difficult to determine, the average amount of information per file is still more so. Files actually encountered by the author in the course of this research have contained, on the average, the subject's name, address, spouse's name, telephone number and employer, job title and salary, plus three or four entries describing credit accounts, litigation or the like. Statistics published by TRW Credit Data suggest an average of about three credit transactions per file in that system. Informants with experience in the industry agree that such estimates are at least as good as any, but they are obviously far from rigorous. If this really were the average of information held per person, however, the consumer credit reporting system would be very roughly comparable in this respect with Britain's National Insurance; in both systems, of course, the amount of data kept per person varies enormously.

Finally, in so far as one can compare them, the information collected and disseminated by credit bureaus would seem to depict a broader portion of each client's life than is the case in the three preceding systems. More than elsewhere, one feels in reading a credit file that one can develop a mental picture of the person concerned. True, the British police do aim to compile something like a composite portrait of their clients' lives in the 'antecedent history' sheet presented to the courts, and maintained for further reference, but credit files probably possess a slight edge over these. In any case, like the police information, credit files never ultimately fulfil their essentially 'open-ended' tasks. Almost invariably, there exists more relevant information on the subject of a credit file than the file contains – more credit accounts, more current detail on employment status, fuller information from previous places of residence, and so on.

Also uneven is the *subtlety* of decision-making afforded in this system. Many firms employ the simplest possible decision-making rules in determining whether to grant credit applications. There mere absence of any derogatory credit information, for example, or the attainment of a given income level may in itself be sufficient for the extension of credit. But such simplistic procedures are by no means the rule, and some firms manage to use all of the information presented in even very detailed credit reports. Highly skilled credit officers, with the benefit of considerable experience, can meaningfully interpret not only the promptness and fullness of past credit payments, but also the nature of the goods or services purchased on credit, and the timing of credit purchases in relation to other events like the change of job or the birth of a child, so as to reach highly subtle conclusions about the credit applicant. The screening procedures followed by the BankAmericard system, described in the following chapter, represent a case in point. These uses of surveillance are all the more impressive in that they involve judgements about what the individual is likely to do in the future, as well as of how he has behaved in the past.

With respect to the *speed* of information flow, credit reporting also presents a mixed picture. Credit bureaus are uneven, but generally slow in gathering information for inclusion in their files. That is, the elapsed time between when pertinent information comes into existence and when it enters bureau files may be considerable. Some bureaus, as I have noted, regularly collect data on members' delinquent accounts only once per year. Indeed, the collection of public record information is even less predictable, probably governed in most cases by the extent of other demands on the bureau staff. Thus there can be little assurance, in most bureaus, that information pertinent to a credit application will immediately be available for use by the credit-grantor. The opposite is true, however, in the steps taken to draw up a report: this process may work very quickly. In-file reports are generally available within about a minute over the telephone, or within a day in writing. Up-dated reports may take two to five working days to prepare, depending on the amount of detail required. With the spur of a request for a report on a specific person, the bureau often manages to extract relevant information from its sources much more rapidly than would otherwise be the case, telephoning member businesses for account data which otherwise might take months to reach bureau files, if it did so at all.

With respect to the centralization of information, the conventional forms of consumer credit reporting are as little developed as any system studied here. And, for the reasons cited in Chapter 1, this dispersion of available information reduces the effectiveness of the system in carrying out its tasks of surveillance. This is true, for one thing, with respect to the added time taken to obtain credit information stored in a 'foreign' bureau. More important is the fact that the dispersion of credit information into thousands of locations throughout North America, and the concomitant fractioning of reporting areas among these bureaus, results in the 'loss' of all sorts of relevant data which happen to accumulate outside the area in which the subject resides. The discussion has noted the social forces which have helped to bring about this situation, as well as the effects of the new computerized credit reporting systems in eroding this regionalism and building more comprehensive, centralized files.

Finally, consider the *points of contact* between the surveillance systems and the members of its clientele. Here consumer credit reporting partly compensates for the dispersion of information with a well-articulated array of channels through which information flows into and out of the system.

In comparison with the systems studied in the preceding chapters, this breadth and flexibility of information intake is especially impressive. Any credit transaction – and one must remember that Americans rely very heavily on credit – has the possibility of generating information to credit files. Indeed, in the absence of other data, even information on the consumer's payment of rent or utility bills may serve to establish his credit standing. At the same time, most bureaus rely very heavily on information from employers, both past and present; often these data are as important as any 'credit' information in the narrow sense. Finally, discussion has also shown how credit bureaus avail themselves of legal institutions and other sources of information on financial and family affairs relating to consumer credit. None of the systems discussed in preceding chapters manages regular intake of information from such a wide array of disparate sources.

By the same token, discussion has shown just how wide can be the access to information kept in credit files, how readily consumer credit data thus collated can come to bear on future decision-making. Reports are readily purchasable by any credit-granting firm, and indeed by other firms as well. It is my opinion that credit reports are in fact available virtually to any well-informed person or agency with patience and the resources to pay for them. The main obstacle to the flow of information out of credit files is not so much the availability of the data as the ability of the would-be user to know where the relevant file is located. Here it is clear that the decentralization of the system and the uncertainty of its identification processes do allow information to be misplaced, with the result that it does sometimes fail to come to bear, or to bear fully, on decision-making. Similar difficulties pose problems for the collection of bad debts. In these respects the contact between system and clientele is uneven, and sometimes undeniably weak.

With respect to positive identification of clients, consumer credit reporting is distinctly weaker than either the British police system or that of National Insurance. Credit bureau staff base their identification of consumers whose records they encounter primarily on name and date of birth, corroborated where possible by address, spouse's name, occupation, and so forth. Credit-grantors increasingly ask for applicants' Social Security numbers as a means of identification, and provide such information in turn to the credit bureau. But observance of this practice remains very uneven. The point is, the full array of identifying information is not always available to the bureau when needed. Credit files generally begin and grow with the accumulation of single scraps of data, for example, a credit account record taken from a bureau member, or the record of a lawsuit culled from court records. The amount of identifying information accompanying such data varies greatly. Moreover, names are subject to change, variation and duplication, and even the recording of date of birth can be affected by error or misrepresentation. Under these circumstances, it is not surprising that information is sometimes misplaced, and that bureaus occasionally attribute both whole credit records and single items of data to the wrong person. Wider review of credit records by the persons to whom they pertain, envisaged under the new legislation, should reduce the rate of such mistakes.

Consumer credit surveillance, then, like the other cases studied here, presents a mixture of relative strengths and weaknesses in terms of surveillance capacity. In general, both its strengths and its weaknesses stem from its dispersed internal organization and from the 'free market' auspices under which it operates. The occasional tendency to lose information, to incorporate mistaken data, or to mis-associate persons with 'their' data must be understood in this context. For the credit-grantor, the imperative is not so much to get all his facts precisely correct on all his credit applicants all of the time. Rather, it is to obtain enough information at a reasonable cost to maintain high volume and acceptably low rates of default. In other words, a single 'wrong' decision, either in favour of or against the credit applicant, is not in itself so serious as an over-all rise in default or in the costs of decision-making. The credit bureau, serving the interests of the buyers of its reports, will likewise be more concerned to produce a volume of reports at acceptably low cost than to make sure that these reports are correct and complete in every detail. These circumstances conduce to a high rate of information exchange, and especially to a very wide sharing of relevant data among sources, compilers, and users of information. But the same forces which have conduced to the growth of a very extensive, well-articulated and resourceful system of information exchange also lead the system to neglect the occasional malfunction or mistake.

※

THE DEVELOPMENT OF THIS RESEARCH

My original acquaintance with consumer credit reporting dates to 1967 and 1968, the time of my doctoral research. That early research also led to the preparation, in collaboration with David Caplovitz and Pierce Barker, of a brief published study on these practices.* Caplovitz is a gifted survey researcher with considerable knowledge of the sociology of consumer behaviour. Barker is a social psychologist with the distinctive credentials of once having run a credit bureau. Among the three of us, we visited credit bureaus in Illinois, New York, Massachusetts, Georgia and California in order to gather material for that study. I also visited, in the spring of 1968,

* James B. Rule, David Caplovitz and Pierce Barker, 'The Dossier in Consumer Credit', in Stanton Wheeler, ed., *On Record*, New York, Russell Sage Foundation, 1969.

the headquarters of the Associated Credit Bureaus, Inc., in Houston, Texas.

The material in that earlier study has been reorganized, up-dated and enlarged for presentation here. In 1971 I revisited the ACB headquarters in Houston and spent a day at the headquarters of TRW Credit Data in Southern California. I also made a briefer visit to the TRW Credit Data installation in San Francisco. Officials from both these organizations have reviewed preliminary drafts of this chapter. The chapter has also received a careful and thoughtful reading by Mr Harry Chapman, manager of the Credit Bureau of Gainesville, Georgia, and by Pierce Barker. All these readers checked and sometimes corrected my statements of fact and generally offered many valuable suggestions which I have incorporated in the final version. In some instances they have taken exception to statements of opinion and interpretation contained in this chapter, and the responsibility for these is of course wholly my own.

It is a great pleasure to acknowledge my debt to Caplovitz and Barker for their collaboration in the early research, and to thank Pierce Barker, especially, for his continued interest in this project. I am also extremely grateful to Mr Harry Chapman and the officials of the Associated Credit Bureaus, Inc., and TRW Credit Data, both for the help which they extended and for their tact in handling our very occasional differences of opinion over issues raised in this chapter.

6

The BankAmericard System in America and Abroad

It would be foolish to suggest that the five systems studied in Chapters 2 to 6 represent the only possible choices as case studies. Many systems of mass surveillance, in the sense intended here, are to be found throughout the industrialized world; the selection of these five has been constrained both by their being known to the author and by their accessibility to study. Nevertheless, the choice has been far from arbitrary. Considerable care has gone into selecting cases which correspond closely to the idea of mass surveillance developed in Chapter 1. Further, in the process of selection many possibilities were ruled out because the capacity of the relevant system was not great enough to warrant close analysis. Finally, the choice of these five represents an effort to find systems which differ sufficiently among themselves – in internal organization, social context, behaviours submitted to surveillance and forms of compliance enforced – to enable each case study to make a unique contribution to the tasks of the book.

This chapter is the last of the case studies. It deals with the BankAmericard system, a remarkable, far-flung credit card plan whose operations are centred in San Francisco but whose surveillance activities increasingly extend throughout much of the world. One reason for the selection of this system is its relation to the consumer credit reporting industry, in that the reliance by BankAmericard upon that industry should help to emphasize the impact of consumer credit surveillance upon individual consumers. Another reason has to do with the surveillance capacity of BankAmericard. For although the consumer credit reporting industry is largely, though decreasingly, decentralized, and although it tends to ignore or 'lose' vital information as a result, the BankAmericard system leaves very little to chance in its use of information. Over-all, in the amount of usable information which it keeps, the speed with which it marshalls its data, the centralization of its accounting practices, the points of contact between system and clientele and the ease of apprehending defaulters, this is perhaps the most sophisticated of the five systems studied here. Perhaps even more important, its increasingly international organization points significantly to the continuing extension of the *scale* of surveillance activities.

Origins and Organization of the BankAmericard System

Credit cards have become such a standard accoutrement of consumption habits in the United States that American readers will find any explanation of what they are or how they work gratuitous. Although just coming into use in Britain and other industrial countries, these small plastic badges, imprinted with the name and number of the holder, are virtually universal among middle- and upper-middle-class Americans. Their main use is to authorize the holder of the card to make credit purchases from a specific firm or series of firms.

By having the raised number on the card imprinted onto a sales slip and signing the slip, the card-holder obtains the sale on a credit basis, and receives the account usually within a month. Firms issuing credit cards include petrol companies, department stores, airlines, hotel chains and an ever-increasing variety of companies offering goods and services to private consumers. In addition, certain organizations specialize in providing the credit card service itself, and these include BankAmericard. The effect of all credit cards is the allocation of some form of 'blanket' credit to the card-holder. By providing the card, the issuing firm authorizes credit not just for a single transaction but for an indefinite number of further purchases probably not contemplated at the time the card is issued.

Probably the first firms to issue credit cards on any scale were large department stores in the United States. Early this century such firms found this method useful to encourage their 'good' customers to purchase as extensively as possible. Another major issuer of credit cards during the 1930s were petrol companies, which issued the cards in hopes of encouraging their holders to patronize their affiliated service stations. During the 1950s and 60s a number of other American firms followed suit – retail merchants, hotel chains, airlines and a wide variety of others, including the telephone company and car rental firms. Part of the reason for the popularity of this means of extending credit, of course, was the increase in business which it was felt to promote. Another impetus was the fact that most credit card schemes levied high rates of interest on the unpaid balances in their accounts. It is very common, for example, to extend 'revolving charge' privileges, whereby the customer need only pay a given amount of his accumulated debt each month – often five per cent of the total outstanding balance. This feature obviously has its appeal for the user, enabling him to defer payment and spread the costs of major purchases over considerable time; at the same time, it maximizes the interest charges accruing to the firm at rates running between twelve and thirty per cent per annum.

One might say that the growth of credit card plans has entailed a growth in the subtlety of the relations of trust implicit between creditor and consumer. By this I mean that the firm issuing a credit card contracts a potentially greater risk than if it simply approved a single credit transaction. For a delinquent credit card-holder can theoretically run up an astronomical series of charges before he is apprehended, or the use of his card otherwise curtailed. Matters are especially difficult when the card is good for purchases at a wide array of locations, since the issuing firm must then prevent a continuing flow of bad charges at far-flung points, charges which the card-holder may never intend to honour. In the light of these problems it has only been the growth of sophistication in credit surveillance which has allowed credit card plans to flourish as they have.

This sophistication has grown, as the previous chapter

emphasized, and with it the extent and complexity of credit card plans. The most significant qualitative innovation in credit card schemes after the credit card idea itself was the development of the multi-use card, valid for the purchase of a wide variety of goods and services from a wide array of different firms. These systems separated the management of the credit card scheme itself from that of the firms honouring the card.

The first major representative of this specialized form of credit granting was the Diner's Club card, first issued in 1950 in New York City. Its inventor's original inspiration was to alleviate the need to carry large amounts of cash to cover meals in that city by providing a single credit card for 'charging' bills in a number of restaurants. The plan was so popular, among both the relatively affluent businessmen who used the cards and the restaurateurs who honoured them, that it rapidly spread both to other cities and to other forms of transactions.

The astonishing success of Diner's Club gave rise, in 1958, to two imitators, the American Express Card and Carte Blanche. All three proceeded to make substantial profits by following what amounted to the same basic plan: first, to issue cards to a select, prosperous category of business and professional persons, especially those who travel a great deal; second, to secure the participation in the scheme as card-honouring businesses of a large number of firms offering goods and services to persons in these categories. Especially common among these were firms associated with travel, like airlines and hotels, and those selling goods and services expensive enough to discourage their purchase with cash. The rapid development of these cards from a novelty to a commonplace element in American life is evident in that American Express and Diner's Club now claim, respectively, 3.5 and 2 million card-holders throughout the world.

Besides catering to the same market, the three credit card systems also work very much according to the same plan of operations. Cards are issued very selectively upon application, and on the payment of a fee of about fifteen dollars. Card-holders charge purchases in the customary way, by having the merchant imprint the sales voucher with their credit card and signing the voucher. The card-holder pays no interest on the credit extended him if he makes good the charges to the credit card firm within a specified period of time, usually twenty-five days from the date of the account.

The contract between the credit card firm and the merchant honouring the cards is a bit more intriguing. The merchant accepts no risk in honouring the card provided that he makes the sale according to the rules set down by the system. The latter pay the merchant for all transactions, even if the card-holder ultimately defaults.

In this respect, the merchant enjoys the benefits of credit business, in terms of the increased sales volume supposed to result from his honouring the card, without the administrative costs and risks involved in setting up his own credit system. The merchant, however, does not receive the full value of his credit sales from the credit card firm. Instead, the latter takes a discount of approximately two to five per cent on all purchases, and sometimes more, the exact amount depending on the credit card firm and the merchant. So, on a transaction of $100 charged through one of these cards, the merchant usually receives only $95 to $98. Thus the advantage to the merchant of participating in the scheme lies strictly in the increased volume of business which he expects to do by virtue of honouring the card, along with the absence of costs associated with running a credit system on his own. Judging from the rapid growth of these systems, it seems obvious that a great many merchants have found the advantages attractive, and that a great many others have found it wise to participate in the schemes to forestall the losses of business which they fear would result if they remained outside it.

These three credit card systems – often designated as the 'prestige' cards within the industry, because of the limitation of their appeal and availability to a strictly upper-middle-class clientele – show some of the distinguishing qualities of mass surveillance systems. They entail, after all, relationships of control between the agencies which run them and the clienteles who use them. The element of control lies in the need, first of all, to exclude from participation in the systems those who would be unwilling or unable to make good the charges which they accrued through the use of the cards. And along with this pre-emptive or preventative form of control goes the need to obtain payment for purchase by the users of the cards, and to curtail the use of those cards which have clearly 'gone bad', either in the hands of their intended holders or elsewhere.

Nevertheless, these three systems are not quite comparable to the other systems of mass surveillance and control studied here. First, the clienteles involved are rather small by comparison. Second, the surveillance maintained over the use of the cards, once they are issued, is generally less close than its counterparts in the other systems. Although the screening of applications for credit cards is quite stringent and involves the collection of considerable information on the applicants, the rates of default from these credit card-holders are relatively low. For the screening is so stringent, and the financial positions of those issued with cards so secure, that relatively little supervision is needed to ensure that the obligations contracted with the cards are met.

If the 'prestige' cards lack certain features which might qualify them as systems of mass surveillance, such features are far from absent in their near-kin, the bank credit cards. The operations of these schemes are largely similar to those of the 'prestige' cards, but their clienteles are much larger and there is much closer surveillance over the use of the cards. While they have by no means replaced the previous three, the bank cards have grown larger than the others by catering to consumers of considerably lower incomes and by recruiting merchants offering a wider array of goods and services.

BankAmericard is the earliest-founded of the several bank credit card schemes now operating in the United States.* Like many another social innovation of the 1960s, it had its inception in California, and from there has spread its activities to the rest of the country and, more recently, throughout the world. Wholly owned and operated by the mammoth Bank of

* BankAmericard was not the very first bank card scheme to begin operations, but it was the first to be successful on a large scale.

America at the time of its inception in 1959, its world-wide operations are now the joint responsibility of many banks.

Because of its determination to extend credit privileges on a mass basis, BankAmericard has always made it as easy as possible to obtain cards. The consumer simply completes a short application form, shown on page 234, which he submits without an application fee. The system in turn bills the card-holder each month for the accumulated charges which he has made with the card. The card-holder pays no interest on these charges, nor any other fees to BankAmericard, provided that he discharges his full monthly bill within thirty days. If he chooses to delay payment, or to pay a large bill progressively over a period of months, he incurs an annual interest on the unpaid balance which ranges from ten to eighteen per cent, depending on the size of the debt and the bank issuing the card. These instances of extended payment are obviously highly profitable to the system.

The conditions governing the participation of merchants in the system are much like those involved in the 'prestige' cards. Each merchant is assured payment of all sales made with BankAmericards, provided that the sales voucher is completed and signed by the customer according to the rules set down by the system. This assurance holds regardless of whether or not the purchaser ultimately pays BankAmericard for the purchase, even if the purchaser proves to have stolen the card. Like the 'prestige' cards, however, BankAmericard generally pays participating merchants only a percentage of the face value of BankAmericard sales. The three to five per cent commission usually charged by the system thus represents its second major source of profit.

The bank card schemes have expanded extremely rapidly since their inceptions, both in numbers of card-holders and sales, and in geographical areas of coverage. While the largest of the 'prestige' cards at present numbers about three and a half million users, the users of BankAmericard rapidly came to number tens of millions, as Table 11 shows.

As their name suggests, the bank card schemes are financed and managed by banks and operate through banking institutions. Originally, BankAmericard operated through the 992

Table 11. *Number of BankAmericard Card-holders, Worldwide, By Year (in millions)*

1961	1.0
1963	1.3
1965	1.3
1967	6.7
1969	29.0
1971	28.2

The number of valid cards outstanding, shown here, is always somewhat greater than the number of active accounts. BankAmericard extended its operations to other states and countries in 1966, and the rapid increase in total card-holders shown in 1967 reflects this fact.

Source: National BankAmericard, Inc.

California branches of the Bank of America. Now the system, after expansion to national operations, involves the participation of many banks, in complex patterns of cooperation and competition.

Every card-issuing bank participating in the scheme must work to enlist the participation of merchants to honour the cards and of card-holders to use them. The latter will be drawn largely, but not necessarily exclusively, from the bank's depositors and customers. The former will usually be merchants in the area of the bank's operations, often customers of the bank, as well. The merchant agrees to deposit his sales drafts with the nearest branch of the relevant bank within a few days – usually three days – after sale; the branch credits the merchant with the face value of the drafts minus the discount imposed by the system. The card-holder usually does not deal directly with any local branch bank in matters connected with the bank card, but with the headquarters of its bank card operations.

For BankAmericard, every participating bank has at least one of these headquarters, where most of its bank card activities take place. These processing centres, as they are called, take responsibility for dealing with credit card applications, for keeping the individual accounts up to date, and for controlling the use of the cards. Such centres are scattered around the

United States and, indeed around the world.* One constraint upon their operations is that they must handle all transactions made on BankAmericard, no matter where the particular card was issued. Thus the New York BankAmericard processing centre may well find itself called upon to deal with sales drafts generated by a card-holder whose card was issued in California. This feature is significant in that it enables the various participating banks to work as a single interlocking whole, so that the user of the card can avail himself of Bank-Americard services throughout the world. Some implications of this interlocking system will receive fuller discussion at the end of this chapter. Although BankAmericard and its competitors maintain very similar surveillance systems, I have chosen to concentrate upon the practices of the former. The reason for the choice is the special sophistication of certain BankAmericard practices, though all the systems are impressive by comparison to the others studied in this book. Moreover, the detail of the following remarks must be taken to refer to California BankAmericard practices rather than any of the other 327 card-issuing banks participating in the system.† For while the national organization of the system does enforce a measure of uniformity of practice among participating banks, the system prevailing in California is the oldest and from all accounts the most sophisticated of these. The following pages, then, will concentrate on what appears as the surveillance system with the highest capacity, but will attempt to distinguish, from time to time, where these practices differ from those carried out by other elements of BankAmericard, or by its main competitors.

* In Britain and South Africa, the BankAmericard affiliate is Barclays Bank, whose Barclaycard is negotiable at firms honouring BankAmericards, and whose participating merchants in turn honour BankAmericards.

† Surveillance over BankAmericard use in California is carried out from two processing centres, one in San Francisco and one in Southern California. The former has direct responsibility for approximately 800,000 accounts and the latter for about 1,130,000. The research on California BankAmericard activities presented in this chapter took place in San Francisco, but the two centres work very closely together and maintain uniform practices, so that statements about the one may be taken as valid for both.

Information Flow and Decision-making

Like virtually all consumer credit schemes, and indeed like most of the other systems studied in this book, BankAmericard relies primarily on preventative or pre-emptive forms of social control. That is, the system is designed to secure compliance by making sure that misdeeds do not occur in the first place, more than by pursuing delinquent clients once the violation is a *fait accompli*. The step in this never-ending process is the screening of BankAmericard applications.

The Screening of Applications

Like all credit-grantors, large and small, this system faces the endemic dilemma mentioned in the previous chapter: stringent decision-making rules lower credit losses dramatically, but curtail volume; liberal policies, on the other hand, raise volume but also increase the proportion of defaulting accounts. BankAmericard, since its inception, has aimed at high-volume operation, extending credit to a much wider sector of the populace than the prestige credit cards. To achieve this without prohibitive default rates, however, it has had to rely on sophisticated discrimination practices. Indeed, BankAmericard ran very seriously foul of this dilemma when it began its operations in 1959. Without any precedent for the mass issuance of credit cards, it allocated large numbers of cards without proper discrimination. Names were drawn wholesale from lists of Bank of America account-holders, credit bureau files and a various assortment of other sources. The results were nearly disastrous. 'Irresponsible' use of the cards was so great that the system took enormous losses, and very nearly had to be discontinued. A number of similar bank credit card schemes begun at about the same time did in fact suffer this fate. Having survived its disastrous beginning, however, BankAmericard went on to profit from its mistakes by developing the shrewd system of screening and surveillance which makes it currently the most profitable of all elements of the mammoth Bank of America system.

Like its competitors, BankAmericard makes it as easy as

possible to apply for a card. Every branch of every bank participating in the programme displays the postage-paid application
forms prominently, as do many of the merchants who honour
the cards. Page 234 shows a copy of the Bank of America's
application form completed as though by a typical applicant.
The telegraphic information contained on the application
forms a crucial element of the data used in deciding whether
to grant the card. During the year 1970, the San Francisco
office received about 147,000 application forms and issued
cards to about 89,000 of these applicants, or about two thirds.
In general, the full processing of an application requires about
a week at San Francisco, and the manufacture and dispatch of
new credit cards an equal period.

The basic steps in screening BankAmericard applications
are very similar to their counterparts in other large consumer
credit-granting institutions. In the San Francisco centre, a
staff of about twenty-six devote all their time to the constant
stream of applications, handling them according to a highly
routinized set of procedures. The first step is to give each
form a cursory inspection so as to exclude the manifestly
unsuitable; between five and ten per cent of incoming applications are rejected at that point. The next step is to draw a
credit report on each of the remaining applications as a means
of both checking the veracity of the data provided on the
application form and obtaining some crucial supplementary
data. The credit report, for example, should verify employment, family status, income, place of residence, and a number
of the other facts provided by the applicant. Perhaps more
importantly, it should provide a fuller version of the applicant's
financial position than that available in the application, including data which the applicant himself might prefer to conceal –
bad credit accounts, bankruptcies, lawsuits and tax liens.

Usually it suffices to draw just a single 'in file' credit report
for each application. In these cases, the credit application and
the credit report together show the applicant either clearly
eligible for a BankAmericard or clearly ineligible, and the
staff act accordingly without gathering any further information.
But – as in other decision-making processes studied in this
book – a minority of instances require an inordinate amount

BankAmericard Account Application

BRANCH NUMBER [ ]

1. APPLICANT: Family Residence and Educational Background

LAST NAME (Please Print)	FIRST NAME	INITIAL	AGE	HOME TELEPHONE	SOC. SEC. NO.
Mr. ☒ Mrs. ☐ Miss ☐ SMITH	JOHN	D	25	251-7682	325-14-1215

STREET ADDRESS	SPOUSE'S NAME	INITIAL	AGE	SINGLE ☐ WIDOWED ☐ DIVORCED ☐
123 FIRST ST	BETTY	A	24	MARRIED ☒ SEPARATED ☐

CITY	STATE	ZIP CODE	DRIVERS LICENSE NUMBER(S)	NO. OF CHILDREN
SAN JOSE	CA.	95402	Z 617195	1

AT PRESENT ADDRESS		FORMER ADDRESS		
YRS 1 MOS 10	RENT ☒ OWN ☐ WITH PARENTS ☐	Street / City FORT ORD	State CA.	YRS 1 MOS 4

EDUCATION (Check One)	College Graduate	NAME AND LOCATION OF COLLEGE
Under 12 Yrs. ☐ 13-15 Yrs. ☒	Yes ☐	SAN JOSE STATE - SAN JOSE CA
12 Yrs. ☐ 16 Yrs. & Over ☐	No ☒	

NAME OF NEAREST RELATIVE NOT LIVING WITH YOU	COMPLETE ADDRESS	RELATIONSHIP
MR. F.W. SMITH	234 SECOND ST S.J.	FATHER

2. OCCUPATION: If applicant is Self-Employed, attach Current Financial Statement and/or Latest Income Tax Return

POSITION	EMPLOYED BY	YRS	MOS	BUS. TELEPHONE
COMPUTER OPER.	ABC Co.	1	9	252-2867

BUSINESS STREET ADDRESS	CITY	STATE
456 OAK ST.	SAN JOSE	CA.

PREVIOUS OCCUPATION	PREVIOUSLY EMPLOYED BY	ADDRESS	YRS	MOS
U.S. ARMY	U.S. ARMY		3	

SPOUSE'S OCCUPATION	EMPLOYED BY	ADDRESS	YRS	MOS
TYPIST	ACE INSURANCE Co.	111 MAIN ST. S.J.	—	8

MONTHLY INCOME (APPLICANT)	SPOUSE	OTHER INCOME (SOURCE)	AMOUNT	TOTAL
850.00	450.00	—	—	1300.00

IF IN MILITARY SERVICE, MILITARY ADDRESS	RANK	ENLISTMENT EXPIRES

3. DEPOSITS: Name of Banks, Savings & Loan Associations & Credit Unions

	Bank	Branch & Location	Account No.
CHECKING	BANK OF AMERICA	MAIN OFFICE	0351-1211
SAVINGS	" "	" "	0352-2644
SAVINGS & LOAN			
CREDIT UNION			

4. LOANS AND CREDIT INFORMATION

Home Mortgaged To	Address
RENT	

		Purchase Date of Home	Purchase Price	Current Market Value Approx.	Loan No.	Balance Due	Mo. Payments
						$	$

Auto-Make	Yr	Model	Financed By and Address	Balance Due	Mo. Payments
FORD MUSTANG	71		BANK OF AMERICA MAIN	$2300.00	$115.00
CHEV.	62	2 DR.	OWN	$ -0-	$

5. CREDIT REFERENCES

List other loans and charge accounts: (Banks, Finance Co.'s, Credit Unions, Stores, etc.) Attach separate sheet if necessary.

PAYMENTS BEING MADE TO: (Name & Address)	Type of Loan	Loan Number	Balance Due	Mo. Payments
1. SEARS SAN JOSE	REV.		$265.00	$15.00
2. MACY'S S.F.	"		$136.00	$10.00
3.			$	$
4.			$	$
		TOTALS:	$401.00	$25.00

BANKAMERICARD AGREEMENT

10-18-71	John Smith	Betty A. Smith
Date Signed	Signature of Applicant	Signature of Other Applicant

Molsten and seal. Thank you.

8. A typical but fictitious BankAmericard application.

of time. If the case is ambiguous, or if some fact or circumstance seems suspect, the staff will attempt to bring further information to bear on their decision. One of the commonest means to this end is to purchase a second credit report, from another reporting firm, to supplement the first. Another is to engage in 'direct checking', that is, for the staff of the San Francisco centre to verify crucial facts through telephone inquiries of their own. This may mean telephoning the applicant's employer to verify his employment, its duration, and his salary. It may mean contacting some of the creditors listed on the application, seeking up-dated information on the applicant's pattern of payment. In general, the staff prefer to avoid direct checking, since it requires more time than they like to spend on any single application.

Chapter 5 provided a brief résumé of the significance attached to various forms of credit information, noting that most credit-grantors are unanimous in favouring applicants with high incomes, stable residential, occupational and family patterns, and consistent records of conscientious payments of past credit obligations. BankAmericard policy embraces virtually the same views presented there. But what makes Bank-Americard and every other credit-granting policy distinctive is the ways in which these various characteristics are orchestrated within the decision-making system, that is, the weights and emphases ascribed to each of these conditions in forming an over-all credit-granting policy. These decision-making policies are geared to solving the characteristic problem inherent in BankAmericard operations as described above – the problem of extending sweeping credit privileges to a mass clientele, while minimizing default. This the system accomplishes by setting rather generous standards in terms of the incomes of its applicants, but insisting at the same time on considerable evidence of 'stability'.

The first consideration is, inevitably, the applicant's solvency. Will his income, as noted in the credit application and verified in the credit report, allow him enough beyond his present commitments for rent, food, and so on to pay for his credit purchases? In general, the system does not issue cards to those whose monthly income falls below $650 – a fairly low figure, when one considers that the average annual income per employed person in California was about $9,000 in 1969. Income is not the only consideration in determining solvency, however. Other assets are also important, including real estate, bank deposits, and other evidence of solvency. Credit accounts outstanding, including both mortgage debt and other obligations, also enter into consideration here, in that they help to assess the over-all demands on the applicant's financial resources.

After solvency, the next broad consideration is the applicant's past history of consumer credit accounts. For many applicants there is no better indication of likelihood of meeting future credit obligations than past performance in this same respect, so the BankAmericard staff look very closely at the information on this point. Best of all, from the point of view of the system, is a clean record, with all accounts 'paid as agreed'. Failing that, a few slightly late payments in past accounts, in the context of generally conscientious payment record, should not in itself be fatal to the application. But where delinquency becomes the norm in the applicant's past credit accounts, and where these delinquencies continue over several months without being rectified or, worse still, where the account is 'written off' altogether by the creditor and turned over to a collection agency, the application is rejected. Bankruptcy, as in nearly all other credit situations, automatically results in rejection. Naturally, the over-all process of weighing and interpreting these various data follows an unwritten set of rules much more complex than those just stated. The staff may regard certain forms of hardship like the applicant's illness as sufficiently extenuating to outweigh the effects of temporary delinquencies in payment of accounts, for example. Likewise, the screening process must also take into account all sorts of 'special cases', like applicants too young to have accumulated a 'credit history', or divorced persons whose past records are embroiled with those of their former mates. Such complicating factors, and many others, conspire to make the decision-making process in its entirety quite complex. But the considerations just cited do form the basis for most decision-making.

Neither solvency nor good credit history is in itself more

than a necessary condition, however. Unless the applicant possesses that crucial quality of 'stability', both of the former may be dubious guides. An applicant with considerably greater income than the rule-of-thumb minimum, yet showing erratic marital history, sporadic employment and/or frequent changes of address may be refused a card no matter how solvent he is at the time of application. On the other hand, applicants falling below the usual minimum income level but showing unmistakable signs of 'stability' along with a good credit record are often seen as good candidates for cards. Thus a working man earning only $100 per week, but having long tenure of a responsible job and a record of long and faithful payment of his home mortgage would be quite likely to receive a card. The ultimate question, after all, is not how great are the applicant's resources, but how willing and able he will be to devote those which he has to meeting his BankAmericard debts.

The business of establishing 'stability', then, is crucial, and the staff direct their attention very earnestly to the search for evidence of this much valued quality. The clues which they pursue are roughly of the same sort described in the preceding chapter. Stable marital history is highly desirable. So are stable residential and occupational patterns. So too, as one might expect, is consistency in paying other credit obligations. Ownership of one's own home and of an automobile and, curiously enough, the maintenance of a telephone listed in one's own name are likewise evidence of the desired attribute.

Probably various occupations carry their own connotations of stability from the standpoint of the decision-makers. Bankers and lawyers, for example, are probably seen as *prima facie* stable, while entertainers and construction workers, if only because of the special vulnerability of their employment to fluctuations in the economy, are bound to be viewed with some reserve. Certainly these inchoate impressions of the stability, and hence the creditworthiness, associated with different occupations figure importantly in many firms' credit policies, even if not in those of BankAmericard. Some readers may be dubious about the relevance of these considerations, as well as matters of telephones and years of formal education, to the question of whether a given applicant is apt to pay his bills. In some cases the relationship may indeed be fanciful. But statistical analysis often does show relationships between these apparently unrelated data and final performance as a card-holder, and it is reasonable to think that veteran credit personnel over long experience in the business often develop accurate instincts for these relationships.

It would be wrong to conclude, from this description of the processing of BankAmericard applications, that the exercise of fine discretion by senior officials is the norm. The opposite is the case; the highly routinized screening processes have been designed in such a way that low-level staff can process the great bulk of applications in a matter of a few minutes. Most applications are so obviously either acceptable or unacceptable to BankAmericard that a relatively inexperienced clerk can review the application, obtain the necessary supporting documentation, and take the decision. Only in rare ambiguous cases will the staff shunt the decision-making process upward to a more senior official.

Some Checks on BankAmericard Use

I have already suggested that BankAmericard has had to pay a price for choosing to operate a 'mass' credit card service rather than a 'prestige' credit card scheme. Part of this price, I have said, is the care necessary in screening the applications, so as to separate those low- and middle-income applicants who will prove willing to pay their BankAmericard bills from those who will not. But additional mechanisms are also necessary, once the cards are in the hands of their intended users, to maintain control over their use.

One of the most important and simplest checks on the use of the BankAmericard is the 'floor limit' governing the size of sales by participating merchants. 'Floor limit' is actually a term taken from department store credit practice, where this was the largest credit purchase which could be authorized by the most responsible clerk 'on the floor' at any given time. For the BankAmericard system, the floor limit is the size of the largest transaction chargeable by a particular merchant without a telephone check to the BankAmericard headquarters.

This telephone check, referred to as the 'authorization' of a sale, enables the system to exert control over categories of transaction which would otherwise generate large losses through unpaid charges. Thus the system generally requires the authorization only of larger charges, which obviously generate greater losses, when unpaid, than do smaller ones. Likewise, BankAmericard imposes especially low floor limits on those participating merchants thought to be most susceptible to fraudulent charges. These include firms in areas where crime rates are especially high, and those selling merchandise which is particularly easily resaleable, like liquor or jewellery. Setting the floor limit for any particular merchant is the responsibility of the bank which enrolls that merchant, and this differs according to the bank involved, the location of the merchant, and the type of product or service. For most merchants in California, the floor limit is $50 for most BankAmericards, or $100 for specially marked cards.

The second basic check on the individual's use of his card applies to the total amount of charges which he is allowed to accrue at any one time. Part of the process of screening the application for a BankAmericard is the setting of a 'credit limit'. This figure, which in California ranges from $100 upwards, is adjusted according to the means of the card-holder, and represents the maximum of accumulated charges which he is allowed to accrue at any one time. This means that unpaid balance in the card-holder's account must never exceed this figure, either from a series of charges accumulated all at once, or through the slower process of making more cash purchases than he pays off.

What makes these checks viable is a highly efficient computerized accounting system by which the San Francisco staff maintain exceedingly close surveillance over the activity of each account. This system relies in turn on the rapid processing of records of each BankAmericard transaction. Participating merchants in California are required, under the terms of their agreements with the system, to deposit all sales slips with their local branch of the Bank of America within three days of the sale. This means simply turning over all the sales slips which have accumulated within the last three days and receiving payment for the approximately ninety-seven to ninety-nine per cent of their value which accrues to the merchant. Slips are then returned immediately from the branch bank to the San Francisco centre. Each slip bears the imprint of the card number, the signature of the card-holder, the merchant's identification number, the date, some notation of the kind of merchandise sold, and the amount of the sale. Thus, within three to five days after virtually all sales made in California, the BankAmericard centre enters the charge in the card-holder's account. Payments from card-holders are likewise entered within twenty-four hours of receipt in San Francisco.

The rapidity of the posting of sales vouchers to individual accounts is significant for the surveillance capacity of the system. It means that only five days, in most cases, are necessary before an irresponsible 'spending spree' registers with the agencies whose responsibility it is to control such behaviour. The BankAmericard computer constantly checks the outstanding balance of each account against the credit limit assigned to it. If the account exceeds this limit, the machine automatically prints out a warning to this effect, to be forwarded to the credit department, whose job it is to deal with these delinquent accounts.

Authorization

For the merchant, the inducement to obtain authorization is clear enough. BankAmericard assumes no responsibility for any charge unless the merchant carries out the sale according to a precise set of written rules – and these of course include authorization of charges in excess of the floor limit. Every participating merchant in California has the telephone number of the 'authorization centre' of the BankAmericard headquarters, and the business of obtaining authorization quickly becomes a matter of routine. Every foreign and domestic bank participating in the system maintains at least one of these offices, essentially a communications centre devoted to the rapid checking of information and decision-making on these requests. The San Francisco centre responds to authorization requests every day of the year from eight in the morning until midnight. There may be as many as twenty authorizers, persons empowered to make decisions on these requests, on duty at a single time, depending on season and time of day. It is their task, on receiving such a request, to interrogate the computerized record of the card-holder's account and, using this and any other relevant information, arrive at a decision as to whether the transaction should be permitted.

Each authorizer wears a telephone headset and sits facing a keyboard computer console and a computerized screen; she communicates with the inquiring merchant by telephone while interrogating the computer memory from the console. On receiving an inquiry, the authorizer immediately asks for the merchant's identifying number, the buyer's card number (which is also his account number), the amount of the requested sale, the expiration date of the card, and the nature of the merchandise or services to be sold. All these data the authorizer taps into the computer memory through the console. The computer then automatically analyses the information on the account in question to determine whether the transaction is 'safe', from the standpoint of the system. In about three quarters of all cases, the account shows no irregularities, and the purchase, when added to the credit balance, remains within the credit limit. Under these circumstances, the machine automatically flashes an instruction to this effect to the authorizer via the screen, and the latter relays to the merchant permission to make the sale. The machine's response is conveyed in the form of an 'authorization number', which the machine subsequently 'remembers' and which the merchant must add to the sales slip. The use of this number acts as a control over subsequent claims by merchants that unauthorized sales were in fact authorized. Authorization exchanges of the kind just described, including the transmission of the authorization number, usually take less than one minute.

In the remaining cases, however, where the advisability of authorizing the transaction is not obvious, the machine turns the decision over to the discretion of the authorizer. This it does by presenting on the screen, instead of the authorization number, the entirety of the data stored on the account in question. These are as follows:

The high balance (the largest dollar value of charges which the card-holder has ever allowed to accumulate)

The credit limit (as assigned at the time the card was issued, subject to subsequent revision)

The present balance (or accumulated charges now outstanding)

The number of months the card has been held

The date of the last month in which the account was delinquent

The total number of months in which the account has been delinquent

The date of entry of the last payment (the day on which the card-holder's last payment was credited to his account)

The amount by which the account is delinquent (if any)

The authorizer must use this information to answer the single question of constant concern: will the proposed purchase be excessive in relation to the person's willingness and ability to pay? The first step therefore is to judge whether the proposed purchase will raise the balance of the account into a figure greater than the credit limit. Theoretically, of course, every card-holder should bear his credit limit in mind, and limit his purchases so as to remain within it. But in practice card-holders seem to pay little attention to their limits until reminded of them by the system. Each card-holder, moreover, is allowed at least a minor amount of leeway over his limit. In most cases, for example, the authorizer receiving a request for a charge which would bring the total to within ten per cent of the credit limit would grant authorization. In such cases, the authorizer simply instructs the machine to produce an authorization number which she relays to the merchant.

The nature of this transaction obviously leaves a good deal of discretion in the hands of the authorizer. The system makes every effort to authorize as many sales as possible, even certain ones far exceeding the credit limit; large sales and high credit balances, on a basis of ten to eighteen per cent annual interest, can obviously be highly profitable. But the profits come only from authorizing sales which the card-holder is willing and able to pay. It is the authorizer's art, therefore, to use the available information as skilfully and as fully as possible to discriminate between the transactions which should or should not be allowed.

So, faced with a request for authorization of sales which would considerably exceed the card-holder's credit limit, the authorizer will make a careful analysis of the other account information before deciding. Perhaps the first question which she will ask is how long the card has been held. Short tenure guarantees very little, and will conduce to denial of the authorization. But if the account is of long standing, the authorizer will also note the date of the last delinquency, and the total months during which the account has been delinquent. An old account with no record of delinquencies may be allowed sales considerably in excess of the stipulated limit. Still better if the account information shows a large high balance, without any recent delinquencies. But if the data present a picture of chronic delinquencies, such that the requested sale shows little promise of speedy payment, the authorizer will certainly decline the request. The date of the last payment by the card-holder can also be useful, for it helps to verify the card-holder's common excuse that an excessive balance has already been paid off.

The availability of this account information, then, obviously provides the system with some extremely flexible and useful tools for its decision-making activities. But this is really only the beginning of the immensely resourceful use which Bank-Americard makes of its information during the course of authorization. The main object of the system in making these decisions is clearly to use as much relevant information as possible about each account every time there is a request for authorization on that account. The system especially seeks to avoid authorizing further charges if a 'spending spree' is under way, either by the intended card-holder or by someone who has obtained the card illegally. The difficulty here is that one to five days are required for sales drafts to make their way from the merchant to the San Francisco centre, so that this much time may elapse before the behaviour in question comes under surveillance. But over-floor-limit charges are recorded as they are authorized, so that the system maintains an instantaneous and complete account of these, even including charges within the previous few minutes. Thus the purchase of a portable television for a sum in excess of the floor limit automatically results in the increase of one's credit balance, and hence in a limitation of the further amount one can spend.

Nor is the immediate entry of the amount of the purchase in the card-holder's account the only check which the authorization process affords. For the information which the authorizer initially feeds into the computer memory – including the nature of the goods or services purchased, the amount of the sale and the identity of the merchant making the sale – remains available for scrutiny between the time of the sale and the point at which the sales voucher arrives at the San Francisco centre and is added to the account. This is extremely important for the surveillance capacity of the system, for it means that any spurt of large purchases is immediately apparent to the system, and can form a basis for responsive action.

This feature of the system is immensely useful for purposes of social control. One form of misbehaviour which it serves to curb is the use of stolen BankAmericards. For the staff of the San Francisco headquarters, having dealt with tens of thousands of such cases, can readily spot patterns of use of stolen cards, which usually involve a large number of purchases within a short time, and preferences for specific kinds of merchandise. Whenever the system authorizes a charge on any account, data on the previous authorization immediately appear on the screen if another authorization should be required within twenty-four hours. At the same time, the system warns the authorizer if *any* other authorization data are recorded, that is whether there have been any authorizations for which sales slips have not yet reached the accounting department in San Francisco. Data for all such authorizations are accessible to the authorizer. Thus, if there is anything questionable about any authorization request, the authorizer may check the detail of every authorization held in the computer memory, which can readily number up to a dozen, depending on the amount of recent activity of the account.

The ability to scrutinize the detail of recent sales enables the system to curtail both fraud and many other forms of misuse of the BankAmericard. In the case of fraudulent use, it is relatively easy for an experienced authorizer to spot the characteristic pattern of sales made by someone who has obtained the card illegally. A pattern of rapid authorization of sales of highly portable, readily re-sold items is very distinctive. Thus when an authorizer receives a request for authorization of a sale of a portable television, only to find that the same card has been used to purchase four other portable television sets of the same type within the last hour, she will certainly take action to curtail the use of the card, no matter what the credit status of the account. On the other hand, the same system may serve to allow purchases which otherwise would appear as dangerously excessive. On an account whose credit standing is good, for example, a large series of over-limit purchases which seem to involve some 'legitimate' purpose, for example luggage and airline tickets, may be allowed as readily as a highly suspect series of purchases would be denied. The effect of the availability of this authorization information is thus greatly to enhance the sophistication of the system in deciding which charges should and should not be honoured.

Nor is this the extent of the information which the computer can provide the authorizer to guide her decision-making. There are also a series of 'blocking instructions', capable of being entered against any account, which act as *prima facie* checks on the authorization of any sales through that particular card. One such block, for example, is a code which indicated that the card has been reported lost. When this instruction appears, the authorizer can ask the merchant, who is supposed to retain the card while seeking the authorization, to withhold it from the customer. This the merchant is usually more than willing to do, since BankAmericard offers a minimum reward of $25 for the return of cards in fraudulent use.

But usually the process of reclaiming such cards is more involved than this, for the system makes serious and frequently effective attempts to secure the arrest of fraudulent users. Thus the first task, when a blocking instruction appears indicating that the card has been reported lost or stolen, is to make certain that the would-be user is not simply the authorized user, who may simply have found the previously mislaid card. This the authorizer does by obtaining the original report of the loss or theft, stored near by, and asking the would-be purchaser a few pertinent questions, either directly or more often via the inquiring merchant: Has the purchaser reported the card lost or stolen? If so, under what circumstances did the loss or theft occur? What is the card-holder's current address? All this information is collected and filed at the centre when the card-holder originally reports the loss or theft of the card, and is unlikely to be provided by a fraudulent user. By asking these and a few other questions, the authorizer can form an accurate opinion as to whether the would-be user is guilty of fraud.

Once the authorizer is convinced of attempted fraud, she invokes an elaborate routine of stalling questions to the would-be purchaser, again usually via the merchant. This highly rehearsed routine can go on virtually indefinitely. Meanwhile, another staff member telephones the police in the locality where the attempted charge is taking place, informs them of the situation, and asks them to send an officer to make the arrest. Often, of course, the party flees before the police can arrive – in which case, however, the merchant usually still retains the stolen card. But arrests under these circumstances are by no means uncommon; California BankAmericard reports bringing about 450 arrests by means of identifications through the authorization process during 1970.

But it would be wrong to leave the reader with the impression that the only use of blocking instructions is as a check against fraudulent charges. Their main use is in the much more common instances where the system has reason to deny the intended card-holder the use of his own account. Here, too, the various blocking instructions allow the authorizer a variety of possible choices of how to deal with the request. There are actually about thirty-four different blocking codes, and these appear in pairs. Some of them require the merchant to retain the card, but most do not. One blocking instruction, for example, reads 'MARDIF', and is entered in the accounts of card-holders estranged from their spouses, in cases of disputes over responsibility for BankAmericard charges. When an authorization is attempted on one of these cards, the authorizer simply relays the message to the card-holder, via the merchant, that use of the card is suspended until the question of responsibility is resolved. The system enters other blocks against charges on accounts whose balance is excessive, or whose payments are seriously in arrears. Sometimes the card-holder can provide information to the authorizer sufficient to justify lifting the block, for example an explanation of some irregularity in payment of the account. Ordinarily, however, the block serves to prevent authorization from occurring, and may also result in at least the temporary retention of the card.

Nor, still, is this the extent of the information which the system can bring to bear on authorization requests. For it also has recourse to most of the original BankAmericard applications completed by each card-holder. All but the oldest of these are filed in a library next to the authorization centre, along with the credit reports originally drawn in the course of screening the application. When, as commonly occurs, a request comes to the authorization centre for a large over-limit charge on an otherwise sound account, the authorizer will often obtain the application form as an aid in the decision-making. The effort, in all of these instances, is to authorize as many sales as possible. For the system thrives on high volume and especially on large sales which take some months for the card-holder to pay off, at considerable interest. Often a review of the application will show that the card-holder's resources and credit history permit a higher credit limit than he has been assigned, and in these cases the authorizer will grant permission for the sale.

There is also one additional option open to the authorizers in dealing with requests for transactions which exceed the credit limit assigned, one which requires more time to carry out than the others. This is the adjustment of the credit limit itself so as to allow for greater amounts of indebtedness in the future. If, for example, the customer requests a transaction so large as considerably to exceed his limit, yet shows a sound record of past payment, the authorizer may ask him to defer his transaction a few days until some further research can be done. He may ask the card-holder to submit a new credit card application, bringing up-to-date the information available to the system when it originally issued the card. The 'limit control' section will handle this new information, perhaps also seeking an additional credit report on the consumer. If the new information seems to warrant it, the limit on the account will be raised so as to allow not only the transaction originally sought, but subsequent large purchases as well.

There are many other checks, as well, on the authorization of BankAmericard purchases. Like the Chicago meat-packer who claimed to use every part of his pigs but their squeal, BankAmericard finds countless ingenious uses for the information which it compiles, uses which serve as cross-checks against unwarranted sales, either through the authorization process or elsewhere. For example, whenever an authorizer refuses a purchase, a record of that refusal and the reasons for it are held in the computer memory, and appear automatically when the card-holder seeks to make a further sale. This can help to establish a pattern of 'irresponsible' use, even in the absence of completed purchases. Then, too, card-holders are required to produce personal identification for all sales over $150, and addresses produced in such identification are checked against the computerized BankAmericard record of the address. Merchants themselves act as a potent protection against certain kinds of unwanted charges, since the reward for the return of 'wanted' cards encourages many of them to phone for authorization in suspect cases even where the charge is below the floor limit. And, in areas where the rate of 'bad' charges is high, the system can and does reduce the floor limit to zero, so that all charges must be cleared.

I wish space permitted discussion of all these various cross-checks and surveillance mechanisms in detail. But it would be wrong to give the impression that these complications and special practices are the rule. BankAmericard spokesmen estimate that seventy-five per cent of all authorization requests are approved automatically, without even the necessity of a discretionary judgement from the authorizer. Of the remaining twenty-five per cent, only ten per cent are ultimately denied.

But the San Francisco staff also note that approximately sixty-five per cent of accounts on which new authorizations are requested are already near their credit limit, so that some discriminating decision-making is clearly called for. In this system, then, as in all the others studied here, it is a small proportion of would-be disobedient clients who command a disproportionate amount of the resources of social control.

This is hardly the place to enter a verdict on the moral rights or wrongs of the operations of BankAmericard or any similar system. But it is interesting to reflect on the workings of this system in light of the frequently heard complaint that systems of mass surveillance, and computerized operations in particular, pursue their clients with relentlessness and unforgiving recollection of their past mistakes, real or imagined. The BankAmericard system, it is clear, is undoubtedly relentless in surveillance and control over the use of its cards, but one could hardly accuse it of gratuitous meanness or unforgiving stringency. For many of the practices just described have no other object than to enable the system to continue to extend credit to those who have, at least by the letter of the law, broken the rules set down for the use of the credit card. The careful examination of transactions too large for the assigned credit limit, for example, would be unnecessary if the system were willing simply to disallow these transactions out of hand. But the system flourishes on volume, and goes to the greatest lengths to keep that volume high, in terms of both the dollar value of sales and the numbers of transactions. To do so, it maintains exceptionally close surveillance over its clientele, using every atom of available information with maximum efficiency. This surveillance is not gratuitously stringent, but coldly discriminating in its generosity. The only reason for declining some credit transactions, after all, is to be able to realize the substantial profits which derive from the rest.

Action Against Delinquents

In general, preventative or pre-emptive forms of social control are much cheaper means of ensuring compliance than coercive forms. The use of physical intimidation which people readily associate with the action of social control is almost always unacceptable to controlling agencies as a continuing, everyday policy. For the costs of routinely carrying out such measures, even when they are successful, is apt to be prohibitive in relation to the benefits forthcoming from compliance. Certainly the management of BankAmericard has always predicted its practices on this assumption. The careful screening of applications and the sophisticated monitoring of credit transactions are preventative rather than coercive forms of social control. If the effectiveness of these procedures should begin to slip, so that delinquencies requiring an active, coercive response were to rise even a few percentage points, the whole system would rapidly take notice, since profits would drop distinctly. For no matter how expensive may be the business of preventing people from doing the wrong thing in the first place, the costs of apprehending them once they have 'gone wrong', or of setting right the damage they have done, are much greater.

Nevertheless, it is doubtful whether any system of social control can avoid coercive measures altogether, if only as a means of demonstrating to its clientele that more forceful sanctions are available, should disobedience occur. With BankAmericard, some accounts do become seriously delinquent, and some cards are used by persons who were never intended to hold them and who intend never to pay. At these points, more coercive measures are applied. In the case of bad debts, the system must take action to ensure that the cardholder ultimately pays or, failing that, turn the account over to a collection agency. At the same time, it must take especially energetic measures to deprive the customer of his chance to use his card, which may mean accosting him personally to obtain it. These practices are expensive, as the BankAmericard management is acutely aware. But they are regarded as necessary to prevent still further losses, and the system has developed ways of carrying them out which, characteristically, maximize the returns obtained for the trouble and expense involved.

The system divides its activities with respect to delinquencies into two categories – those dealing with 'credit' violations, and those concerned with fraud. The former are those violations carried out by persons intended to have cards;

Table 12. *Losses Sustained by United States BankAmericard Operations as a Result of Credit and Fraud Delinquencies, for Quarter Ended 30 June 1971*

	Average Loss per Delinquent Account	Percent of Total Liquidations (card-holder payments) Represented by Each Form of Loss
Credit	$430.00	1.47
Fraud	$464.00	.30

Source: National BankAmericard, Inc.

the latter, violations by persons who have obtained cards through loss or theft. The procedures used in dealing with the two categories are distinctly different. The former it handles, at least initially, with considerable patience, in hopes of 'rehabilitating' its delinquent account-holders into paying, profit-generating customers once again; the latter receive coercive treatment from the beginning. Table 12 shows the financial losses stemming from these two forms of deviance.

The treatment of credit delinquencies meshes closely with the accounting and surveillance practices described in the previous section. A special collection department in the San Francisco centre, staffed by fifty-one 'collectors', keeps careful watch over delinquent accounts, and deals with them according to a highly specified set of rules. Most of their contacts with delinquent card-holders are by telephone. Accounts become delinquent if unpaid thirty days after the date of the first monthly statement, and the collectors make routine telephone calls to card-holders fifteen and thirty days after the date of delinquency. After sixty days' delinquency, a file is opened on the case, and telephone contact becomes more frequent and less standardized after that. The collector's first task is always to obtain an explanation of why the delinquency has occurred. In most cases some unexpected financial stringency, like an unexpected medical expense, proves to be the immediate cause. The collector, gently but firmly, next seeks a commitment from the card-holder of payment of a given amount by a specified date. The card-holder's file is then reopened one week after the promised date to determine whether payment has been received. By pursuing delinquencies in this way, the staff insist, they quickly establish a pattern either of payment or of non-payment.

During the first period, when a promise to begin repayment is pending, the collection section place a block in the computer against the use of the card, and request the card-holder not to use it until his account is once again in good standing. In most cases, the payment is forthcoming as agreed, and the account gradually returns to a 'healthy' condition without the necessity of more forceful steps than these. If the delinquency is quite serious, however, or if the card-holder does not make good his promise to begin repayment by a specified date, or if he fails to reach such an agreement with the collector, the latter will request him to return his card. In approximately ninety-five per cent of these cases the cards are returned freely. Nor does even this recourse count permanently against the card-holder, since approximately half the cards obtained in this way are returned within a year, once the credit delinquency has been rectified.

If the card-holder remains recalcitrant, however, and appears apt to make further use of the card, the system does not hesitate to resort to more forceful measures. BankAmericard then takes recourse to what must be one of the more extreme examples of the division of social labour in modern America – the credit-card repossessing firm. For $5, this firm sends one of its agents to the home of the delinquent card-holder, to demand the card; if successful, the firm collects an additional $15 for its trouble. The agent has no special legal standing, and certainly no power to enter the premises of the card-holder against the card-holder's wishes, but he nevertheless obtains the card in the great majority of cases. And, by the report of the collection department staff, even those who refuse to yield the card still do not use it, once they have had a call from one of the agents.

There still remains, however, the problem of recouping the financial losses to the system in those cases where the card-holder shows no inclination to pay voluntarily. The policy is never to follow any delinquent account for more than 180 days, unless a convincing pattern of repayment has been established. If the debt shows no signs of being paid at that point, the account is apt to be assigned to a collection agency. The agency will then attempt still more forceful and persistent measures to ensure payment. Otherwise, the matter will be turned over to the Bank of America's legal department for civil or criminal action, much in the same way as delinquent loans from the various branches of the Bank of America. In either case, the matter passes outside the BankAmericard system.

The measures applied against fraudulent users of lost or stolen cards are much more stringent. The San Francisco centre maintains a security staff of seven former policemen, who specialize in the curtailment of fraud. These agents retain their status as special officers with the police forces with which they were formerly affiliated – all cities in the immediate San Francisco Bay Area. This gives them both the advantage of close working relations with these bodies, and the power of arrest.

Information on the fraudulent use of cards comes to the attention of the security department in a number of ways. Very commonly, a card-holder will himself report the loss or theft of his card. When this occurs, the details of the loss or theft are taken down and held in readiness as described above, and a block against use of the account is entered. In other instances the intended card-holder will be unaware that the card is missing, so that the first signal to the system is a rapidly mounting series of charges which quickly spill over the credit limit. Many fraudulent users, it is true, appreciate the surveillance capabilities of the system well enough to use the card only once, in which case there is little chance of apprehension. But elsewhere there will be a rapid series of charges, usually either centred on a specific geographical location or describing a path in a single direction. It is these cases which receive the most assiduous attention from the security staff.

Whatever the other difficulties faced by the security staff, they always can identify the places where fraudulent use of any card is taking place from the transaction records. The first task is to interview, either in person or by telephone, staff members of the establishments which honoured the cards, to attempt to develop a description of the user. The agent then approaches the police in the localities in which the card has been used, in hopes of identifying the suspect. Often the suspect proves to be someone known or sought by the local police, who will make the arrest on the strength of the agent's report. But, failing this, the agent will at least be able to alert the police to his search. In other instances, it will remain for the BankAmericard agent to establish a pattern for the use of the card, perhaps making inquiries about the suspected user at places where he is thought to reside or frequent.

Another weapon at the disposal of the security department is what they call their 'hotcarding' technique. This entails circulating the number of the card under fraudulent use to a number of merchants considered likely targets for such use. The merchants are offered the $25 reward for the return of the card, and denied payment for any charges made on the card. The practice is advantageous to BankAmericard, in that the sum offered as reward is considerably less than the losses to which fraudulent use of a single card can subject the system. In a small minority of cases, cards involved in credit delinquencies also receive this treatment, but its main target is the professional criminal. The principal constraint upon this technique, however, is that the management of BankAmericard consider it undesirable to circulate more than ten cancellation notices to the same establishment. Such circulations represent something of an obstacle to the desired quick consummation of sales.* Thus, to be effective, the choice of which merchants to approach requires great predictive skill in determining where the fraudulent user is apt to strike. The security staff, it must be said, possess considerable accumulated expertise in such decision-making, having reclaimed a total of 1,020 cards this way during 1970. And, even where the card is not reclaimed, the security staff insist that knowledge of the hotcarding practice among professional users of stolen cards effectively discourages their use.

---

* In this respect the system possesses a distinct advantage over certain of its competitors who circulate listings of thousands of not-to-be-honoured cards to all of their participating merchants. The necessity of checking all these listings before making a sale is bound to be irksome to the latter.

Sometimes, too, the user of the card will be identified when he attempts to make a purchase subject to the authorization procedure – although professionals in the business are generally too sophisticated to attempt this. When such an authorization is sought, of course, a block appears with coded instructions making it apparent to the authorizer that the card is stolen. When this happens, the authorizer employs the highly developed routine of stalling described above, meanwhile alerting the security staff. Either the police or the security agents will attempt to arrest the would-be user of the card before he leaves the establishment.

Exchange of Information with Other Agencies

For the consumer credit reporting industry, as the preceding chapter noted, the purpose of collecting and collating information is its ultimate dissemination to other organizations. Britain's National Insurance system, on the other hand, collects information almost exclusively for use within the system, and its provision to outside bodies, though it does occur, is exceptional. BankAmericard stands somewhere between these two extremes. True, it has designed most of its record-keeping procedures to fit its own internal needs of accounting, authorization, collection, and so on. But this same organizational machinery also serves to provide information on BankAmericard accounts to outside agencies, primarily credit bureaus, which require its use. And the symbiosis between BankAmericard and these agencies is in fact vital to both parties.

In these respects, BankAmericard differs little from other very large consumer credit granting firms, such as banks or large department stores. All such firms rely on information from one another – either directly, or indirectly via consumer credit reporting agencies – in deciding to accept or refuse credit applications; and all must, by the same token, provide information to one another. Most consumer credit reporting agencies require their members to provide account information for their files. In some cases, *all* account information is regularly incorporated into bureau records. In addition, credit agencies regularly make single inquiries to the San Francisco centre concerning the status of specific accounts. BankAmericard routinely honours such requests, from both credit bureaus and other businesses. For not to do so would endanger the principle of reciprocity which governs these exchanges, and probably result in the subsequent denial to BankAmericard of information badly needed for processing applications or for reassessing card-holders' credit limits.

In the San Francisco centre, the provision of information is accomplished in conjunction with the authorization procedure. Along with the authorizers, the authorization centre contains seating space for three staff whose sole function is to provide account information for credit inquiries. For this purpose they use the same equipment used by the authorizers – telephone headset, computer console and viewing screen – and to the outsider they appear to be doing the same job. But the task of providing credit information is considerably simpler than that of making authorizations. The clerk simply obtains from the caller the card-holder's BankAmericard number, taps this into the machine with the appropriate coded instruction, and the account data appear on the screen. This is the same account information used in making authorizations, and consists, the reader will recall, of the high balance, the credit limit, the present balance, the number of months the account has been open, the total number of months during which the account has been delinquent, and the date of the last delinquency. The policy of the centre is to report no delinquencies from more than two years in the past, effectively providing a little extra latitude for those delinquent card-holders who 'rehabilitate themselves'. The information thus provided by the San Francisco centre, telegraphic though it is, is sufficient for the purposes of most credit-grantors.

Is there any foolproof way of controlling the destination of this information? Not under the present arrangements for handling it. The situation of BankAmericard is much like that of credit bureaus in this respect. The most conscientious bureaus do succeed in selling reports only to authentic credit-granting businesses, but there is no positive means of ensuring that an employee of such a business will not order a report for purposes of his own. Likewise, BankAmericard faces an ultimately impossible discrimination task in accepting requests for account information from other credit-grantors. As a matter of policy it does provide the above-cited information for such firms, but there is in fact no certain means of identifying 'inauthentic' requests from these sources. The practice of the San Francisco centre is to ask the caller for the card number of the person on whom information is sought, on the assumption that the card number is unlikely to be available unless provided on a credit application. But there are obviously other ways of obtaining such card numbers, and no other means of identifying the 'wrong' requests than to seek such numbers. The existing safeguards, then, probably deter whimsical or capricious inquiries, but it is doubtful that they can be effective against concerted, persistent 'illegitimate' efforts to obtain account information.

International Organization and Future Trends

I have already mentioned that the operations of the San Francisco centre are not necessarily identical to those of other BankAmericard centres throughout the United States and the world. It now remains to explain a little more specifically the similarities and differences between the California operations and the others, and the patterns of competition and cooperation among the participating banks. This will make it easy, in turn, to cite some probable directions for future development of the system.

Originally the BankAmericard system operated only within the state of California. For the first seven years after its inception, it was the sole property of the Bank of America which, under Federal law, was empowered to do business only in that state. But since 1966 the parent bank has sponsored the introduction of this highly profitable element of its operations to the rest of the United States and, more recently, to other parts of the world. This it has done by selling the right to establish new systems elsewhere, and by extending the advice and know-how necessary to establish and operate these systems. The other participating banks in turn issue BankAmericards in their own right and recruit merchants within their areas of operation to honour these cards. In so doing, however, they also honour BankAmericards issued elsewhere and join together in competing with other large-scale credit card systems. Since 1970 the coordination of United States operations of Bank-Americard has passed from the Bank of America itself to the hands of a legally autonomous membership corporation, National BankAmericard Incorporated. Outside the United States, however, the Bank of America licenses other participating banks, enforcing certain uniform practices among all participants.

Thus, although the system maintained by the Bank of America in California is large, the entire world-wide enterprise represents a surveillance system of staggering proportions. But the California business remains a disproportionately large element of the total picture. Table 13 shows a rough comparison of the two.

Table 13. *Size of California, United States and Worldwide BankAmericard Operations, 30 June 1971*

	California	United States (excluding California)	Other Countries
Card-holders* (millions)	3.0	19.5	5.7
Participating Merchants	98,000	672,000	222,000
Member banks	1	3,901	80
Gross Sales, first half of 1971 (millions)	$390	$1,097	$280

Source: National BankAmericard, Inc. All figures are approximate.

In California only the Bank of America operates the Bank-Americard system; in each foreign country, one or more banks, or a Bank of America branch, take responsibility for the system. In other areas of the United States, the system's rules permit more than one bank to serve a single territory, and this occasionally happens. Under these circumstances, two or more banks will sometimes compete with one another to a limited extent within that area. They compete, for example, to enrol persons

* The number of card-holders is always greater than the number of accounts, since several members of a single family or firm may hold cards on a single account. In California the ratio of currently valid cards to accounts is approximately 3:2.

as BankAmericard holders. For every card-holder is tied to a single issuing bank, and it is that bank which must take responsibility for screening his application at the start and servicing his account thereafter. Member banks likewise compete to recruit merchants to participation in the system. In the first case, the actual terms of agreement between card-holder and bank vary rather little throughout the system. But the contracts offered participating merchants vary significantly in relative advantages they offer to the two sides, especially with respect to the size of the discount on sales claimed by the bank.

Nevertheless, despite this element of competition, National BankAmericard Inc. does set down certain binding rules which govern practice among participating banks. Each card-issuing bank must, first of all, maintain a processing centre along the lines of the one in San Francisco – although the latter is from all accounts much the most sophisticated. It must impose a floor limit upon participating merchants. It must establish an authorization procedure, observe accounting procedures roughly similar to those observed in California, and also maintain similar security and collection procedures. The rules of the national organization do allow for a good deal of variability in practice in all these respects – for example, the accounting and authorization procedures of one participating bank still rely on a paper-and-pencil ledger system, rather than computers. But practice among all banks, foreign and domestic, must be similar enough to allow for the easy use of cards issued by any one bank throughout the world.

It is this easy usability of cards throughout the various participating countries which holds the greatest interest here, for it is full of implications for the *scale* of this surveillance system, both present and future. As the preceding chapters have shown, surveillance systems face characteristic problems when they grow large. As any system attempts to deal with clients over greater social or geographical space, it faces difficulties of organization and communication which make it difficult to bring the full weight of its clients' records to bear on its decision-making concerning them. If it fails to do so, it exposes itself to the characteristic dangers of evasion through clients' flight from the scene of past misdeeds. On the other hand, there are often great premiums on these forms of expansion of scale – and that premium, in the case of BankAmericard, is the increased business which results from offering consumers a card usable as widely as possible. Thus mechanisms which ensure the extension of scale in this system deserve some special note here.

Perhaps the most important and interesting of these is authorization procedure. One point of a special vulnerability in any large-scale credit card system, of course, is the possibility that a 'bad' card might be used wildly outside the jurisdiction in which it was issued, without the issuing agency being able to curtail that usage. The first 'line of defence' against such abuse is the system's interlocking authorization procedures. Any 'foreign' card, that is any card issued by a bank outside the merchant's region, remains subject to the same authorization procedures as any other card. When a merchant telephones his authorization centre to make the charge, that centre must in turn contact the authorization centre of the issuing bank. Within North America, participating banks usually do this by telephone. For other countries, requests are generally by telex, though there is no firm rule. Once contact is established between the merchant and the appropriate authorization centre, the authorization transaction continues very much as if it were occurring in the same city as the sale.

Still, there are often problems. Both telephone and telex lines do sometimes fail, so that the authorization cannot be completed. More importantly, differences in time zones intervene when the distances between transaction and authorizing centre are great. Few centres remain on duty around the clock, and an early-morning request in New York will find the San Francisco centre off-duty. Thus, when contact between the merchant and the authorization centre is impossible, a complex series of rules, set down in detail by National BankAmericard Inc., governs responsibility for the sale. Under some circumstances, for example, the merchant himself must take responsibility for the charge, as though he had requested no authorization at all. Elsewhere, the responsibility lies either with the bank which issued the card or the one which accepted the original phone call. In some instances, the card-holder is asked to wait several hours to complete the transaction. These are awkward circumstances for the system. The most desirable thing, it is agreed, is to bring the full weight of each card-holder's record immediately to bear on the authorization decision, no matter where in the world he should attempt to use his card.

Other points of cooperation aimed at strengthening the collective system of social control have to do with hotcarding policy and the pursuit of fraudulent and delinquent card-holders. To prevent unchecked use of a 'bad' card in 'foreign' areas, any participating bank can request any other to apply the 'hotcard' technique to any or all participating merchants within its area. There is, however, a charge for granting these requests, a charge set and enforced by the national organiza-tion. Likewise, cooperation prevails with respect to the pursuit of delinquent card-holders across the jurisdiction of different banks. If a card-holder seriously in arrears in his payments moves from San Francisco to Chicago, the San Francisco centre forwards his account records to its Chicago counterpart for action by the latter, and *vice versa*. Or when a fraudulent user crosses the jurisdiction of various banks – usually, as it happens, leaving a trail of charges in his wake – the various security services treat the case with the same earnestness as if it were their own.

These patterns of cooperation, then, help to secure the net of social control, even though different participants may hold different corners of that net. Still, as I have suggested, the efforts of the various systems do suffer by virtue of the dispersal of the centres of social control throughout America and the world. Another way of putting this is to say that the capacity of the system is reduced by the *imperfect centralization* of information, with the resulting difficulty of using the full content of a client's records once he is outside the relevant jurisdiction.

BankAmericard officials are well aware of these limitations, and attempts to eliminate them are under way at the time of this writing. Under consideration at present are a series of alternate plans envisaging either a number of regional authoriza-tion centres, or possibly a single comprehensive national centre for all participating banks within the United States.

Such centres would remain open around the clock, and contain full information on all accounts throughout the region or throughout the nation. Any of the plans would, of course, involve the difficulties inherent in centralizing somewhat diverse and hitherto semi-autonomous activities. Conflicts among participating banks would be inevitable over such questions as how, if at all, to preserve the unique standards and techniques of authorization and data storage when all such activities take place within a single centre. But the message is plain: this system, like the others studied here, continues and will continue to develop fuller and fuller capacity. Whatever obstacles may stand in the way, the forces pushing against them seem at least for the time being superior.

The Capacity of BankAmericard Surveillance

Once again the time has come to formalize these observations in terms of the criteria for surveillance capacity set down in Chapter 1. Let me briefly review the various measures of the over-all effectiveness of BankAmericard operations as a system of surveillance.

First, the *amount* of usable data. The world-wide BankAmericard system deals with a clientele of staggering proportions, maintaining surveillance over the affairs of some twenty-eight million card-holders. This work, of course, is allocated among some eighty-six processing centres. But it is worth remembering that, even with this distribution of responsibilities among the various centres, the close cooperation among them makes this a more unified, centralized system than, say, the North American consumer credit reporting network. And the number of accounts under the jurisdiction of the two California centres alone – some two million of them – makes the system comparable in numbers of files to the criminal records system maintained by the British police.

The other main consideration, with respect to the quantity of information used, is that of how much data is filed on each client. As we have seen, the information stored is terse. Basically, as maintained in San Francisco, it consists of the original application and credit reports and the past record of the account, including amounts of credit used and the merchandise purchased. Occasionally, if the card is lost or stolen, or if there have been difficulties with payments, there may also be notes and forms resulting from conversations between the card-holder and the BankAmericard staff. These data represent a highly pertinent, succinct body of facts, useful for a variety of organizational purposes. The credit application, for example, not only provides information for the decision as to whether credit privileges should be granted in the first place, but also information on how the system can reach the card-holder once the card has been issued. As the discussion has shown, the credit application and report also serve to supplement authorization decisions, as do the accumulated data from past transactions and payments. Thus, although the information stored on any specific account may not amount to much more than two or three sheets of discrete facts, the resourcefulness of the system makes these data very potent indeed.

This is to say that *subtlety* of decision-making based on this information is considerable. As much should be clear from the discussion of authorization procedures. The success of the BankAmericard operation turns on nothing less than a continuous assessment of the future behaviour of the card-holders – most specifically, whether a given client, in light of the total information available to the system, warrants further credit. This is a considerably more delicate business, say, than a simply binary decision as to whether a specific suspect is listed on a register of persons wanted for crimes.

With respect to the *centralization* of surveillance, the organization of the San Francisco operation is the most efficient of any studied here – and, indeed, the effectiveness of the over-all nation-wide system does not suffer grievously from the allocation of headquarters about the country. Viewing the system in Northern California in isolation, its centralization is perfect. All of the relevant account information for all the card-holders in this area is stored in full at the San Francisco headquarters, and all decisions about how to deal with the accounts are made from that centre. This full centralization helps considerably to enhance the *speed of information flow and decision-making* within the system.

The slowest information on sales to reach the San Francisco headquarters takes no more than five days from points within the Northern California region, and this represents the period necessary for the system to respond to 'irresponsible' charges. From points outside of Northern California, the elapsed time is only slightly greater. And the speed of reaction to transactions requiring authorization is all but instantaneous, even taking into consideration the most recent changes in the card-holder's balance. This speed, and the fullness of the intelligence which it brings to bear, enables the system to curtail violations of the rules which it sets down for the user of its cards very rapidly indeed.

Seen as a national or international system, BankAmericard is not quite so strong in these two respects. The authorization process suffers on account of the lack of national or international centralization, in that sales are lost or 'unwise' sales allowed in the absence of full access to the relevant filed data. Nor is communication so rapid or so certain between participating merchants and authorization centres in other states or countries as it is within California. One disadvantage of this, from the standpoint of the capacity of surveillance, is the delay in processing sales vouchers at the centre responsible for a given card. Because of this delay, valuable time may be lost before the system can respond to an irresponsible spending spree far away from home. Nevertheless, with the use of telephone and telex for inter-state and international checking on the use of 'foreign' cards, the system manages to keep deviance to a minimum. The proposed further centralization of authorization and processing activities, with its attendant increase in the speed of information flow, should wear away at these limitations even more.

Finally, the *points of contact* between client and system. Here, too, BankAmericard is impressive. At the beginning, of course, when the credit application receives its initial screening, there are only two points for the intake of data on the applicant – the application itself, completed by the applicant, and the credit report. But the latter in effect gives the system access to a very wide array of relevant sources – as the previous chapter showed. And once the account is activated, every participating merchant represents a potential point of contact between the card-holder and the agency control. Every transaction is a source of information on the card-holder, not only with respect to the amount charged, but also the date, the nature of the purchase, and the merchant who made the charge. All of this information is subsequently usable for controlling the individual's use of his BankAmericard – for example, by enabling the authorization department to judge whether he should be extended further credit. The discussion has shown how fully and skilfully the system uses this information, as well as the other account data generated through the card-holder's use of the card, in its decision-making. In some cases, where the authorization process is used, this information enters the files instantaneously, as soon as it is generated. Elsewhere, it takes no longer than a week to reach the central accounting system from points in Northern California. And any of the participating merchants can also serve as a point through which the system 'reaches out' to make the effects of its decisions felt – through either refusal of credit, repossession of the BankAmericard or, in the most extreme cases, through arrest.

One element of the contact between system and clientele, of course, is the ease of establishing positive identification of clients. Here BankAmericard presents a mixed picture of strengths and weaknesses. Certainly the system has nothing like the virtually foolproof tool of fingerprinting which the police can often rely on. Indeed, one category of deviance which poses a most serious threat to the system is the fraudulent use of cards – something which would be quite impossible if means of identifying card users were really fully effective. Still, considering the fact that any BankAmericard is usable at hundreds of thousands of different establishments, identification of card users works remarkably well. Especially cunning is the cross-checking, via the authorization procedure, of information provided by would-be card users against data held in file at the relevant processing centre. The previous discussion has cited a number of points where the system relies on this sort of double-checking of information in order to establish the identity of those with whom it deals.

The thing which makes the BankAmericard system impressive from the standpoint of this book is, above all, the closeness and intensity of surveillance which it maintains over its card-holders' use of their credit privileges. No other system studied here, nor indeed any other known to the author, manages to trace the movements of so many persons so continuously, rarely allowing geographical mobility to stand as a barrier to the application of the full weight of their 'records' in its decision-making concerning them. And that record is almost always quite up-to-date, given the minimal time-lag between use of the card and the entry of charges in the BankAmericard accounting system. Thus the possibility of evading the effects of one's past record is minimized, and the ability of the system to carry out its decisions *vis-à-vis* the card-holder is greatly enhanced.

To a large extent, of course, this sophistication of surveillance requires the compliance of the clientele. People willingly tender their cards when they wish to make purchases, thus providing immediate identification themselves and enabling the system to link them readily with their past records. The task of the system would be impossible, needless to say, if it entailed maintaining surveillance on the same millions of card-holders without their cooperation. Still, it is worth remembering that there are ways of compelling such cooperation, as the use of identity cards in many countries demonstrates; the positive inducements of the benefits of the BankAmericard simply represent a more pleasant form of encouragement than certain alternatives.

The system does entail limitations, of course, most of which are vividly apparent to the BankAmericard staff. Although the flow of information from participating merchants to the San Francisco centre is rapid, most of it is not instantaneous. Even the three to five days required for most vouchers to reach headquarters allows either a fraudulent user or a delinquent card-holder to evade the system to some extent before his disobedience can register. True, the authorization procedure mitigates this delay, but it can do no more than cut the losses resulting from especially large transactions. And although many cards are collected, and some arrests are made, through the use of the authorization procedure, really shrewd opponents of the system are often well enough informed to avoid authorized transactions altogether. Nor is this the only shortcoming of the system. It goes without saying that some authorized transactions are never paid, some approved BankAmericard applications go to card-holders who ultimately cause losses to the system, and so on. Still, as surveillance systems go, this one loses very little information, and leaves very little in the way of decision-making to chance.

Finally, however effective and efficient, the system does largely confine itself to one area of persons' lives – their use of consumer credit. With the exception of its attention to matters like occupational and family stability at the time of application, the system bases its decisions about the treatment of its clientele strictly on their behaviour within the system – what they buy, when, and how well they pay. To date, the use of the BankAmericard is not a prerequisite to a job, to marriage or divorce, to freedom of movement – although it could make the pursuit of any of these things more pleasant and more feasible. Nor is the card subject to withdrawal because of conflicts between the card-holder and his family, or the government, or his employer. To this important extent, then, the BankAmericard system falls far short of any threat, or promise, of total surveillance.

THE DEVELOPMENT OF THIS RESEARCH

My first direct contact with the workings of BankAmericard came in December 1968, when I paid a visit of several hours to officials at the San Francisco processing centre. The purpose of that visit had been simply to supplement my understanding of the uses of consumer credit reporting, but by the end of the discussion it was clear that the sophistication and scope of these operations warranted special attention.

The preparation of this book provided the opportunity for such attention. The material presented here was gathered in two concentrated spurts of interviewing, one of about three weeks in March and April 1971, the other of one week during August that same year. The bulk of the interviews took place in the San Francisco processing centre, but there were also several interviews at the National BankAmericard, Inc., headquarters in that city. I also carried out an interview at a BankAmericard processing centre in an East Coast city and a number of interviews at the headquarters of another bank card system. The latter two served to help clarify my thinking about BankAmericard, but are not directly reported in this chapter.

BankAmericard officials were extraordinarily helpful with all aspects of my inquiries. I enjoyed free access to the San Francisco processing centre and spent hours simply observing its operations, in addition to interviewing. The staff at all levels were extremely patient and thorough in explaining their work. I am especially grateful for their provision of pertinent statistics and other documentary information used in this chapter.

A first draft of this chapter was prepared after the first series of interviews in 1971; the second series of interviews in August provided the opportunity to double-check and enrich this material. Officials from the two San Francisco offices reviewed a preliminary version of this chapter in the autumn of 1971 and made valuable corrections and suggestions. Over-all they expressed satisfaction with the manuscript.

Interviews were conducted with at least twenty persons in the BankAmericard system, including encounters ranging between brief conversations of fifteen minutes to repeated meetings totalling several hours. This does not count time spent simply observing the day-to-day routines of work. Here as elsewhere it is impossible to thank by name all those who helped. But I should like to thank Mr Anthony Laudari, Vice-President and Manager of the San Francisco processing centre, all his colleagues and staff, for their openness to this research and for their conscientiousness in helping me.

7

Internal Dynamics of Surveillance Systems

To paraphrase Marx, surveillance systems grow, but they do not grow just as they please. However spare in analytical content, the preceding chapters should have suggested that the evident growth in these five systems is subject to regular constraints, both from inside the systems and from the social contexts in which they are embedded. This chapter starts the work of studying the forces propelling the growth of surveillance, and those which constrain and channel such growth. Discussion begins with perhaps the simplest observations stemming from the case studies – a summing-up of the broad patterns of change in surveillance capacity. From there, the analysis builds more elaborately on the empirical material to chart specific patterns of organization and process within systems of mass surveillance. Throughout this chapter, and throughout the balance of the book, I aim to offer conclusions not only about these five systems, but also about systems of mass surveillance and control in general.

The Development of Surveillance Capacity

Each of the five case studies has ended with a brief evaluation of the surveillance capacity of the system under study. This has amounted to a summary of its strengths and weaknesses as a surveillance system, reckoned in terms of the standard criteria. This section aims to use these evaluations to formulate some comprehensive judgements on the direction of change in the capacity of mass surveillance.

The Advantages of Increased Capacity

The first summary observation is a simple one: all of the five systems studied here show signs of over-all development of increased surveillance capacity. Moreover, such increases are evidently taking place along all the various dimensions of capacity.

Consider first the *size* of the various surveillance operations. In terms of the size of clientele in relation to total population, at least four of the five systems have shown marked growth, over say, the last twenty years. National Insurance may stand as an exception, since its coverage has remained roughly static since the beginning of the system in 1948; one must remember, though, that a major innovation of the system at that point was increased participation in relation to its predecessors. But the vehicle and driver licensing system has grown steadily with the increase in motoring; police surveillance has kept pace with both the rise in crime and the increased ability of that system to absorb information. Consumer credit reporting files have grown with the increase in consumer debt generally. And, of course, the clientele of the BankAmericard system rose from nothing to some twenty-eight millions between 1959 and 1971.

Also evident, though generally less dramatic, is the tendency for the systems to grow in the amount of *useful data kept per client*. The licensing system, static for most of its existence in this respect, will take on one small but significant additional datum with the introduction of the new, centralized system. This will be the birth date of drivers, needed for positive identification because of the growth in numbers of files kept in one place. National Insurance, though showing no clear-cut changes in the records involved in its flat-rate scheme, has supplemented this with the graduated contributions scheme involving additional, computerized record-keeping on each client. British police surveillance is problematic, because of the dispersion of the system and the consequent variety of different record-keeping practices. Growth in the amount of data per client within the last twenty years is certainly not clear-cut throughout the system, though it must certainly have occurred in some centres. Similarly, consumer credit files have certainly become more extensive on average since the inception of the system early this century in the form of simple blacklists of bad credit risks. It would be rash, however, to judge how much of this change has taken place, for example, during the past twenty years. It is probable that TRW Credit Data files, on average, contain more usable data per client than do conventional files, because of that organization's policy of full incorporation of its members' account records. Finally, it is unclear that there has been any major increase in‘ amount of data kept in the California BankAmericard system since its inception; but it is certain that more of this information is actually used by the system in decision-making.

The question of the *subtlety* with which systems use filed information in decision-making is itself a subtle one, and changes over time are difficult to register. None of the three British systems has shown clear-cut change in this respect, independent of changes in the amount of data available. It is quite possible that the police have become more sophisticated in using available information in responding to 'stop check' requests as the latter have become frequent. But real evidence on this point is unavailable. Consumer credit surveillance in America has probably become more sophisticated in this respect, as the use of credit reports has become more common and more subject, in large firms, to well-developed bureaucratic routines. And the BankAmericard system, starting from the gross unsophistication of its discrimination practices at the time of its nearly disastrous beginning, has grown extremely resourceful in its use of filed data.

There is nothing particularly subtle about the press towards *centralization* of surveillance files, however, and here the movement towards increased capacity is dramatic in four of the five cases. The possible exception is National Insurance, though its institution effectively centralized the operation of several predecessor systems. The remaining four have been undergoing centralization as this study took place. The licensing system, of course, is in the throes of conversion from extreme dispersion to almost total centralization. Much the same thing is happening with police surveillance, although without quite the same extreme contrast between old and new. This step on the part of the police reverses the limited decentralization of their records which took place in the mid-1950s, a step which nevertheless served to increase surveillance capacity in other respects. In the case of consumer credit surveillance, the movement towards centralization set off by Credit Data Corporation in the mid-1960s has so infected the industry that, perhaps by 1980, the majority of credit files will probably be located in a handful of centralized, electronic repositories. Finally, in the case of BankAmericard, one notes a movement from a system which in California already comprises nearly as many files as the criminal records section of the Metropolitan police, towards an even fuller, national centralization.

Several of the systems also show signs of increased capacity with respect to the *speed* of information flow and decision-making. This is largely the result of computerization, but by no means wholly so. British police surveillance is as impressive as any in this respect. Under the new, computerized system, information on wanted and missing persons, and on drivers and vehicles, will enter the system daily from the respective sources. This information, and other filed material, will be available within about ten seconds to police officers requesting it, at least according to the predictions of those developing the system. Consumer credit surveillance, with the centralization and computerization of its operations, shows a similar decrease in the time required for incorporation of information from outside sources. The new systems are also probably quicker, though only marginally so, in the speed of provision of data to callers. California BankAmericard, computerized from its inception, reports having decreased the time necessary to process applications for cards and, even more important, to authorize sales during the twelve years or so of its existence. National Insurance has shown no major changes in speed of information flow and decision-making since the time of its inception, but such changes are conspicuous in the vehicle and driver licensing system. There the centralization and computerization of surveillance operations will markedly speed both internal information processes and exchange of information with the police.

Finally, most of the five systems have increased their capacity in terms of the effectiveness of *contact between system and clientele*. One element of such contact is the number of points of intake of useful information on clients, and of points through which the system can make its measures of social control felt. Perhaps the development of BankAmericard system has been the most dramatic in this respect. There the very growth in size of the system, specifically the growth in numbers of participating merchants, has represented a major advance. For every business honouring the cards automatically provides information on the client with every sale it makes, whether or not the sale involves 'authorization' of the charge. At the same time, these are points through which the system can act against those who have broken the rules. The same sort of extension has been evident in British police surveillance, through the increase in use of personal radios by patrolling constables, and in the growth in the number of traffic wardens providing information on untaxed vehicles to the licensing system. Again, all of these persons represent both potential points of intake of information and potential agents of control. Similarly, with the general increase in use of credit reports, consumer credit surveillance has come to avail itself of more and more sources of credit information. And finally, National Insurance has developed an important further source of data in its system of collection of graduated contributions. The contributions themselves, and the information about their collection, enter the system through the Inland Revenue system of income tax collection.

The proliferation of such contact points between system and clientele, coupled with rapid information flow, has important implications for the intensity of scrutiny possible over any one client. A system possessing many such points and rapid intake of information from them can potentially use them to build a continuous, minute-by-minute account of the activities of any one client – or at least of certain of those activities. The most extreme case among these five systems is BankAmericard, where the trail of transaction records left by a free-spending card-holder can effectively chart both his movements and his consumption habits. The same possibility exists for the police system of stop checks, although such close monitoring does not occur except in cases of extraordinary interest in the movements of a suspect. Similar trends are evident in consumer credit surveillance, where some American firms hope soon to market a device enabling any cashier in any store to obtain an immediate reading on a customer's credit standing. So far, however, the continuousness of such contact depends largely on the willingness of the client voluntarily to bring his presence and his actions to the attention of the authorities.

Finally, most of the systems also show signs of increased sophistication in identifying their clients and in linking them to their records. The British police rely on fingerprints, physical description, and name and date of birth as they have traditionally done, but their development of computerized means of identifying fingerprints promises a considerable advance for the near future in the efficiency of such procedures. BankAmericard has grown more sophisticated in identification procedures during its brief history, especially with respect to comparing information provided by would-be purchasers to data held in file. The consumer credit system, plagued by public criticism and internal inefficiency stemming from its loose identification procedures, has taken tentative steps towards the use of social security numbers and other forms of cross-checking, to ensure that the correct data are linked to the correct files. The licensing system, likewise, is tightening its rather loose procedures in this respect by beginning to require date of birth from driving licence applicants.

Each of these five systems, then, is in the process of movement towards increased surveillance capacity. But the case studies also yield a considerably broader insight. They have demonstrated, I suggest, how increased capacity *in general* enhances the ability of organizations like these to achieve their ends. In other words, (1) whenever a bureaucratic agency seeks to make and enforce discriminating decisions concerning a mass clientele, and (2) whenever these decisions must accord with details of clients' past circumstances or behaviour, and (3) whenever they entail points of potential conflict between system and clientele, it is advantageous to the system to develop the maximum possible surveillance capacity.

It should be evident, for example, that the centralization of filed data allows any systems to bring the full weight of clients' records to bear in any decision-making concerning them, and prevents clients from evading the effects of their records through flight. These advantages, from the standpoint of the system, obtain despite differences in the social setting of the system and in the forms of compliance it seeks to enforce. It should likewise be clear that the extension of points of contact between system and clientele, by maximizing the incorporation of pertinent data and the ability to act agressively towards clients when necessary, helps the task of surveillance. Foolproof means of identification, by preventing clients from evading the effects of their records and ensuring that all relevant data are filed together, strengthen the position of surveillance. Rapidity of information flow and decision-making maximizes the chances of bringing the full weight of filed information to bear on every decision, and minimizes the chances of the clients' escaping before the relevant data can come to light. Finally, the more data kept per client, and the more subtly these data are used, the better the system's chances of making the 'correct' decision. Thus the various dimensions of surveillance capacity are more than just theoretical criteria set down for the purposes of this study. They are also, as the case studies have shown, matters of considerable practical concern to those who rely on mass surveillance to realize organizational goals.

I have tried to make these observations on the growth of surveillance capacity neither too sweeping nor too thoroughly qualified. I have not stated, for example, that the growth of surveillance capacity is inevitable 'in the long run', since the long run is not subject to sociological measurement. Nor have I suggested that the growth of capacity represents a 'tendency' in these systems, since it seems to me impossible to verify a tendency apart from the actual occurrence of the phenomenon. What I do mean to say is no more or less than that, for organizations like those studied here, the increase of surveillance capacity is advantageous. Because such increase helps these systems to achieve the goals which have been set for them, those who control the systems are bound to find such increase desirable. Whether it is practically possible to bring about such growth in any specific case is another matter.

Costs

But why the gap between what is practically possible and what is theoretically desirable? Why, if the increase of surveillance capacity is inherently advantageous to agencies seeking to maintain mass surveillance and control, does one not encounter uniform and relentless movement in that direction? One key countervailing factor is the *costs* involved. It should be obvious that any system of mass surveillance and control is bound to be a highly costly operation. Indeed, in so far as these functions can be separated from the other activities of the organizations studied here – for example the costs for National Insurance of maintaining compliance with its rules, as against the other costs of its operations – the former represents a major element of the total budget. Further, major qualitative innovations in surveillance capacity – centralization, computerization, extension of contact between system and clientele – represent very considerable investments for the organization concerned.

Often decisions on the extension of surveillance capacity take the form of a formal cost-benefit calculation – and such calculations can certainly reveal that sophisticated new measures are unwarranted in light of their cost. The BankAmericard system is undergoing such a phase of critical decision-making precisely at the time of this writing, over the question of further centralization of its surveillance system. The present system of limited centralization, as Chapter 6 noted, does result in some losses through inability to bring clients' full records to bear on authorization decisions. But although full centralization of the system would curtail such losses, it is by no means clear that such a move would pay for itself in light of the capital investment required. Whether it would in fact do so turns on a reckoning of such chancy matters as the rate of growth of business, the expected increase in geographical mobility among card-holders, and the future rate of attempted fraud. At the time of my last interviews with BankAmericard officials the matter remained undecided, but it was by no means clear that the fullest possible centralization would be preferable to a less costly programme of regional centralization.

Still, it should be evident from these five cases that the present trend is towards decreasing costs of initiating and maintaining mass surveillance, and increased benefits of doing so. Part of the explanation for this lies in factors external to the systems in question – matters having to do with changing demands made on them by other elements of society. Elsewhere, the cause is internal, having to do with matters like the techniques of operating the systems. In this connection, people often see the advent of computing as the key explanation for the development of systems like these, and certainly the machines, when used efficiently, can drastically curtail the costs of record-keeping. But it is by no means apparent, in the five cases studied here, that the role of computing is necessarily more crucial than that, say, of an efficient communication system – telephone, telex and the post. No amount of computerization could help either the BankAmericard system or the consumer credit reporting system if they were to lose their advantageous telephone rates, which permit constant long-distance inquiries from customers. Similarly, the bulk of the National Insurance system still relies on manual records, even though its clientele is vast and its decision-making extremely subtle. The speed of service has declined in recent years, but because of decreased efficiency in the British postal system rather than any inherent inability of manual files to do the job. No, the growth of mass surveillance thrives on a variety of increased efficiencies in operations, of which the computer is only one.

Discrimination and Control

In general, then, the capacity of mass surveillance seems to be on the increase. But this conclusion in itself can hardly more than whet the intellectual appetite of anyone interested in the future of surveillance. One wants to know more specifically what forms the new systems are taking, what forces are particularly shaping their growth, and which of their capabilities appear to be developing most rapidly. Discussion now turns to these questions. The balance of this chapter deals with trends and forces in the internal dynamics of surveillance systems, specifically those affecting the organization of filed data, the use of available information, and the contact between system and clientele.

Identification of Deviants

A number of the generalizations put forth in this section of the book are not exclusively my own, but were at least partially formulated by interviewees during the preparation of the case studies. It never suffices, in investigative interviewing, to take the words of one's interlocutors simply at their face value. But when the same bureaucratic folk-wisdoms come up over and over again, it pays to grant them careful attention. Such was the case with people's accounts of the disproportionate attention which they had to devote to a minority of their system's clienteles. More than once I heard comments like 'It's only two per cent of the public who cause ninety-nine per cent of our problems', or 'If it weren't for a few "rotten apples", our job wouldn't exist'. Over and over again, in many different settings, I heard complaints about the inordinate pains necessary to deal with a difficult minority of clients – or expressions of gratitude that this minority created sufficient work to keep my informants in employment.

However inchoate in their original form, I believe such comments reflected accurately a basic fact of life for all these systems. All of them deal with millions of clients, engaging in tens of millions of discrete decision-making transactions every year. Most of these decisions proceed in a highly routine way, according to the rules set down by the system. In a minority of cases, however, the system must act against those who have broken the rules. But although these breaches represent a minority, they are a highly troublesome one which requires an inordinate expenditure of resources. The Bank-Americard operation, for example, would be unrecognizably simpler and vastly more profitable were it not for the need for its vast and continuing effort against credit and fraud losses. Such losses, like the losses of National Insurance to fraudulent claims and failure to contribute, stem from a minority of the clientele. Likewise, for the licensing system, enormous efforts go into checking the activities of a small minority of motorists who should not drive, or of keepers of vehicles who have not paid their tax. In consumer credit, as that chapter emphasized, the rate of serious delinquencies is around two or three per cent for most credit operations. The only apparent exception is police surveillance, since virtually all files kept in criminal record offices refer to people who have in some sense broken the rules. But even here, if one views the task of the police as ensuring compliance with the law from all citizens, the wrongdoers remain a minority.

To state matters formally: deviance – the failure to abide by the rules whose enforcement is sought – is an endemic minority occurrence in these systems. Most clients abide by the rules, and most decisions about clients can therefore proceed in a routine way. Nevertheless, the minority of deviants necessitate the existence of systems of surveillance and control. To be sure, the organizations depicted in the case studies have many other activities besides these two. But it is no exaggeration to say that those elements of these organizations which have received the main attention here, the ones devoted to surveillance and control, exist strictly to deal with this minority occurrence.

As I noted above, the maintenance of mass surveillance and control is a costly business, whether the control consists of sanctioning people when they have done the wrong thing, or preventing them from misbehaving in the first place. In either case, one of the costliest aspects of the operation is narrowing the attention from the whole of the clientele, mainly compliant, to the deviant minority. The discussion of National Insurance emphasized that, however awesome in relation to any single client, the surveillance resources of that system are only just adequate in relation to a persistent deviant minority embedded in a massive, anonymous clientele. A similar observation might apply to any of the systems. Without a cheap means of separating out the deviants, their task becomes impossible. Mass surveillance, in other words, requires constant efforts of *discrimination*.

To effect this discrimination, all five of these systems have developed highly routinized means of 'scanning' available information, so as to identify those who have broken, or are likely to break, the rules. These scanning processes serve to separate out this minority for closer attention, so that they can be prevented from disobeying the system, or punished in some way for having done so. Examples from the case studies are easy to cite. In the BankAmericard system, the authorization routines pre-eminently act as discrimination processes. For the police, stop checks serve as a way of separating out wanted and missing persons from the general run of the populace. In National Insurance, the reconciliation of contributions and credits serves to discriminate those who may be guilty of fraud from the rest. In the licensing system, the main purpose of keeping files on drivers is to screen out those not qualified to drive. And, likewise, the *raison d'être* of consumer credit reporting is to refuse credit privileges to those unlikely to abide by the rules of the game.

For any of these systems, it would be disastrously expensive to devote to every client the attention granted to deviants. Even the costs involved in 'scanning' available data to decide where such attention is necessary strains the resources of many systems, and limits the amount of such checking. Faced with very large clienteles and complicated discrimination problems, surveillance systems often cannot even afford to take advantage of 'available' information in their own files. Chapter 4 noted that National Insurance claims for increased benefit in the light of dependants are not necessarily checked, despite the existence of verifying data in Family Allowance Branch files. Here officials of the system actually carried out a study which showed that these checks cost more money than they save. Nor do the police always check the most comprehensive files for information on the status of suspects, though it is theoretically desirable to do so. Nor, for similar reasons, do local licensing offices check their own vehicle files directly to determine whether the registration of vehicles is current, even though such information is directly pertinent to their concerns. Likewise, BankAmericard in California generally limits its authorization procedures to sales in excess of a certain figure; to check the files in every case would be too costly. Nor, finally, do credit bureaus glean all the information which their customers could theoretically use. All of this serves to emphasize the importance of cost consideration in these routine 'scanning' operations. More specifically, it goes to show once again that 'possession' or 'availability' of information is meaningless unless one takes account of the costs to the system of bringing those data regularly to bear on decision-making.

Harold Wilensky, in his book *Organizational Intelligence*, examines a number of cases of successful and unsuccessful use of information by organizations in critical decision-making junctures.* One of the most interesting of his discussions concerns 'the great salad oil swindle', a notorious disaster in organizational intelligence which cost a number of highly reputable American firms enormous amounts of money.† The fiasco stemmed from a series of loans and credits made on the basis of collateral – huge amounts of salad oil – which in fact did not exist. On dissecting the fraud after the fact, investigators noted that the proof offered for the existence of the oil had always been slender, and that information had been available all along to show that the perpetrator had a shady past. How, Wilensky wonders, could the sophisticated banks, brokerage houses and investment firms victimized by the fraud have failed to take advantage of such readily available, pertinent data? Part of the reason, he argues, has to do with the superficial trappings of normality generated by the scale of the perpetrator's operations – people simply could not believe that such a vast, flourishing enterprise, the likes of which they dealt with all the time, could be faulty. Then, too, most of these firms had a short-term advantage in the *status quo*, in that their relationship to the fraudulent firm was highly profitable until the bubble finally burst. In any event, the glossy exterior sufficed for a long time to discourage inquiry into the complex but thoroughly fraudulent reality.

* Harold L. Wilensky, *Organizational Intelligence*, New York, Basic Books, 1967.
† Wilensky, op. cit., pp. 88–93.

Perhaps the five cases studied here shed some light on the forces which may have conduced to such negligent surveillance practices. Faced with very many points at which delinquency or some other occasion for loss might occur, the firms involved in the salad oil disaster may simply have had their resources for surveillance stretched too thin in all respects. Given a very large number of possible sources of trouble in different aspects of their operations, perhaps they simply could not afford detailed attention anywhere, except in relation to the most serious danger signs. Wilensky points out that such clues should have been evident, but he also observes, '. . . the salad oil case . . . does not tell us how much expenditure on what kinds of search and surveillance procedures would be justified to make such failures impossible or almost impossible.'* The business of determining the 'rational' allocation of resources to intelligence, where the number of points that need watching is very great, the costs of watching are high, and the consequences of any one thing's going wrong are disastrous is bound to be problematic.

All of this should serve to emphasize again the importance, not of possession of relevant data, but of efficient and economical means of bringing it to bear on decision-making. Indeed, many of the most significant innovations in surveillance techniques seem to derive from the development of just such means. A particularly cunning advance in this respect, I am told, has been developed by the United States Internal Revenue Service, with the aim of identifying fraudulent income tax returns. The costs of thorough surveillance over any return – that is, of an audit of the return – are far too great to allow for auditing all returns. On the other hand, the dangers of checking none at all are obvious. One solution envisaged by Internal Revenue officials, but not yet put into general practice at the time of my conversation with them, was to carry out a thorough statistical investigation of a small random sample of returns. IRS officials audited all of the sample, and took careful note of which proved to be fraudulent. By noting the statistical determinants of fraud, the IRS staff were able to develop discriminant analysis equations to predict what they deliciously

* Wilensky, op. cit., p. 93.

term 'audit potential'.* Thus by computerizing the statistical operation and feeding in basic statistical data – the size of income, number of dependants, numbers of deductions in different categories, for example, from all new returns – the system could identify the minority of returns most likely to involve deviance. This sophisticated means of narrowing the 'attention' of the surveillance system is precisely the sort of mechanism which systems of mass social control require. Without them, they are lost in a mass of 'available' but unusable information.

Condensation of Filed Information

These questions of the costs of checking filed information, and of the ease of making it available at decision-making junctures which require it point directly to consideration of the organization of data itself. Although the case studies have described broadly how, where and in what form relevant data are kept, these matters have not yet received any analytic attention.

Of specific concern here is the variation in the *standardization* of data storage. Almost any information on persons can be recorded either according to patterns unique to the single occasion, or in a format which also guides the storage of information on countless others. An example of the first extreme might be a letter of recommendation, written by someone who had never written such a letter before, on behalf of someone applying for a job whose qualifications were unique. An example of the second might be a student's record of scores on a series of tests also administered to many others. Examples of the first end of the continuum are apt to be kept in discursive prose, while those at the second are apt to be brief, telegraphic and coded. Although adaptation to computerized storage places a premium on standardization, it by no means necessitates it. Highly standardized, condensed data can be stored manually, and the computer record can also store discursive prose.

By nothing more than an intuitive reckoning, the five systems studied here seem closer to the standardized extreme

---

* Discriminant analysis is a statistical technique for predicting certain properties of persons or things by virtue of other statistically measurable properties of the same individual.

than to the other. In nearly all cases, their files are condensed, telegraphic, and coded. Some consumer credit files, it is true, are still kept in a kind of modified prose, but even in that system computerization is making the use of coded data more and more common. In fact, among the files noted here in any detail, there is only one clear-cut and glaring exception: the antecedent history sheet kept in criminal record files by the British police. While the other major files studied in that chapter are standardized and terse, this sheet remains stubbornly discursive and unstructured. Although antecedent history sheets do show some similarity of concern – the home life and occupational background of the criminal, for example – the details of their contents and the form of presentation are anything but fixed.

But this document is actually atypical in its uses, atypical in a way which may help to explain the premium on standardization elsewhere. It is prepared in the first place for the use of the court in sentencing, although the police may later also have recourse to it. Once an accused person is convicted, the police present the sheet, along with a copy of his criminal record, to the court as an aid in setting an appropriate sentence. The use of these documents, however, is highly unpredictable and discretionary from one magistrate or judge to the next. The police, indeed, believe that many courts take little account of the information transmitted by the antecedent history sheet, and consequently take few pains preparing them in those cases. Elsewhere, the sheets are quite detailed. The important point is that there is no one-to-one correspondence between the contents of the sheet and the decision of the court; the latter may use the information in any way it deems suitable, or may ignore it altogether.

The reverse is true of the demands made on the other files depicted here. There each recorded datum is supposed to have a known and circumscribed significance in the decision-making process. Under such circumstances it will not do to allow for uncontrolled variations in the form in which data are recorded. This is especially the case where, as in most instances studied here, the organization concerned with recording the information and transmitting it also takes responsibility for the decision-making process. There the pattern of bureaucratization runs its full course, since there is no means of ensuring uniformed decision-making unless the recording of the data is itself uniform. The most extreme development of this is found in the case of National Insurance, where information recorded in any office of the system must be usable at any other, and at any subsequent point in time, to reach identical decisions. This system does in fact make good its aims of extreme uniformity and predictability in recording and use of information, by requiring its approximately 29,000 local office employees to work to an extremely detailed, multi-volume set of written instructions.

Another factor conducing to the standardization of the recording of data is the fact that, in settings like these, such data are apt to be subject to contest. Systems of social control, by definition, engage in decision-making which may be contrary to the interests of the client, and the clash of interests leads to the demand for justice in such decision-making. Ensuring justice, like ensuring other forms of uniformity of decision-making, requires control and hence standardization of data processes.

Other considerations conducing to standardization of filed data have to do with the speed and efficiency of information flow and decision-making. One of the most terse files studied here is the wanted and missing persons index kept by the police, whose use requires both quick and unambiguous transmission of information. Similar considerations have conduced to the streamlining of the data used in BankAmericard authorizations, and in that transmitted in 'in-file' reports in consumer credit reporting. In these cases, the transmission of rich, discursive, unstructured data, however pertinent to the decision at hand, would take more time than the systems can afford. One imagines that it would also confound the decision-making process through varying and inaccurate interpretations of the data transmitted.

Finally, the condensation and standardization of filed data greatly facilitates the quick 'scanning' of files involved in checking for deviance. I noted above the considerable costs involved in such discrimination procedures, and the resulting inability, in many cases, to check even the information already in file. It is the rendering of income tax data into a standardized format for all returns, for example, which makes it possible to carry out the sophisticated, statistical scanning described above. Similarly, it is the condensation and standardization of BankAmericard data, along with computerization, which enables that system to identify so readily those accounts which show preliminary signs of deviance.

This press towards standardization in recording practices, however, does exert certain constraints on the ability of the systems in question to maintain surveillance. The use of these rigid formats and circumscribed coding schemes for the preservation of information often does not permit the inclusion or use of information in novel or innovative ways, and it may thereby heighten the difficulty of coping with irregular, unanticipated situations. The computerized account information used in the California BankAmericard system, for example, does not permit the addition of marginal notes relevant to future transactions except in previously coded formats. Likewise, the standardized recording of criminal record information does not, in itself, make it possible to note extenuating circumstances or other relevant ancillary data along with the details of convictions and sentences. To be sure, there are ways of circumventing these difficulties. Under the new law, consumer credit agencies are required to include statements from consumers about disputed entries in their files, statements which may seek to provide fuller information than the files themselves. This requirement prevails, incidentally, even where the credit files are computerized.

Whatever limitations the streamlining of information may create in this respect, however, it would be wrong to think that it prevents surveillance systems from increasing the subtlety of their decision-making. Most impressive in this respect, perhaps, is BankAmericard, which uses its highly standardized data in extremely flexible and indirect ways. Likewise, in the computerized scanning venture of the United States Internal Revenue Service, it is highly standardized bits of data which, when assembled and used cunningly, yield the statistical identification of deviants described above. Similar observations might be made about the use of other highly standardized information by these five and other systems of mass surveillance. When the information is highly pertinent to the decision-making task at hand, and when the decisions are made by highly experienced, shrewd persons or immensely pertinent statistical techniques, standardization does not prevent resourceful use of data.

Rates of Deviance and Viability of Control

Let me now return to the costs of surveillance and the frequency of deviant behaviour. Earlier on, discussion noted that the need for expensive surveillance systems seems to rest only on the activities of small minorities of their respective clienteles. To this observation one might add that the viability of these systems would rapidly come into question if the rates of those disobedient activities rose sharply. The matter is clearest where it can be reckoned in terms of profit-and-loss. If the rate of persons making major BankAmericard charges without intending to pay rose, say, to ten per cent of that clientele per annum, the system almost certainly could not sustain a profit. The same observation, *mutatis mutandis*, could apply to other credit-granting systems. If credit surveillance could screen out no more than ten per cent of serious bad risks, most merchants and lenders would have to curtail or suspend their credit activities.

The issue is more ambiguous in the cases of the other systems, because the point at which public non-compliance would render them unviable is less clear-cut. But such a point certainly does exist. The continuation of National Insurance would become politically and administratively unviable, if say, a quarter of the insured made every possible effort to evade contributions and to claim benefits for which they were not entitled. It may be true that such rates of deviance could be combated and even curtailed by the application of more and more organizational resources to surveillance and control. But those responsible for policy-making in these organizations are rarely able, let alone willing, to muster such resources.

I wonder if this strikes the reader in the same ironic way as it does me. These enormous agencies of control, so powerful in relation to any single client, actually exist at the sufferance of their clienteles as wholes. No matter how sophisticated, no matter how forceful in their everyday dealings, all five of these systems would be in serious trouble if they faced serious, simultaneous resistance from, say, a quarter or even a tenth of their clients. Officials of these bodies, in the course of discussions with me, made much the same observation, in phrases like 'Without the honesty of ninety-nine per cent of the public, our work would be impossible'. Again, the matter turns on the costliness of identifying and responding to serious, major breaches of the rules. It is only the compliance of the majority which leaves resources free to meet the activities of this small minority.

This paradoxical situation suggests a fascinating heuristic question. What would happen if the activities of the minority of evident deviants in any system could somehow be magically neutralized? How would BankAmericard fare, for example, if all those at present inclined to use cards without paying were deprived of cards, and no further cards were accessible to those like them? Could the whole system of surveillance and control then be scrapped?

On first consideration, one's inclination would probably be to answer affirmatively: without deviants, there should be no necessity for social control. But the question turns, in fact, on a judgement of the forces which ensure conformity from the majority who generally abide by the rules. To what extent, one wonders, does the conspicuous presence of the surveillance system, visibly at work identifying and curtailing people's misbehaviour, represent a deterrent? To what extent are the actions of the system against the deviant minority a necessary encouragement to the majority who never break the rules? This question, in its broadest form, has a long pedigree in sociological thought. Durkheim and his followers have stressed the importance of punishment as symbolic vindication of the legitimacy of social norms; Malinowsky and others have emphasized the more concrete deterrent effects of the fear of punishment.* All these authors have assumed that the effects

* Emile Durkheim, *The Division of Labor in Society*, Glencoe, Illinois, The Free Press, 1960 (first published 1893); esp. pp. 96–110. Bronislaw Malinowski, *Crime and Custom in Savage Society*, London, Kegan Paul, Trench, Trubner and Co., 1926; esp. Chapter 11.

of punishment go considerably farther than just to the punished. One wonders to what extent similar principles operate in systems like those considered here.

It is important to remember that the clienteles of these five systems generally do not have an accurate idea of their surveillance capabilities. Indeed, the systems encourage ignorance on this point, in hopes that such ignorance will itself deter attempts at deviance. (This calculated obscurantism, incidentally, did nothing to endear the officials of these systems to the research undertaken here.) National Insurance forms for increased benefit for dependants note conspicuously: 'WARNING: TO GIVE FALSE INFORMATION MAY RESULT IN PROSECUTION', even though the information provided by clients is not necessarily checked. Similar warnings are conspicuous on the forms submitted to local licensing offices by drivers and vehicle owners, though there is very little checking of this information. Likewise, many American consumers certainly predicate their debt-paying behaviour on exaggerated estimates of the surveillance capacity of consumer credit reporting. *Mutatis mutandis*, one could just as well make the same point for the other systems.

And while this point represents a major theoretical concern to sociologists, it is at the same time a goading practical issue to policy-makers in these systems. For there are many processes of surveillance and control whose expense in the short run exceeds any direct savings from the curtailment of deviance, yet which are kept for their supposed exemplary effect. I would judge, for example, that the expenses of checking certain difficult forms of National Insurance fraud, like widows' cohabitation, may well exceed the savings resulting from curtailed benefits. Likewise, it seems apparent that the costs to BankAmericard of pursuing and prosecuting certain categories of fraud – not by any means all fraud – are excessive in relation to the amounts of money recovered. But, as one BankAmericard security official told me, 'The day it gets around that BankAmericard doesn't prosecute, we're finished.'

This issue figured directly in one of my conversations with officials of the British Ministry of Transport, in connection with the conversion of vehicle registrations to centralized, computer storage. In preparing for this change, some planners had raised the question of the stringency of measures to be taken against keepers of vehicles who fail to pay their tax. Since the expenses of pursuing these people are considerable, in relation to the revenue resulting, there was some feeling in favour of considerably relaxing the enforcement. The counter-argument raised the question of the effects which such a relaxation might have on the over-all rates of compliance and whether, specifically, it would encourage the majority of the law-abiding public to relax their compliance. The latter argument won out, and energetic enforcement practices, considerably shored up by centralization and computerization, will be part of the new scheme.

The nature and likelihood of such second- and third-order consequences of relaxed surveillance and control are matters which would repay careful attention from sociologists. Undoubtedly the best means of proceeding with such a study would be to effect such a relaxation in a given system under otherwise static conditions, and note the results over time. But given the disastrous consequences to any system of a drastic rise in deviance, those in charge may not be willing to propose their organizations as guinea-pigs. One imagines that the results of such an experiment would differ according to the organization, the clientele and the social setting. But so far as the systems depicted here are concerned, neither their managers nor I would be willing to assume that the workings of social control are felt only by manifest deviants. On the contrary, the opposite assumption seems inherent in the policies which guide their operation.

Contact with Clientele and Staging of Control

The first section of this chapter dealt with the growth of surveillance capacity generally, along all the various dimensions. The preceding section took a closer look at the form taken by the growth of capacity in terms of the amount of data held per client, the subtlety of decision-making, and the speed of information flow and decision-making. This section, which also concentrates on the internal dynamics of surveillance systems, is concerned with still another dimension of capacity, the contact between the system and its clientele.

Points of Contact

The case studies have demonstrated how advantageous it is, for systems of mass surveillance, to extend their points of contact with clientele. Because such extension provides the opportunity of incorporating more and more recent information on clients, for example, it may enable systems to sharpen the discrimination of their decision-making. Consumer credit reporting, for example, becomes more sophisticated and effective as any bureau maximizes its sources of data – credit-grantors, periodicals, other bureaus, court-house files, collection agencies, and so on – and the frequency of recourse to these. For similar reasons, the frequent inability of the licensing system to make the sort of discrimination against medically unfit drivers stems from its lack of an independent source of medical data on them. This premium on maximizing the intake of information, I maintain, characterizes not only these five systems, but also all other systems of mass surveillance and control.

The case studies have also called attention to the difficulties involved when an agency of control must actively seek out a delinquent client to apply some corrective measure. All five of these systems can and sometimes do dispatch representatives to locate and accost clients for these purposes. National Insurance inspectors, for example, spend a good deal of time attempting to locate those whose contribution records are unsatisfactory. The licensing system has its force of former police officers who devote their time to tracking down keepers of untaxed vehicles. These apprehension activities have their counterparts in the other three systems, too. But such actions are expensive and problematic in their results, compared to other techniques of control; hence they usually represent a last resort. Perhaps the main difficulty in these operations is the fact that no system manages to keep its address data as fully up-to-date as its managers might desire. Though all attempt to file addresses for their clients, this information is quickly dated, especially where the client is bent on evasion.

True, any one of the systems stands a good chance of tracking down someone who has really done something serious, if it is willing to invest heavily enough in the operation. But this sort of investment is one which cannot be made too frequently.

In general, systems of mass surveillance find it advantageous to avoid recourse to such direct means of contacting their clients, and to rely instead on more streamlined techniques. Specifically, it is usually much less costly to maintain regular, predictable junctures through which many clients pass, and where measures of social control can come into play when necessary. In the case of BankAmericard, this is the authorization procedure, which acts as a giant net capable of catching card users who have broken the rules of the system in some way. Likewise, the National Insurance system uses its system of granting claims, and its system of enforcing contributions through employers, to identify and locate those contributors whose cases warrant some corrective action. For the licensing system, the net is the system of checking vehicles by traffic wardens and policemen. For the police, it is the routine stop check. All these points represent junctures where agents of the surveillance system come directly into contact with members of the clientele, and where some sort of forceful action can be taken towards those who warrant it. Because they represent means of dealing with large numbers of persons at once, through highly routine procedures, they are much less costly than actions in which an agent must make a special effort to seek out and deal with a delinquent client. Moreover, by maximizing the points of possible encounter between system and clientele, these developments may increase the ability of the system to make its strictures felt.

In the case studies, the term 'points of contact' has applied both to the first kind of juncture, where systems incorporate data on their clients, and to this second one, where they may act against them. In many cases, the two points are combined. Thus the BankAmericard authorization procedures both generate useful data for further decision-making and provide the system with the opportunity to control the use of the card. Or a policeman's sighting of an untaxed vehicle both provides evidence that the latter was illegally on the public highways and enables the policeman to accost the vehicle's driver. In general, these combinations of function are advantageous for the systems in that they facilitate what Chapter 1 termed the *staging* of social control. That is, they bring relevant information to bear on decision-making about the client at precisely the point where the latter is most vulnerable to action from the system.

No matter how numerous the points of contact with agents of control, nor how fully these agents have access to the relevant data, systems still require some means of obliging clients to place themselves in touch with these points. Among these five systems, the police are probably strongest in this respect. For their agents can move about freely and make persuasive requests to clients for identifying information about themselves. The same patrolling constable, of course, can also make an arrest. The other systems are in less forceful positions, and generally must offer some positive inducement to their clients to put themselves in touch with the system. In the case of National Insurance, for example, that juncture comes when a delinquent contributor applies for a benefit or takes up employment on a Class I basis. For BankAmericard, the inducement is the desire of the person holding a card to make a purchase which will activate the authorization procedures. Inducements do exist, then, and serve to strengthen the position of the agency. But in most of the cases studied here, clients still possess the option of remaining out of contact if they are willing to pay the price of doing so. When this occurs, the only choice is for the system to mount the expensive effort necessary to seek out the client individually, or to hold his case in abeyance until he surfaces again.

One way around this dilemma, from the standpoint of the system, is somehow to link the client's contact with the agency of control to some different point of contact which he cannot afford to avoid. I am told that one of the New England states in America recently scored a cunning success in this direction. In this state the enforcement of traffic and parking fines was badly failing; the mechanisms of enforcement simply did not suffice to track down the recipients of citations and to oblige them to pay. In response to the situation, the appropriate agency of the state government installed an on-line computer terminal at entrances to the state's extensive system of turnpikes. As every entering vehicle passed through the access gate, its licence number was tapped into the central computer memory of outstanding citations, which responded in turn by listing any fines outstanding on the vehicle. No car was allowed to continue until all arrears were paid. One could scarcely imagine a more effective means of bringing clients into contact with the agency of enforcement at a point highly advantageous for the latter. Whereas sending a representative to seek out the client places the burden of success very much on the system, the opposite is the case when, as here, the staging is favourable to the interests of control. Discussion will return to this matter in the following chapter.

Positive Identification

Throughout this book, the ability of surveillance systems readily and accurately to identify members of their clienteles, and to link the client quickly to his record, has figured as an element of the contact between system and clientele. It should be obvious that no extension of information intake, or of points of action against deviant clients, is helpful without some means of effecting identification. In general, numbers are superior to names for internal purposes, since they are less subject to misinterpretation or duplication, and more amenable to quick transmission and easy filing. The majority of the files depicted in the case studies are organized numerically. But the problem of linking the client with his number, and hence with his data, remains a very difficult one. None of the solutions adopted by the five systems studied here is altogether satisfactory.

One of the simplest, and still widely used means of identification is the client's presentation of distinguishing information about himself. All five of these systems rely to some extent on this technique. National Insurance manages to identify most of its clients most of the time using only their reports of their name and date of birth. But National Insurance is fortunate in that the nature of its operation makes it rare for clients to attempt to impersonate other clients, or to deal with the system without revealing their identity. The licensing system, using virtually the same data for identification of drivers, is hard pressed to deal with those who falsify such information. BankAmericard, as usual, is more sophisticated. When it does rely on information from the client himself, in processing certain authorization requests, it requires the client to provide information so recent and idiosyncratic that others would be unlikely to know it. But even these exchanges are not wholly satisfactory, because they require too much time to be used regularly. And more generally, it is apparent that the provision of information by clients on themselves, because it is subject to falsification, is an unsafe bet where major interests turn on positive identification.

Other systems, in an effort to avoid the difficulties involved in clients' self-identification, may rely on the use of documents. This is obviously satisfactory only where the clientele is motivated to cooperate, and among these five systems only BankAmericard relies heavily on documentation for this purpose. The use of the credit card carries one advantage, in that the card itself is embossed with the client's account number, thus speeding and simplifying the linkage of client and filed data. The trouble with using credit cards, or any other documents, is that they are subject to loss, theft and counterfeiting. Were this not true, the whole of the security operation in the California BankAmericard headquarters would be superfluous. One check on these forms of fraud is in the inclusion of the applicant's signature on the card, which can be compared against that on the sales draft. Other credit card firms have attempted to circumvent the problem by printing the photograph of the card-holder on the card. But all these techniques require the cooperation of participating merchants, who may not be motivated to question the sale, and the cards themselves remain subject to loss and counterfeiting. The use of documentation, for whatever benefits it entails, also involves unavoidable drawbacks.

One way around the difficulties inherent in the use of both information and documentation is to base identification on physical characteristics, which are not so easily susceptible to modification or transfer from one client to another. The police rely on this means, both in their fingerprinting system and in their routine quests for wanted and missing persons. In the latter case mistakes do sometimes occur. The Wanted and Missing files give only name, date of birth, and a very brief physical description of the person, and it remains for the individual police officer to take responsibility for identification. Fingerprinting is virtually foolproof, however, and it forms the key link between persons and their criminal records. Indeed, fingerprinting might be an optimal means of positive identification were it not for the time required to process fingerprints through comprehensive fingerprint files, and for the fact that people cannot always be constrained to produce them.

Thinking of the strengths and weaknesses of these various techniques, one can, with a little reflection, easily envisage the ideal means of positive identification for purposes of mass surveillance. It would have to be based on some characteristic quite unique to each client, and inalienable from him. It should be readily interpretable by the agents of surveillance and unsusceptible to falsification. Finally, if should be amenable to rapid communication back and forth to the centres of surveillance – preferably in the form of a number which could also serve as the number of the client's file. In this light, the optimal solution is a system of tattooing all members of the clientele with a unique number, in some conspicuous part of the body. To be absolutely effective, of course, such a system would have to involve the participation of everyone, so as to prevent impersonation by feigning someone else's number. It is true that public opinion, at least in Britain and America, may not yet be ready for such a dramatic advance, but the effectiveness of such measures has already been demonstrated in situations where the necessity of efficient social control is imperative.

In the long run, aesthetic or sentimental objections to physical marking may not prove a serious obstacle to progress in this field. For equally efficient means of identification may soon be developed which bypass such objections altogether. British government agencies have recently been working on computer programmes which will, when perfected, reduce the time necessary for matching an incoming set of fingerprints against the entire police central collection to about ten minutes. If inexpensive means are available for projecting fingerprints by telephone to a central computing installation, the problem of positive identification should be largely solved. Another possibility, which has received considerable discussion in consumer credit circles, is the use of voiceprinting. It is argued that voices can be identified as reliably as fingerprints, so that credit-grantors could link consumers with their files simply by having them speak into a telephone receiver linked with a surveillance centre. Either one of these techniques, if the costs of their operation can be sufficiently reduced, would be as efficient as physical marking if not more so. And, of course, they would circumvent the necessity of imposing an authoritarian and coercive measure such as tattooing.

Conclusions

The aim of this chapter has been to move from the detailed empirical material presented in the case studies to generalizations, about both these five systems and other systems of mass surveillance and control. Now it is time to review and reiterate some of the main conclusions which have emerged.

In the opening remarks on surveillance capacity, there were three main observations drawn from the case studies. One was that the five cases showed a clear-cut trend towards increased capacity. This increase was evident both in all five systems and along all the dimensions of capacity, though not along every dimension in every case. Second, discussion noted that increased surveillance capacity is bound to be advantageous not just for these systems, but for all systems of mass surveillance pursuing similar objectives. Finally, I noted that the costliness of increasing surveillance capacity prevented such increases in many practical situations. But I also suggested that, because of economies in internal operations and other considerations, the over-all trend at present seems to be quite clearly in the direction of increased capacity.

This dialectic between operating costs and surveillance capacity has formed one of the main themes of this chapter. All the subsequent observations about specific trends in the internal organization of mass surveillance also noted the constraints on these trends exerted by cost factors. The need for rapid means of separating deviant from compliant clients, the importance of low rates of deviance in the viability of social control, the condensation of filed information, and the emergence of new patterns of contact between system and clientele – all these trends are directly shaped by cost considerations. This was especially dramatic in the discussion of rates of deviant behaviour. That discussion suggested that, no matter how sophisticated, none of these systems could cope with the costs of a drastic rise in deviant behaviour. Nor, again, are these observations meant to apply only to these five cases. From all one can tell, the problems of matching limited resources against a troublesome minority embedded in a compliant majority are endemic in the position of systems of mass surveillance.

These observations on the patterns of growth organization place some of the popular images of imminent total surveillance and control in an ironic light. None of these five systems shows any signs of incorporating and using full, discursive accounts of the movements and behaviour of their clients, in the model of *1984*. Indeed, it is evident that all the five systems must sometimes renounce the use even of 'available' information in decision-making, because of the costs of such use. Techniques of the sort described here may be capable of maintaining something like continuous surveillance over handfuls of clients at one time; but nothing like this is yet possible in mass surveillance. Thinking of the worst thing which could possibly happen to systems like these, one imagines their suddenly being inundated with complete, discursive accounts of all the behaviour of all their clients, instead of their usual intake of data. The resulting glut of information would paralyse their operations.

Nevertheless, there can be no doubt that these five systems, and others like them, are moving in the *direction* of total surveillance, even though the movement may not take the forms that popular imagination might envisage. Instead of the incorporation and scrutiny of discursive reports on every aspect of their clients' lives, these systems seem to be moving towards more and more sophisticated use of condensed, telegraphic information. The potency of these data does not lie in their voluminousness, even where the assembled information does provide something like a full sketch of the person concerned. Rather, the strength of the data stems from its ability to bear meaningfully, unambiguously and quickly on decision-making problems faced by the systems. Specifically, the files are most useful where they enable the system quickly and unerringly to single out the minority of their clients who warrant some measure of social control. In their most refined form, these discrimination procedures involve highly subtle judgements, often predictive ones about the client's future behaviour, based on imaginative and interpretive use of the discrete facts on file.

The press for economy in the compilation of data is matched in the patterns of its application to social control. Any of these systems can, for example, dispatch a representative expressly to accost delinquent clients; but as a regular measure this technique is difficult and expensive. Instead, the emerging pattern appears to be the extension of possible points of routine contact with the clientele, points through which clients must pass for their own purposes. At these points, the systems seek to develop means of quick identification and rapid information flow to enable them to bring the full weight of people's records to bear in decision-making about them – and, where necessary, in action against them. As the inducements to place oneself in touch with these points becomes more potent, the efficiency of these operations increases.

Thus the increasing power of these systems lies above all in the increasing sophistication of allocating surveillance resources precisely where they are needed. Instead of voluminous documentation of every act and movement of every client, one notes the importance of condensed, highly pertinent descriptions of those facts and behaviours which matter most to the system. Instead of an agent ready to knock at every door, inducements to clients to place themselves in touch with the system, with the possibility of more direct and aggressive attention where urgently needed. For the immediate future, at least, these patterns seem to be the ones dominating the internal organization of mass surveillance.

8

Mass Surveillance Within the Social Structure

Systems like those studied in this book are creatures of their social contexts. No idea has more formed this research than the notion that systems of mass surveillance are distinctive of certain social orders, and that their continued growth is closely tied to other changes in their social structural contexts. Some of these connections have been so obvious as to require little mention – for example the evident dependence of systems like these on technologies peculiar to industrial society. Others are much more subtle, and warrant special comment and analysis in light of the case studies.

This chapter aims to review some of the more important aspects of the dependence between systems of mass surveillance and control and the social contexts of these systems. This task runs parallel to the one undertaken in Chapter 7. There the goal was to chart certain similarities in the structure and workings of mass surveillance systems as they arise from similar internal constraints. This chapter, too, searches for common patterns in the development of mass surveillance and control, only here the interest centres on the effects of forces emanating from outside the systems themselves. As before, the concern lies both with identifying the forces which have shaped the growth of these systems so far and with noting the likely directions of further change in the near future. Unlike the preceding chapter, however, this one must also concern itself with the reciprocal effects of the development of surveillance upon the rest of society. For there is no reason to assume that causality is simply one-directional here, and some evidence suggests that the perfection of systems like these itself induces further changes in social structure. The first of the three sections of the chapter deals with the relations between the development of mass surveillance and control and the growth of social scale. The second deals with the evident tendencies towards exchange of information and other forms of symbiosis and cooperation among systems. The last part treats the social conditions which conduce to the growth of mass surveillance activities.

Surveillance and Social Scale

Throughout this book, social scale has served as the main criterion for comparing the 'development' or 'modernity' of social forms. The scale of a social unit, whether a whole society or some smaller element of social life, has been understood as proportional to the number of persons participating in that unit, and to the intensity of their involvement in that participation. Such a notion, of course, is but one of many possible yardsticks for comparing the modernity of social structures, and clearly it requires further specification so as to deal with the subtleties of concrete cases. But it is especially useful here in that both elements of the concept – numbers of participants and closeness of involvement – point directly to problems of social control. For changes in social scale conduce to, and in the final analysis demand, qualitative and quantitative changes in social control. And the perfection of new forms of social control can, in turn, lead to the birth of social units of increased scale.

On a number of counts the growth of scale and the extension of surveillance capacity virtually presuppose one another. One aspect of surveillance capacity, after all, is the number of clients over which a system maintains surveillance, and of course the number of participants in any social unit is one of the elements of the notion of scale. Thus as the number of participants grows, in social units requiring mass surveillance over those participants scale and hence the capacity of the system likewise grow. Moreover, in both the amount of useful data maintained per person and the increased contact between system and clientele, the growth of surveillance capacity and that of social scale go together. For both these dimensions of capacity reflect the closeness of involvement between system and clientele. The more details of the client's life the system deals with, and the more frequent or likely the encounters between the two, the more intensely one would say that the client is involved in the system.

But nowhere is the link between the growth of social scale and surveillance capacity so clear-cut or so closely articulated as with regard to the *centralization* of surveillance activities. Here most clearly one notes the constraints exerted on mass surveillance by the growth of scale, constraints pressing directly towards increased capacity. These constraints derive from the fact that any surveillance system suffers to the extent that it fails to hold its clients as fully as possible responsible for their actions. Because of this, every surveillance system must aim to accomplish two things. First, it must strive to collect the most 'complete' information possible on its clients. And, second, it must make sure that clients cannot easily escape measures of control based on such information.

The ability of any system of surveillance and control to shape the behaviour of its clients depends very much on the certainty with which it manages to bring information generated in one social and temporal setting to bear elsewhere. In law enforcement, both the deterrent effects of a 'criminal record' upon the criminal, and the usefulness of that record in determining the 'correct' sanction later on, turn on the likelihood of the record's being available to the police and the courts in case of subsequent conviction. Similar observations could be made about any other system of this type.

Most such systems, after all, order their activities within a well-defined jurisdiction. They aim to persuade their clients that they are prepared to enforce their rules throughout this jurisdiction, whether it may be a bounded geographical space, like a state, or social space like a bureaucracy or a social movement. Rules to be enforced accordingly pertain to clients' behaviour within those boundaries. Frequently, but not necessarily, the jurisdiction of a system corresponds to the area in which it systematically gathers information on clients. The three British systems studied in this book, all agencies of the state, aim at the enforcement of uniform or virtually uniform rules throughout the boundaries of Great Britain. To this end they gather information mainly from points within these boundaries. Any of the three has at least the possibility of incorporating information from elsewhere – for example, in the case of the police, from foreign police forces. But such intake serves more to fit the requirements of special, unusual cases than to sustain the routine regular inflow of information. Similar boundaries exist for the BankAmericard system and for the consumer credit reporting system, although the looser organization of the latter makes its boundaries more ragged.

Any system must arrange its boundaries so that both its surveillance and its control activities cover a sufficiently broad area to prevent clients from escaping their pasts simply by moving outside the relevant jurisdiction. One sees this principle at work to the detriment of law-enforcement in very tiny principalities. No matter how forceful or efficient police activities in such a situation, their effectiveness is bound to be compromised if a violator need only cross into the next jurisdiction to escape responsibility for whatever he has done. For some systems facing this problem, the solution lies in arriving at extradition arrangements, whereby other regimes join in the enforcement efforts by helping prevent flight to escape the consequences of past actions. Other systems adopt the solution of making exit from the jurisdiction very difficult indeed, so that the deviant client has no choice but to confront the system. But perhaps the most useful solution, in terms of the systems studied here, is to extend the jurisdiction of the system so as to cover the greatest possible area in which clients are likely to circulate.

Much the same principle is involved with respect to clients' 'escaping' from information which the system has incorporated concerning them. Over and over the case studies showed that powerful enforcement mechanisms, even those deployed over large jurisdictions, are helpless without effective means of bringing pertinent data to bear on encounters with clients. The problem is one of arranging for data on each client, wherever it enters the system, to be stored so as to be available for future decision-making on the client, whenever and wherever it occurs. Thus the strength of the BankAmericard system lies in the remarkably speedy routing of relevant information to the single point where information on that account is stored, and in its easy and quick recourse to those data in future decision-making. And, conversely, the weakness of British vehicle and driver licensing in its old form, in that information might not 'find' the correct file, and that subsequent decision-making on a given client might fail to bring to bear all the relevant data. Both in terms of optimal storage of information, and in terms of the administration of measures of social control, the solutions to such problems lie in centralization of surveillance and control activities over the widest possible area. To be sure, Chapter 7 noted that cost considerations may make complete centralization in any given system undesirable, at least in the short run. But it is clear that the coordination of surveillance and control activities over a wide area from a single point, wherever possible, does confer an advantage to the system *vis-à-vis* deviant clients.

To put matters succinctly, the scale of surveillance and control in any system must be commensurate with the life-space of the clientele. Close surveillance and potent mechanisms of control are useless if clients are apt to move readily in and out of its jurisdiction, if their movements continually lap over the boundaries of the system's enforcement activities. By the same token, intensive collection of information within a given area, through a wide array of channels of intake, is useless if decision-making requires the consideration of data generated elsewhere. Again, this is not to say that *unlimited* centralization does any system any good; there is no reward in spreading the net of surveillance and control wider than the paths described by the clientele themselves. But as the scale of social structures change, and those paths become wider, systems must centralize their activities over commensurately wider areas, or fail in their tasks of enforcement.

The case studies provide more than ample illustration of the workings of these constraints. The centralization of vehicle and driver licensing in Britain, taking place as this research was carried out, occurred very much in order to make the sphere of operation of that system commensurate with the life-space of its clients. Similar considerations have impelled the British police to centralize their accounting on criminals and wanted and missing persons. The same principles, again, have led BankAmericard to move towards further centralization of their surveillance and control activities in North America. All these changes represent efforts to make information culled from widely separated sources available wherever needed throughout a very wide jurisdiction. Other considerations have also figured in these reorganizations, since centralization may also bring other administrative advantages. But questions of surveillance and control have been as important as any.

Consumer credit reporting is perhaps most dramatic of all in these respects. There, as in the preceding cases, the necessity of centralization has stemmed from the increasing dispersion of information generated by clients, information pertinent to the decision-making tasks at hand. Especially important in this respect is account information generated with national and other non-local credit-grantors, like airlines and petrol companies. The experience of TRW Credit Data has shown that massive intakes of information from such dispersed accounts can be especially efficient when carried out directly with the large-scale organizations which generate them. But the need for centralization in consumer credit reporting stems not only from the increasing dispersion of individual consumers' account data, but also from the increased residential mobility of credit users themselves. The fact that people move about so readily from one part of America to another reinforces the necessity of centralizing information on them. For centralization makes it easy both to incorporate data on a given client from any point within the system's area of coverage, and to have recourse to such data without necessarily knowing where the client resides at the time. Here as elsewhere, growth in the scale of social structure draws mass surveillance itself into increasingly large-scale organization.

But it would be wrong to think that the causality in this relationship works only one way. For the perfection of techniques of social control also has its own effects in conferring vitality to social units which could not otherwise exist.

Chapter 1 pointed out that most, if not all, social units seem to display 'fault lines' of problematic compliance – points where resistance to rules imposed by the system is especially likely, and the consequences of disobedience particularly dangerous for the vitality of the system. Chapter 7 developed this observation a bit farther, suggesting that even a modest rise in serious non-compliance would probably cast into doubt the very viability of systems like those studied here. Conversely, improvements in the apparatus of surveillance and control may work to secure the position of social units whose existence would otherwise be tenuous. In the creation of ancient political empires, for example, such innovations might have been the improvement of communications to a sufficient extent to enable the capital to keep more effective watch over the provinces, or the creation of a new class of bureaucrats to act as agents of social control on behalf of the central government. In systems like those studied here, where lines of social control go directly from bureaucratic agencies to the members of very numerous mass publics, significant innovations of this kind often tend to include rapid communication techniques and other technological changes like computing. But they may also include innovations in organization techniques *per se* – that is, increasingly shrewd ways of organizing the work of surveillance and control.

Among the five systems studied here, BankAmericard provides the best case in point. Before the inception of that system, many of its constituent social elements had existed for a long time. There had long been the same array of firms desiring to sell their merchandise or services on credit, and the same large public of consumers who would have been pleased at the chance to use credit for such purchases. Many of the firms did in fact offer their own credit programmes to certain regular customers. But these credit schemes were all of relatively small social scale. The fact that any one firm offered credit only to its regular customers and that there was no way of extending blanket credit to all the customers involved made this inevitable. One result was undoubtedly a diminution of sales volume in relation to what it might have been, had credit been more widely and freely available. The crux of the problem was clearly a matter of social control: without some means of controlling the use of credit by the minority of bad credit risks, the firms involved could not afford to do business with the great majority who would represent acceptable risks. The role played by BankAmericard in this situation was to act as specialist in social control, screening out large numbers of bad risks, and controlling the use of credit privileges by the majority of good risks. Advantages of a very high-volume operation, and innovations in the bureaucratic organization and technology of surveillance, enabled BankAmericard to play this role profitably. The result was a new, very large-scale social unit in place of the congeries of smaller credit schemes which had preceded it.

Chapter 7 noted that the very necessity for surveillance and control seemingly stemmed from the activities of small minorities of deviants – though the final conclusion was more complex than this. By the same token, the activities of a minority of participants who resist the rules imposed by any system, or the threat of such activities, can make any social structure unviable. Trade may be impossible between two countries, for example, because banditry along the trade routes causes unacceptable losses to the traders. Or a library may have to curtail its lending privileges because of high losses of books, even if only a minority of borrowers are responsible. Efficient systems of control, by insulating the system from misbehaviour on the part of deviants, or by constraining the latter to comply, make possible the sustained cooperative behaviour which assures the vitality of the system. And this is simply to say that the development of social control makes it possible to extend the scale of social relations by enabling larger numbers of people to carry on sustained relations with one another.

It would be no exaggeration to describe all social units as maintained by their own peculiar arrays of social control mechanisms. This is true whether that unit involves only a handful of participants or millions, whether their involvement in it is fleeting and inconsequential or profound and all-important. In all social behaviour, some temptation not to do the 'right' thing is endemic. This is not the same as saying that disobedience is inevitable, but only that every viable, ongoing social unit must develop its own mechanisms of control. When the social world is operating smoothly, and one can afford to take compliance for granted, one hardly averts to these matters. But any act of participation in a really large system of social behaviour – posting a letter, depositing money in a bank, boarding an airliner – in fact implies confidence in quite an elaborate series of mechanisms of control. Such mechanisms are necessary to encourage large numbers of unseen others to do what they may well be tempted not to do. The more participants involved in the working of any social unit, and the more demanding the behaviour required of them, the more formidable the task of social control.

Among the institutions of contemporary industrial societies, the trend for the immediate future seems to be the continuing increase in social scale. Both state institutions and others promise to continue to draw together larger and larger numbers of participants, and to bind these participants in more demanding, more complex forms of dependence upon one another. At the same time, one may expect new means of control to emerge to ensure compliance among the participants in these larger-scale social units. In many cases it may be difficult to determine whether the perfection of control techniques itself has led to increase in social scale, or whether the growth of a larger-scale social unit spurred the development of new means of control. But one may be certain that the increase in social scale will not proceed any faster than the development of means for assuring compliance within the new social structures. And the development of those techniques will, where mass clienteles are involved, entail growth in the capacity of mass surveillance and control.

Symbiosis among Surveillance Systems

In the day-to-day work of carrying-out this research, no aspect of record-keeping practice proved more volatile or more difficult to explore than the disclosure of filed information and its exchange with outside organizations. No topic evoked less candour on the part of my interlocutors or gave rise to more vivid displeasure when I insisted on pursuing it. These reactions should come as no surprise when one takes account of the social setting of such issues. For it has been precisely over these issues which the most animated public controversies concerning mass surveillance have developed.

These controversies are scarcely misplaced. For questions of disclosure of filed information and cooperation among surveillance systems go to the heart of certain endemic conflicts between the systems and their clients. Systems like these develop, at considerable expense, unique powers of remaining in contact with numerous members of their mass clienteles, and of developing information on these clients even when the latter might resist it. Such facilities are bound to be attractive to other interests in society, and above all to other systems of mass surveillance and control. In many instances, this mutual attraction officially or unofficially gives rise to systematic cooperation among surveillance systems. The effect of such cooperation, when it does occur, is distinctly to enhance the position of the systems of control *vis-à-vis* their clienteles, to increase their surveillance capacity, and to conduce to change in the relations between agencies of surveillance generally and the public at large.

There are a number of reasons for the special usefulness to mass surveillance systems of shared information on clients. One is the 'interactive' quality which items of data referring to a single person can manifest when used in conjunction with one another. Two bits of information on the same person may, in other words, have an effect when combined quite different from the effect of either one alone. In consumer credit reporting, for example, it may be useful but unremarkable for the user of a credit report to note that a consumer's instalment debt obligations amounted in a single year to six thousand dollars. At the same time, the income tax authorities may take little note of a tax return from the same person reporting a total taxable income of five thousand dollars. But the two items together may have potent significance in either or both systems, since they establish that the person is either living vastly beyond his means, or drastically underreporting his income for tax purposes. Similarly, the fact that someone in Britain changes his vehicle registration to a new district is ordinarily of no more than routine interest to the licensing personnel there. But it may be of the greatest interest to the local police if they know that he has a history of a serious crime – and all the more so if a rash of similar crimes occur subsequently in the area. Similar interactions in the significance of two or more items of data may equally well occur in data collected by a single system. The principle is quite the same; the intersection of two disparate data, each unremarkable in itself, may be all that is required to single out a particular individual for special attention or corrective action. And discussion has already emphasized the extreme importance of processes which narrow the attention of systems like these to a limited, manageable number of deviant or potentially deviant cases.

The usefulness of such supplementary information is especially great when it derives from a source quite independent of the first source, and when the supplementary source is one not susceptible to falsification on the part of the client. The British National Insurance system relies very heavily on such techniques, in its use of 'credits' as cross-checks against fraudulent claims for Sickness Benefit. Insured persons may sometimes falsify facts sufficiently to present what appears to be a legitimate claim for Sickness Benefit while they actually continue to work. But it is much more difficult for claimants to interfere with the flow of information from employers, in the form of National Insurance contributions. And the receipt of such contributions for a period in which Sickness Benefit is claimed is an automatic signal of possible fraud. Equally automatic is the flow of data to National Insurance from the Registry of Births, Deaths and Marriages, information bearing decisively on entitlement to benefit and, of course, information quite outside the control of the insured. Finally, under the new system of computerized surveillance to be inaugurated by the British police, information provided by keepers of vehicles to local licensing offices will be available to policemen to corroborate the identity of drivers. And this information, too, will be but minimally subject to falsification by clients. Information generated in social settings quite independent of the actual workings of social control, and thus freer from pressures to falsification inherent in those settings, can be an immensely useful tool for systems like these.

The reliance on these forms of corroborative or supplementary data, like many another important feature of systems like those studied here, stems from the potentially conflicting interests of system and clientele. This is not to say that open conflict is universal between agencies of control and their clients; the case studies have shown that this is hardly true. But the very necessity of the existence of systems like these arises from the tendency of a resistant minority to break the rules. The result is that all systems must use information so as to protect the interests which they represent. In such situations, information is never a neutral commodity, but entails advantage or disadvantage to one side or the other. This is none the less true of data originally collected under the most routine or benign circumstances. Few people, for example, any longer contest the collection by the state of information on births, deaths and marriages; indeed, attestations of these facts are so widely required that people actively seek to register them as they occur. But such documentation may later serve to enable agencies to protect themselves against unwarranted claims from clients, as the case of National Insurance demonstrates. It is of course fortunate from the standpoint of the system that the original creation of such certified documentation is not the subject of conflict or of manipulation by the client. For this makes the information more authoritative and trustworthy – highly valued qualities, both.

Other reasons for exchange of data among systems are more mundane. One consideration is simply the expense involved in repeating or replicating bureaucratic operations of information collection already carried on elsewhere. If the British police had themselves to collect and keep current information on the registration status of every motor vehicle licensed in the land, instead of relying on licensing files, the expense would be so great as to render the operation unfeasible. Nor would the clientele of vehicle keepers have such a potent inducement to provide correct and current information. Likewise, if credit reporting agencies could not rely on bulk receipt of account information from member bureaus and others, their task would be much more difficult and expensive. For all of the systems studied here, intake of relevant information, and especially the task of assuring intake from all relevant sources, represents a major operating expense. Regular cooperation with other systems, so that relevant data arrive *en masse* on a regular basis, reduces these costs of intake significantly.

Because of the potentially conflicting interests involved in the collection and use of information, it is easy to see why clients may resent cooperation among systems. For such exchange may place the client in a disadvantageous position which he could not have anticipated when he originally yielded the information to another agency. The credit applicant may feel stung when he finds that information provided to one credit-grantor has found its way into credit bureau files, to be used elsewhere in a context where it was not freely offered. Or people may resent the fact that vehicle licensing information, generated in their contacts with the local licensing office, may become the basis for action by the police or the Department of Health and Social Security. No matter what one thinks about the justification of these forms of exchange, it is clear that the exchange of data among systems enhances the position of the latter in making discriminating decisions concerning their clients. And the fact that such decisions favour some clients means that they elsewhere work to the disfavour of others.

Another press towards symbiosis among surveillance systems has to do not with the use of information in decision-making, but with means of 'getting back at' those clients whose cases warrant corrective action. Chapter 7 emphasized the expense of sending an agent expressly to locate and accost delinquents. The five systems studied here all resort to such steps in the most urgent cases, but other means are considered preferable. And even under the most urgent circumstances, such recourse is bound to be difficult, for it is extremely hard to keep the addresses of all members of a mass clientele current, especially for those clients bent on evading the system. The preferred solution in these instances is to encourage members of the clientele to place themselves in contact with the system, in such a way as to make themselves accessible to corrective action. Perhaps the best example of all in these respects is the Bank-Americard authorization procedure, which, besides providing direct control over sales, often makes it possible to apprehend and sanction delinquent card-users. Steps like these change the apprehension and sanctioning of deviants from an expensive, extraordinary activity to one which can be carried out routinely, in settings maximally advantageous to the system.

Nevertheless, reliance on such means for contacting clients does pose problems. Specifically, it means that the system cannot act until the client voluntarily places himself in contact with it. Under these circumstances, the system requires some form of inducement to encourage such contact, something to attract clients and make them willing to make their whereabouts known. Of course, this is by no means impossible to arrange. In Britain's National Insurance, there may be minimal efforts to contact clients delinquent in their contribution record or suspected of benefit fraud. But such persons cannot take up employment on a Class I basis, or file claim for any further benefit, without coming to the attention of the system. Likewise, in Britain police surveillance, wanted or suspected persons may be able to avoid being caught in the net of 'stop check' encounters but to do so they must avoid the highways and other public places, and generally stay away from all settings where the police might notice them. For the Bank-Americard holder, the price paid for remaining out of direct contact with the system is renunciation of purchases activating the authorization procedure. In many of these instances, one must remember, clients are not well informed about the system's surveillance capabilities, so they do not necessarily realize the consequences of making contact. In any case, the strength of inducements to contact is extremely important, because it very largely shapes the ability of the system to enforce its rules.

In pursuing their own advantage, then, systems of surveillance find it useful to strengthen the inducements which bring clients within range of social control. One way of doing this is for several systems to 'pool their resources' in this respect, so that contact with one system exposes the client to action from another. The use of a state's highway system as a means of trapping persons delinquent in the payment of fines, mentioned earlier, represents a case in point. Inducements to contact were weak in the enforcement of fines, but the administration of that form of control in concert with control over highway use tips the balance of advantage in the direction of the authorities. One can see limited examples of such cooperation in some British systems. In so far as National Insurance occasionally provides information to the police, for example, the inducements to contact with the former represent inducements to contact with the latter, as well. Both the police and National Insurance, in turn, make their surveillance resources available to the armed forces in tracing deserters, so that contact between either agency and a deserter is apt to result in the latter's apprehension by the military. This means in effect that the deserter exposes himself to the forces of control if he should encounter a police stop check, or if he should register for Class I employment or otherwise make his presence known to National Insurance. These forms of cooperation have the effect of increasing the contact points between the armed forces and this particular clientele and in so doing strengthen the capacity of their system of social control.

There are other examples to the same point. One might regard one major purpose of the credit reporting industry as linking the surveillance activities of one credit-grantor with those of others. Thus, if it is efficient, a credit bureau-cum-collection agency should make it possible for someone's application for credit in one setting to lead to the collection from him of a debt contracted elsewhere years before. In general, the more potent and more numerous the inducements of any system for clients to place themselves in contact with it, the greater its powers of enforcement. Britain had an especially forceful asset in this respect in the identity card system used during the Second World War and up until 1951. Food was so scarce as to be unavailable without rations, and rations were available only to persons registered in their area of residence and provided with an identity card. Registration was all but universal, and the continual need for rations forced people to keep the authorities apprised of their current addresses, so that they could present a valid identity card. The cards were nationally indexed, so that the police could immediately find the address of any person throughout the country. As long as food remained virtually impossible to obtain without rations, the inducements to keep contact with the authorities remained highly persuasive. As a result, the police and other state agencies had ready access to people whom, for any reason, they wanted to contact. Two of my interlocutors, close to police affairs at the time, mentioned that some police circles had attempted to develop arguments against discontinuing the system, hoping to maintain this highly useful aid to police surveillance. But another figure, a civil servant, noted that the system in its old form would have quickly become unworkable without the inducement of rationing to keep addresses current. In any case, for political or administrative reasons, or for a mixture of the two, the identity card system was discontinued at the end of rationing.

At the time of this writing, British public opinion seems quite mixed in its attitudes towards the use of state surveillance powers in the exercise of control over private persons. In particular, the use of any form of mandatory police registration and identification – for example, an identity card system – seems to be regarded as subversive of British liberties.* And attitudes towards the state surveillance agencies studied in this book, and especially those towards cooperation among surveillance systems, often seem quite sceptical, among both the general public and their elected representatives. It was a Parliamentary question by a Labour MP noted for his critical stance towards such practices which led to the statement by the Secretary of State for Social Services quoted in Chapter 4 on page 161. There, the reader may recall, the reply stressed that 'records concerning individuals' were generally 'strictly confidential', but added that data were 'exceptionally' disclosed 'in the public interest'. The occasions for such disclosure, of course, were discussed at some length in that chapter.

But another variety of Parliamentary questions, and no

* Comments in the press noted during the course of this research seemed generally to view such measures in this light. See the *Guardian* story on trade-union opposition to identity cards in the edition of 5 July 1971, and the equally critical editorial appearing the same day.

doubt another significant element of public opinion, have tended in the opposite direction. Here the demand has been for fuller and more efficient use of government surveillance facilities for tracing persons, in cases where 'the public interest' required it. On 13 May 1971, just two days after a series of Parliamentary questions criticizing negligent disclosure of personal information kept by state agencies, the Prime Minister had to give assurances that the government was doing enough to help trace breadwinners who had absconded from their families. He then stated:

In England and Wales, when the courts request it, information is made available for this purpose from the central social security records and the records of the National Health Service, the Passport Office and the Ministry of Defence.

He went on to note some other measures also being taken. But another questioner remained unsatisfied. Was the Prime Minister aware, it was asked, that 'although these arrangements look well on paper, they are not working in practice? A large number of families are being maintained by the State simply because the breadwinner cannot – or will not – be traced?' No doubt feeling himself walking a very thin line, the Prime Minister replied,

It is possible that there are cases in which even with the use of all available machinery it is not possible to trace the persons concerned, which I regret. On the other hand, we are going to the utmost lengths to enable people to be traced without giving away confidential information. From recent events which we discussed in the House last Tuesday, it must be apparent to all that there is a delicate dividing line between the provision of the information which will allow these problems to be dealt with and the withholding of information, in circumstances in which it would be quite wrong for personal details to be made available.

One could not say that British government policies in these respects testify to any clear-cut, coherent set of guiding assumptions on the principles involved. But one must admit, as well, that the basic moral and social issues are themselves far from straightforward. A case can be made, consistent with many people's principles, that National Insurance ought not to provide information to the armed forces on the whereabouts of deserters. Perhaps some would argue that National Insurance data should never be available to any outside agency. But would such an argument be held to apply even in cases where National Insurance data might help to capture a murderer who had proclaimed his intent to kill again? And if not, what about cases in which the police claim that murder is imminent, but no crime had yet occurred? The Parliamentary remarks of the Secretary of State are ambiguous on this last point, since he states only that information is provided 'to assist the police in the prosecution of cases other than trivial crime'.

And what principles account for the differing standards covering release of information from different agencies? Why are data on persons' whereabouts freely available to the police and others from vehicle registration files, but only on a limited basis from National Insurance? Does the answer lie in some quality of the relationship between client and agency, such that a higher threshold of urgency is necessary to justify disclosure from National Insurance files? If so, what about the doctor–patient relationship? An employee of the National Health Service Central Register once told me that those records are occasionally used to help the police trace persons in connection with serious crime. Should this information be held sacred simply because the inducement to the client to provide it is tied to his need for the vital and personal services of medical care?

On occasions when I have discussed this research with left-wing friends and colleagues, they have often interpreted its main aim as that of unmasking the authoritarian purposes guiding the development of mass surveillance and control. People who mistrust the large institutions administering these forms of record-keeping seem to view cooperation among such systems as evidence of a specific political content as the inspiration of such policies. Such a view misses the point. The dilemmas involved in cooperation and exchange of data among systems like these are endemic in the role of such systems in any society. No matter what political system predominates, the difficult question of whether information gathered for one purpose should be used for enforcement elsewhere is inevitable. It is easy to reject the use of medical information systems for overtly political purposes, but the question of whether such information should be used to forestall a serious crime against a private person defies solution in partisan political terms. Regimes of all political complexions have considerations which they interpret as overriding in such matters, and there is no guarantee that a regime of the left can transcend the underlying ethical dilemmas any more readily than a liberal or a conservative one.

It is hardly the intention of this study to whitewash the policies and practices uncovered here. But the fact remains that a case can be made for virtually all the practices of disclosure and cooperation noted among the five systems covered. I do not mean that these would be cases which I could accept, but that they would be cases acceptable to significant segments of public opinion in the country concerned. Consumer credit reporting practices, much as they disturb many liberals and civil libertarians in America, seem to be widely accepted among American consumers, especially those eager to take advantage of credit. The disclosure of information from persons' criminal records to current or prospective employers, so energetically denied by the Home Office in Britain, would probably be endorsed by large elements of the British public. Many other people, of course, would like to see such practices curtailed. But the facts do not permit even the most emphatic opponents to suggest that these practices are solely the result of the self-interested manipulations of the agencies which carry them out. Not only corporate bodies, but also the general public have interests in the purposes which guide the use of mass surveillance. There is no reason to expect unanimity on either side as to which purposes these should be.

No system which develops the capabilities of those studied here can avoid pressures to share those facilities with other interests. The collection of data on a significant share of the general populace, and the maintenance of access to this clientele, are invariably tempting to other persons and organizations, especially those dealing with surveillance and control. The time and expense involved in developing these facilities, and the resistance of clients to providing information which may subsequently work to their disadvantage, inevitably place systems which succeed in these tasks at a premium. Given the difficulties posed by large-scale societies for discriminating social control, any system which succeeds in keeping touch with its people will inevitably be called upon to assist in other functions of control. However one feels about the justification of these attempts at cooperation and sharing of information among systems, it would be wrong to see their origin other than as endemic in the role of such systems in their broader social context.

Total surveillance, under anything like the present state of technology and social organization, is impossible. One simply cannot envisage how it would be feasible for any regime literally to watch everyone all of the time, to digest the resulting information continually and fully, and to remain eternally ready to respond. It is possible, however, to imagine what one might call a 'central clearing house' for mass surveillance and control, without straining the limits of present-day technology and organizational skills. Under such a system, all major agencies of mass surveillance and control within a single society would render unlimited assistance to one another. Information generated in the relationship between a client and any one system would automatically be available to any other system, whenever it might bear on decision-making in the second setting. Furthermore, the access of any one system to its clients would be fully shared by the others, so that the client's contact with one would have the effect of contact with all. Finally, in such a system, no favourable decision from any agency would be implemented while there remained a dispute between the client and another agency. Thus it would be impossible to obtain National Insurance benefits if delinquent in paying one's motor tax, or impossible to register one's car if wanted by the police. Such a system would certainly call for ambitious organizational rearrangements, but it would by no means be sociologically impossible. And clearly any such technique of 'pooling' the resources of systems for social control – resources of information, of access to clients, and of decision-making power itself – would enhance the capacity of all the systems involved.

Opposition to a programme such as this stems not from doubts about its efficiency so much as from feelings that such unlimited symbiosis among systems is morally wrong. But the underlying moral issues are in fact complex and problematic, and the policies actually observed in this connection do not seem to reflect a single universally-accepted set of principles. Discussion has noted that in many settings exchange of information and other forms of cooperation occur very widely indeed, while elsewhere quite different attitudes prevail. So far as the two American systems studied here are concerned, cooperation between the consumer credit reporting system and credit-grantors like BankAmericard is very nearly total, and in fact vital to both. Among the three British systems, cooperation ranges from the easy and extensive to the extremely guarded. Other systems of mass surveillance and control in Britain and America seem to show the same wide variation between unquestioned exchange and virtually total reserve. In terms of the moral principles guiding such exchange, a case can be made that the exchange of any information or cooperation against the interest of the individual is wrong. Others would make the opposite case: that information made available, say, to the state for any purpose should be used to enforce compliance with any legally binding obligation. Both the forces militating towards extended cooperation among systems and those against it are strong; both for that matter appear to be growing. As public awareness of the importance and power of systems like these increases, conflicts over symbiosis among them seem bound to sharpen and spread.

The Growth of 'Fine-Grained Concern'

So far, this chapter has considered two broad categories of external social forces shaping the development of mass surveillance and control. The first was the growth in social scale among the social structures in which these systems are embedded. The second was the tendency of systems like these to join in symbiotic relations with one another, so as to combine and strengthen their surveillance capacity. To complete these considerations of contextual forces bearing on the growth of mass surveillance, it is now necessary to explore a third issue, one which in a way precedes the other two. This is the question of the social settings in which such systems come into being – the conditions which lead to the development by corporate agencies of 'fine-grained concern' over the affairs of mass clienteles.

The term 'fine-grained concern' in ordinary English hardly carries the exact meaning which one means to give it. I have used it here, for want of something more exact, to describe the situation in which an agency aims to deal with its clientele discriminatingly, according to precise reckoning of subtle differences in each client's circumstances and background. Fine-grained concern in the application of social control is hardly a new development; on a face-to-face basis, people always aim to influence others in ways appropriate to those others' lives, and to the relationship between the two parties. Nor is control over large numbers of people a distinctive product of modern industrial society – one thinks of the subjugation of whole peoples by invading armies, or indeed of the conscription of such armies themselves. But the combination of these two things, such that single agencies both exert control over massive numbers of persons, and adjust that control to fit fine details of each individual's circumstances, does seem to be a product of our own times. For it requires a reliance upon technology in communication and information storage, and a sophistication in bureaucratic organization, which are distinctively modern.

What circumstances conduce to the institution of such ventures in corporate concern over the affairs of mass clienteles? First, obviously, the agency involved must somehow see it in its own interests to maintain the form of control in question. It must already possess an interest in that area of persons' behaviour, or must envisage a way in which the control of such behaviour might come to be profitable to it. Given such interests, the system must then set about developing and maintaining the data on these persons which might form the basis for decision-making on them.

The launching of systems like these *ipso facto* results in the subjection of areas of people's lives previously regarded as private to institutional attention. Opposition to such ventures is likely from those who resent the intrusion of corporate concern into such areas – for example, those who see the creation of credit records on themselves as a manipulative measure, or who regard the institution of a tax on income, with its attendant surveillance measures, as an unconscionable extension of government power. In societies like Britain and the United States, where public opinion does make a difference in these matters, it seems unlikely that systems of mass surveillance and control stand much of a chance without widespread acceptance, or at least acquiescence. People must believe, in other words, that the systems benefit not only the corporate interests which maintain them, but also that more diffuse thing identified as 'the public interest'. Certainly the five systems studied here seem to be regarded with such approval, at least among wide segments of public opinion. People seem to see themselves as benefiting from the services of National Insurance record-keeping or consumer credit reporting, while seeing any unpleasant effects of these practices as confined to a small proportion of deviant others.

One wonders what further areas of people's thus-far private lives are susceptible to mass surveillance, what areas of behaviour might thus be subjected to control in a way attractive both to corporate interests and to public opinion. One possibility might be reproduction. Clearly both the state and the general public have an interest in controlling the quality and quantity of offspring. Moreover, this is an area in which systematic surveillance, throughout people's childhood and child-bearing years, could produce much information bearing on the wisdom of their becoming parents. Such information, concerning health, physical characteristics, intelligence, and many other matters, is bound to become more and more pertinent to decision-making as the biological and social sciences establish more links between genetic inheritance, parental influence during childhood, and adult characteristics. In many instances, one imagines, this form of control would be attractive to potential parents, since it would allow them forewarning of possibly undesirable offspring. But since not everyone could be expected to cooperate willingly, it might be felt necessary to make participation compulsory, and this would necessitate enforcement mechanisms for resistant cases. Needless to say, the initiation of a system like this would face opposition from those holding the areas of life involved to be basically private. And certainly it is true that matters of health, intelligence and reproduction are generally regarded as private – just like information on persons' income, family status, encounters with law-enforcement institutions, medical fitness to drive, and other data collected by the systems described here. But these same data are also clearly more than only private, in that decision-making which could be based on them bears on the welfare of corporate interests, and of the general public.

Another possible new form of mass surveillance and control might have to do with crime and related anti-social activities. Chapter 2 has already dealt with one such system, of course, but British police surveillance confines itself mainly to controlling the behaviour of persons once they have already been convicted of crimes. It is not inherently impossible, however, to envisage a system which would predict the emergence of criminality and take corrective steps before it manifested itself in a specific person. Such prediction might draw on data on persons' social backgrounds, family lives, personality traits and a number of other matters already known to be associated with criminality. The research of sociologists and psychologists is continuing to refine such associations. A controversy broke out in America during the early years of the Nixon administration when it came to light that the President had actually given serious consideration to such a plan. That particular scheme proved to be naïve and crude, but not all forms of such discrimination need be so crude. If it became clear that a sophisticated version of such a plan could work on a large scale and could offer some hope of coping with rising crime rates, public opinion might well favour it.

Perhaps the reader may feel that most people, at least in Britain and America, would not in fact countenance such a scheme. Perhaps not. Perhaps it would be unacceptable to maintain such close surveillance and control over persons without their having actually been guilty of some infraction. But the BankAmericard system, and consumer credit reporting more generally, both work to control the behaviour of consumers before they have a chance to break the rules – that is, by preventing people from buying on credit once they have reached the end of their resources. The British police, too, occasionally rely on such preventive reasoning in dealing with suspects who have extensive criminal records. They may arrest a man who has broken a law if it appears that he is about to engage in some form of criminal activity of which he has already been convicted, yet make no arrest in the absence of such a record. There is precedent, then, for the use of surveillance techniques in order to apply corrective measures before actual deviance can occur. How far that principle will extend in the growth of new systems is of course the crucial question.

The control of reproduction and of criminality are only two possible foci of new systems of mass surveillance and control. There are plenty of others. One could imagine a scheme for identification and control of accident-prone motorists, using a blend of data on driving record, medical history, social background, personality and psycho-motor skills. Such a system might make it possible to curtail the activities of bad drivers before they actually had the chance to do serious damage. Or one could imagine a system of predicting unstable marriages through the use of information on the social background, personality traits and other characteristics of the potential partners. Preventive action could then be taken where a contemplated union seemed certain to end in divorce. In both these cases, increasing sophistication of social science methods could be a key factor in making such surveillance and control feasible. Of course, any of these new possibilities would involve institutional attention to areas of life now regarded as private. But it is also apparent that the behaviour which might be made susceptible to surveillance and control is of eminently public interest.

I can identify no 'natural limit' to the areas of people's lives which might serve as foci of mass surveillance – that is, no inherent, long-term limit in the *possibility* of using such personal information for mass social control. Indeed, it is often the most personal and private areas of life, like health and reproduction, which bear most tellingly on some socially significant result. Instances where comparative data on large numbers of persons are unavailable may serve to protect privacy, since they fail to reveal the connection between predictive states and the result in subsequent behaviour. But statistical manipulation of aggregate data on very large numbers of people can show unanticipated connections between previously obscure variables and some undesirable result. The detection of 'audit potential', as described earlier, is as telling an example as any. Of course, the search for audit potential does not require collection of information qualitatively different from that collected previously. But if some highly-sought-after form of prediction did in fact turn on the use of extremely intimate, personal data not yet freely disclosed, the lines of conflict would be clearly drawn. Chapter 7 pointed out the extraordinary utility of techniques which narrow the 'attention' of surveillance to a relatively few cases where deviance is especially likely. Prediction techniques like these offer precisely this selection. But they work only when the necessary data are available from all members of the clientele.

Chapter 1 expressed misgivings about the tendency of some authors dealing with topics like these to arrive at sweeping and often baleful predictions on the basis of preliminary, tentative indications. In subsequent discussion I have tried to avoid speculation which might seem rash. Thus it is important to note that these remarks on possible future developments in mass surveillance and control do not represent predictions, but heuristic cases aimed at establishing two things: first, that the feasibility of such measures is increasing, and that some of the techniques involved may already be practicable; second, that the ethical and social issues which such innovations would entail are not qualitatively different from those inherent in the workings of other existing systems of surveillance and control, including the five studied here. The fact that such developments are feasible, and that many are apt to hold them desirable, does not amount to a prediction that they will occur. That will depend on those who control institutions capable of maintaining mass surveillance and control.

And it will depend on public opinion – concerning both the desirability of the control offered by the new systems and the acceptability of the measures required to achieve such control.

Conclusions

Over-all, the growing importance of systems of mass surveillance and control within their social contexts appears bound up with the continuing growth of other modern social forms. Directly and indirectly, both as cause and as effect, the growth of more and more powerful systems of the kind studied here is tied to growth in scale of the social units with which these systems are associated. This relationship holds true with respect both to the growth in numbers of participants in such units, and to the increase in what has been called the intensity of their participation.

This second element of the concept of scale, the intensity of involvement or participation in a social unit, has not so far come in for much explicit discussion. It now deserves some attention, in light of the ideas developed in this chapter. Any attempt systematically to reckon how 'intensely' people participate in any social unit is bound to pose analytical problems, and require further specification of notions of 'participation' and 'intensity'. But there can be no doubt that the underlying dimension represents an important form of variation. There must be some means of comparing, say, a political association which demands no more of its supporters than their monthly dues and an occasional evening's or Saturday's participation, to a thoroughgoing political sect counting the same number of adherents but demanding of them total loyalty, exacting discipline and full-time participation. The same kind of difference is implicit in the comparison between the participation of the ordinary person in a loosely organized, feudal state and that in a modern industrial state. The individual is part of both units, but in the first case his relation to the exercise of state power is apt to be distant and indirect, whereas citizenship in a modern state entails all sorts of direct and immediate demands upon the private citizen, including taxation, obedience to a uniform legal code, and so on. Social units do differ, then, in the amount of their participants' social behaviour which they subsume, in the extent to which participation requires compliance with potentially distasteful obligations. This is not to say that participation in highly demanding units need necessarily be oppressive or undesirable from the standpoint of the participant himself; there are many, for example, who willingly yield total commitment to demanding political or religious movements. The point of comparison has only to do with how much of the participant's behaviour is actually structured or shaped by such participation.

With this in mind, it should be easier to understand why numbers of participants and intensity of participation usefully go together in the concept of social scale. For both forms of variability have to do with what one might see, very abstractly, as the total amount of social behaviour shaped or coordinated or subsumed by the social unit. Scale may grow, in other words, either by increasing the numbers of people upon whom certain demands are made, or by increasing the demands made upon those already participating. And both forms of increase quite clearly involve the extension of social control. The growth of systems involving larger and larger numbers of persons obviously requires new techniques of control – including, of course, the sorts of mass surveillance and control techniques studied here. But so, too, does the change from a situation where the social unit requires only limited participation – for example, a reserve army – to one where the demands become total and potentially all-consuming, as in the mobilization of reserve forces in wartime.

The research presented here should have amply illustrated the growth in scale of mass surveillance implicit in the increase in numbers of participants in such systems. The trend towards centralization of surveillance and control over wider and wider areas, for example, involves the inclusion of more and more participants in single units, and hence represents a movement towards greater scale. But a fundamentally similar movement is implicit in the increased intensity of clients' involvement in the systems. If bureaucratic agencies come to submit wider and wider areas of people's lives to mass surveillance and control, then the intensity of involvement of the clientele within the system to that extent increases. And when agencies of control strengthen their position *vis-à-vis* their clientele by measures of cooperation and symbiosis, the 'hold' of these agencies on their people likewise grows. The more thoroughly the agency controls its clients' behaviour, the greater the social scale implicit in the relationship.

The extreme case of such developments, of course, is total surveillance. At that imaginary point, all of men's private lives become subject to public surveillance, and the control of the single master agency over the actions of its all-inclusive clientele becomes not just extensive, but total. I have argued that the interactions between systems like those studied here and their social contexts press such systems steadily towards increased surveillance capacity, which is to say towards total surveillance. The internal operating requirements of the systems themselves, for example, drive them to seek closer and closer symbiosis with other similar systems. Increasingly sophisticated technology promises to make such exchange more and more attractive and feasible, thus enhancing the power of the systems which engage in it. At the same time, other developments in modern societies promise to extend the effects of fine-grained corporate concern over wider and wider areas of men's private lives. Here both improving technology and new understanding of human behaviour itself promise to increase the scope for mass surveillance and control. Finally, some of the most important pressures towards increased surveillance capacity stem from the growth of social scale itself. For as modern social institutions come to bind more and more people in larger and larger social structures, institutions of social control must develop to ensure compliance from these increasing numbers of participants. And as the new, larger social units come to make more and more extensive demands on the behaviour of those who participate in them, the mechanisms which enforce these demands must increase commensurately in strength and effectiveness.

But, again, the fact that these pressures exist represents no guarantee that they will necessarily lead to the growth of a totalitarian social order. Crucial questions remain. Does the growth in sophistication and power of systems like those studied here necessarily amount, in the long run, to growing *repressiveness* in social control? Does such growth necessarily mean that those subjected to it are 'less free' or 'more controlled' over-all than before? And what are the prospects for the countervailing forces which have grown up as a reaction against trends like these? These are questions to be addressed in the following chapter.

9

The Future of Surveillance

These discussions have taken us over a long route. Chapter 1
began with some very general observations about social control, and especially about its changing role in the growth of
modern social forms. Systems of mass surveillance, it was
seen, work to sustain social control required in large-scale
social structures. At the same time, similar systems figure
importantly in the control practices of authoritarian regimes,
thus raising concern over the role of these institutions in 'free'
societies. The case studies in the following chapters aimed at
developing a richness of comparative material on mass surveillance and control which might illuminate these issues.
Chapters 7 and 8, following the case studies, served to organize
some of their findings in terms of the major internal and external
forces shaping the development of such systems. By now, our
journey has taken us nearly back to the point of departure.
What remains is to apply the information and insights developed
so far to some more explicit responses to the questions raised
in Chapter 1.

Privacy

Probably the most common popular objections against mass
surveillance have to do with the effect of such practices on
personal privacy. Certainly systems like those studied here
are subject to frequent complaints that they collect, store and
use information which is inherently 'too personal' for public
attention. People widely believe that the growing appetite of
corporate bodies for personal information on their clients is
somehow related to other broad trends of social change. And

in this they are correct. But are people also justified in fearing that these trends are bound to culminate in ultimate extinction of all personal privacy?

This book has dealt with exchange of personal information mainly in terms of social control. That is, it has traced the movements and uses of such information primarily in order to show how it enables bureaucratic agencies to enforce compliance from mass clienteles. In this context, men's craving for privacy is easy to understand, for the ability to withhold information may mean the ability to escape the reach of corporate control. But men also desire privacy for its own sake, simply for the inherent satisfaction of protection from the idle curiosity of others. Mass surveillance obviously also has implications for the satisfaction of this form of the desire for privacy.

In one sense, the complaint that the growth of mass surveillance entails an erosion of personal privacy is obviously and necessarily so. By their natures, systems like these work to collect, store and use personal information in more far-reaching and systematic ways than would otherwise be the case. If one regards privacy straightforwardly as the total amount of others' ignorance of one's own affairs, there can be no question but that mass surveillance detracts from it. But this is hardly the same as saying that, with the development of systems like these, modern life is becoming altogether 'less private', or that people are on balance more subject to the intrusive attentions of others. For the growth in social scale which gives rise to mass surveillance also brings about many other changes affecting public surveillance over men's private lives. And the same social changes which make *mass* surveillance feasible and necessary may also release men from other forms of surveillance.

There is no reason why a careful investigation could not produce some useful quantitative comparisons between the 'net privacy' afforded private persons in a variety of social settings. One might base the relevant measures on the number of other people typically having access to certain 'private' information. Other possible indices might be based on the ease of control over access to such information and on the importance of those who knew to the person to whom the data pertained. The application of such techniques would turn on some highly interpretive judgements, judgements which would obviously affect one's understanding of resulting comparisons. It would be necessary to weigh, for example, the disclosure of the status of an illegitimate child to social welfare services against similar disclosure to one's next-door neighbour. If competently carried out, though, such comparisons could lead to a highly illuminating view of a difficult topic.

By those measures which would accord most with people's intuitive ideas of privacy, however, it is far from clear that life in contemporary Britain and America is necessarily 'less private' than its counterpart in small-scale societies. Indeed, one can argue that the average Briton or American is no worse off in this respect than his counterpart twenty, thirty or fifty years ago. For besides bringing the advent of mass surveillance, these decades have also seen the relaxation of many forms of small-scale surveillance. The community, the neighbourhood, the extended family and other primary groups have from all accounts grown weaker in their hold over their members, and hence less binding in their claims for personal information. No one who has ever lived in a parochial community, or delved into the sociological or anthropological literature on traditional societies, can doubt the strength of those claims. In larger-scale settings, relative ease of mobility enables people to leave the scene of past misdeeds, avoid those who possess sensitive information about them, and so on. Moreover, the growth of scale may prevent those who possess sensitive information about someone from being in touch with one another, and hence from developing a 'total' picture of the person. By contrast, small-scale communities and similar primary groups collate and compile personal information with a relentlessness which would do credit to any computerized central filing system. Indeed, the very press for development of modern surveillance systems stems at least partly from the breakdown of their traditional counterparts.

Probably any effort to compare 'total privacy' afforded in different social settings is bound to require matching incommensurables. Again, how is it possible to weigh the exposure of personal information to scores of indifferent operatives, in a modern surveillance system, against disclosure to a handful of neighbours in a tightly-knit community? How, for that matter, is one to weigh the discursive but relatively evanescent information transmitted in gossip against the terse, telegraphic but enduring data held in dossiers or computer files? Questions like these seem to mark the limits of simple comparison between what is and what was. Yet it does not seem that one's view of the rights and wrongs of modern mass surveillance should turn on such comparisons. Those who value personal privacy will certainly seek to protect it in the present, no matter what the precedents in the immediate or distant past. Let us then look more carefully at the impact of systems like the five studied here on personal privacy.

One central issue here must be the extent to which information provided to surveillance bodies is made available to other persons and agencies. Every mass surveillance agency which I have ever encountered insists that its files are 'confidential', that its personal data are held 'in confidence'. All this means is that the information is used for some purposes but not for others, for in fact agencies vary very widely in disclosure policies. Consumer credit reporting agencies in the United States are committed to the principle of confidentiality, for example. But their reports are available to any agency or individual who appears to be a grantor of credit. Likewise, information held in criminal record files by the British police is 'confidential' in that it is not available freely to everyone. But Chapter 2 showed that police data are supplied routinely to many employers and professional bodies, as well as accidentally or unofficially to other users. On the other hand, the case studies have also noted instances in which the organizations maintaining filed information manage to protect it quite effectively from outside access.

Certainly there is no reason to believe that systems which collect and use volatile information on mass clienteles must necessarily broadcast those data. Even very large systems may manage to limit the access of their own staffs to sensitive data stored *en masse*. The National Insurance Central Office at Newcastle, for example, assigns contributors' records randomly among some one hundred ledger sections, so that the chance of any one employee's using his position to locate the records of someone else is very small. At a greater extreme of protection of personal privacy, one might imagine a system so thoroughly automated that its personnel virtually never come into direct contact with other people's data. One wonders whether a system violates a client's privacy if it uses 'his' information without actually 'seeing' it. More concretely, there are a number of other sources of variation in the 'confidentiality' of field information. These have to do with organization of the surveillance system, with that of the data themselves, and with the technology involved in maintaining and transmitting the data.

People seem instinctively to fear the accumulation of large amounts of data in inclusive, centralized repositories, and there is some wisdom in these fears. For the centralization of data always solves certain problems for those desiring to avail themselves of it, whether or not their access is 'authorized'. The case studies illustrated how the usefulness of any data depends entirely on the user's ability to determine quickly and cheaply where to find it. Keeping all available data for the whole of a clientele in a single place makes it easy to locate desired information. By contrast, discussion of the older forms of credit reporting and vehicle and driver licensing showed how decentralization multiplies the problems of those who would gain speedy access to data. Similarly, though records of arrests held by the police in America are often quite susceptible to access by outsiders, they are nearly as dispersed as the organization of American policing itself. In contrast to the highly centralized British system, the American practice is often to store this information only with the force which made the arrest. Thus it is easier to conceal a record of arrests in the United States than is generally true in Britain.

Nevertheless, there is no reason to believe that the centralization of personal information *inevitably* and *necessarily* makes that information 'less private'. To be sure, if security measures are poor, centralization will ease the task of those bent on gaining access. But if the agency concerned is determined to protect its data, centralization may enhance the efficiency of measures of protection. In other words, economies of scale and other considerations may make it easier to perfect security measures in a single location than to maintain them simultaneously over many. Thus, for example, the fully centralized records in the National Insurance Central Office at Newcastle, which is relatively insulated from direct contact with the public, are probably safer from unauthorized access than those same records would be if they were stored, say, in local National Insurance Offices.

Another factor in the accessibility of filed information to unauthorized outsiders has to do with the routine paths through which data flow from file to user. Some surveillance systems entail the creation, storage and use of filed information within the confines of the single organization. Elsewhere the 'producers' of files are not the same as their 'consumers', so that information must routinely cross organizational boundaries. Control of access is probably more difficult in this second case, since recipients within one's own organization are usually easier to identify. Difficulties in these respects are likely to be especially great in cases where sensitive information must be provided quickly, since these situations provide the most slender opportunity to identify the recipient. Consumer credit reporting in America and British police surveillance are cases in point here. On the other hand, the provision of National Insurance information in Britain from Central Office to local offices is less vulnerable. This is both because the recipients are part of the same organization, and because the exchange of data is usually less urgent.

Problems of control are undoubtedly greatest where 'consumers' of filed information have many paths of access to the files. British police surveillance, consumer credit reporting and the BankAmericard system are all vulnerable on this score. If a call on one telephone line fails, or a request on one letterhead is rejected, an unauthorized seeker of information will simply try another approach. In the police system, a request to one police force or to one criminal record office, if rejected, will scarcely discourage any caller from trying elsewhere. In consumer credit reporting, the stricter credit bureaus may not provide information to unknown buyers of reports, but they always do so to other bureaus. Thus the problem is simply to find a single bureau willing to make the request. By contrast, National Insurance Central Office supposedly provides data only to the local office holding the claimant's file. With some exceptions, this system seems to work in practice, and thus places National Insurance in a stronger position against unauthorized requests.

To judge from most public pronouncements on the matter, computerization of filed data represents the single greatest threat of all to personal privacy. This is certainly true in so far as the availability of computing encourages organizations to compile and to centralize more information, including more personal information, than they would otherwise. But beyond this the issue is not so clear-cut. I am not convinced, for example, that electronically stored information is necessarily more vulnerable to unauthorized access than manually held data, other things being equal. If anything, it seems that control over electronically stored information may be easier than that over manual files. I am no specialist in the techniques of computing, and my acquaintance with the uses of the machines has mainly to do with their role in settings like those studied in this book. But it is certainly true that, once data are entered in electronic storage, a machine transaction is necessary for their retrieval. There are problems of controlling the use of the machines by unauthorized persons, but these problems all have their counterparts in manual storage. Computer operations at least require fewer personnel per amount of information stored than manual operations, and both computer personnel and transactions are subject to monitoring. Some specialists in computer technology have suggested exotic means for electronic theft of computer data, but these are in turn vulnerable to electronic countermeasures. And, again, manually-stored data are also vulnerable to theft. In general, it seems to me that *absolute* security of either form of data is an unhelpful abstraction. The problem, for both manual and electronic files, is to push the costs of unauthorized access sufficiently high to exceed the worth of any likely benefits to unauthorized users. The case studies have shown that this is something which many systems, electronic or manual, are unwilling to do.

The purely technological issues have simply received more

publicity than they deserve. The most important variable in determining the protection of any system of personal data is the earnestness of the organization concerned to do so. Certainly careful attention to the technology of privacy is essential whether data storage is computerized or not. But privacy is attainable if sought earnestly enough. The trouble is merely that the measures necessary to ensure privacy are expensive and troublesome in either case, and hence unpopular among those responsible. In the case of British police surveillance, protection against unauthorized inquiries from the outside would require, at the very least, an effective system of identification of callers to criminal record offices. This might necessitate, in the simplest imaginable form, something like the exchange of a password before the release of information by phone. But even this minimal measure would make the processing of stop checks much more troublesome and time-consuming, and would face resistance from working policemen. Nor will the computerization programme now being implemented do much to change this situation. Similar difficulties inhere in the workings of other mass surveillance systems. Existing barriers may exclude whimsical or unsophisticated attempts at unauthorized access, but no more. This situation will not change until those responsible are constrained to regard the issue with much greater urgency than is now the case.

I strongly believe that the agencies which succeed best in protecting personal information are those with the greatest purely selfish interest in doing so. I suspect that the U.S. Census is one of these. Sociologists using data provided by this agency have remarked how careful it is in releasing information, and how information on single individuals, as distinct from aggregate data, is never disclosed. Certainly this fastidiousness towards personal data is not a general characteristic among all American government agencies, any more than is the case in Britain. But the Census is especially at the sufferance of the public with regard to its collection of information. Should people come to believe that their answers were not held in confidence, public resistance to census inquiries would rise, and candour in answering would fall. Under the stimulus of considerations like these, strict security measures are only prudent. It seems that the best way to ensure careful attention to this issue from any agency is to make the issue sufficiently important to warrant a really major application of resources to the protection of access.

Mass Surveillance and Repression

If the erosion of personal privacy represents, for most people, one of unpleasant consequences of mass surveillance, then the abridgement of personal freedom represents the other. People instinctively feel that the appetite of corporate agencies for personal data is not simply whimsical. They feel rather that information so collected is apt to bear on subsequent decision-making, and that such decision-making may work to their disadvantage. The case studies have shown that these perceptions are quite correct, at least as far as they go. The question is: has this inquiry also revealed an over-all trend towards totalitarian repressiveness in the model of *1984*?

Ordinarily, one uses the term 'repression' to describe those situations where a minority attempt to force their way on an unwilling majority. This is hardly characteristic of the five systems studied here. True, these systems exist to constrain compliance from those who would not otherwise comply. But, from all evidence, they enjoy the support or at least the acquiescence both of their clienteles and of public opinion more generally. People feel that the collection of personal information and its use in decision-making serves ends which either are justified by necessity or bring actual benefits to the clienteles. Americans may be uncomfortable at the idea of others collecting information on their incomes, family status and consumption habits in the course of consumer credit reporting. But they regard the system, with considerable justification, as necessary for the relatively easy availability of credit. Some elements of British public opinion are likewise disturbed at surveillance techniques used to substantiate National Insurance claims. But National Insurance is seen as a desirable institution; and the collection of information on eligibility for benefits appears essential to its operations. Moreover, the case studies have shown that a majority of clients do comply with the strictures of these systems. The clienteles thus are apt to see the unpleasant results of mass surveillance as directed against a deviant minority of others, rather than at themselves.

The concern of this book is not just with the present state of mass surveillance, however, but also with its future. Moreover, as Chapter 1 emphasized, this study deals primarily with the organizational form, rather than the political content, of mass surveillance and control. And there can be no question that systems like these, however readily accepted in their present relatively benign form, would also serve for purposes which anyone would consider repressive. The bureaucratic mechanisms developed by Britain's National Insurance for tracking the places of employment and residence of insured persons, for example, could as well serve to control the movements of political undesirables. It is interesting to note, in this connection, that Britain's National Health Service Central Register, listing virtually every British resident, uses the record system originally developed for the identity card system used during the Second World War. Similarly, one can readily imagine using the BankAmericard system for police stop check procedures directed against political dissidents. The computer memory, now used to hold credit account information, might keep up-to-the-minute data on people's standing with the authorities, while the BankAmericard itself could serve as a general identity card. Moreover, techniques discussed in the preceding chapter of 'pooling' the resources of surveillance and control among agencies would serve at least as well in repressive regimes as in liberal ones. An efficiently centralized, master agency of control could enhance its position considerably by making access to National Insurance, or Britain's National Health, or to any of the other systems studied here, contingent on political reliability.

There is one important qualification to this point. Chapter 7 concluded that these five systems require majority compliance in order to maintain control over the deviant minority. Earnest efforts at evasion from even as many as ten per cent of their clienteles, it appeared, would make their operations unviable under present conditions. On the face of it, this would suggest that systems like these could not successfully enforce rules which their clienteles generally opposed. But one must remember that enthusiasm for compliance is not the same thing as willingness to comply, and that authoritarian measures may draw compliance even from resentful clienteles. If National Insurance punished failure to contribute with a stiff prison sentence, for example, compliance might well remain high even in the face of the deepest antagonism to the requirement. Thus a high rate of 'willing compliance' – compliance without the necessity of expensive sanctioning measures – may be forthcoming under proper conditions even from clients whose state of mind is anything but compliant.

Then, too, one must remember that authoritarian regimes may be much more willing than ones like these five to accept very high costs of control. For BankAmericard, the enterprise of control becomes unviable at the point where the operation ceases to make money. For the other four systems, the point at which the maintenance of control ceases to be 'worth the trouble' may be less obvious, but it exists nonetheless. But for a political regime whose very existence depends on the maintenance of certain forms of control, any expenditure may appear cheap. Such regimes may be willing both to take much more drastic action against the disobedient, and to devote much more of their total resources to control, than is true of any of these systems. History is not lacking in examples of regimes which have bankrupted their societies in keeping themselves in power.

There can be no question, then, that surveillance mechanisms developed for relatively benign purposes can also serve the needs of repression. But this is hardly to suggest, as some writers would seem to imply, that the availability of potentially repressive tools in itself engenders repression. On the contrary, the case studies have shown some agencies quite willing and able to resist the appropriation of their resources for purposes other than the original ones. Discussion of the possibility of 'pooling' surveillance and control resources illustrated particularly a willingness to forgo practices which would obviously be advantageous from the standpoint of control. Britain's National Insurance, despite some cooperation with outside agencies, obviously goes to great lengths to resist many possible forms of cooperation with, say, the police. The same sort of resistance would obviously manifest itself against the use of many of these systems for measures of repression – at least, under present political conditions.

But concern over the 'repressiveness' of mass surveillance obviously has to do not only with the purposes it serves, but also with the extent of its penetration of everyday life. That is, the extension of mass surveillance is disquieting partly because of its prospect of corporate supervision of every private moment. The case studies have suggested that the dominant trend is towards increasing the extent and the impact of mass surveillance on men's lives. Moreover, it should now be clear that mass surveillance need not be *repressive* to be *total*.

There is no *a priori* reason why a system of mass surveillance might not extend its attentions to the whole of its clients' lives, while still working to enforce rules which most of them favoured. Indeed, the attractiveness of the systems studied here to their clienteles seems to turn on their ability to enforce rules which most clients wanted enforced. Many sociologists have commented on the growing extent of centralized controls of all kinds in ordering and directing the affairs of mass publics. Some of these observers have taken optimistic views of these developments, while others have viewed them as the beginning of the end of individual liberty. Barrington Moore, Jr, though never one to minimize the role of coercion in any political context, has noted,

Nobody seriously regards the traffic control officer in a busy airport as an agent of social repression. Yet he makes decisions for all the pilots which greatly improve their chances of landing safely. Not every sacrifice of individual autonomy necessarily means a loss of freedom.*

The point is well taken. But this research suggests that changes in modern social structure may place most people on something like a flight plan most of the time. Benevolent or otherwise, the

* Barrington Moore, *Political Power and Social Theory*, New York, Harper and Row, 1965, p. 189.

directions emanating from the control centres are shaping their lives more and more.

Still, it would be wrong to interpret every advance in the development of *mass* surveillance and control as an *absolute* advance in the impact of social control on men's lives. For modern social structures also release men from all sorts of small-scale agencies of control, just as it frees them from many intrusions on their privacy. If bureaucratic, corporate control is growing in importance, the extended family, the neighbourhood and other small-scale, primary groups are losing their grip. Moreover, innovations in the technology of control, so much emphasized by writers on these topics, have as their counterpart innovations in the technology of evasion. Law-enforcement officials whom I interviewed, for example, sometimes complained that their new surveillance techniques could scarcely keep pace with the advantages of modern criminals in terms of rapid mobility, quick communication, and so on. There is no point in taking such complaints precisely at their face value. Quite an ambitious research undertaking would be necessary to show whether a given form of crime, or any other misbehaviour, is easier to perpetrate under modern surveillance conditions than previously. But for all the advances in police surveillance techniques, rates of reported crime have continued to rise in Britain and America over the last several decades. One would be wrong to assume that the growth of social scale and technology have favoured only one side of the struggle between evasion and control.

A particular irony in this respect is that the new social structures supported by mass surveillance may in themselves lead to qualitatively new forms of deviance. The advent of National Insurance in Britain, for example, has obviously involved the penetration of corporate surveillance and control into many previously private areas of men's lives. But the existence of National Insurance itself makes feasible forms of misbehaviour like benefit fraud quite impossible before this institution existed. Likewise, the BankAmericard scheme and its counterparts in the credit card business have spawned what is virtually a new criminal industry. Known as the 'plastics business', this profession specializes in stealing or otherwise obtaining credit cards and using them to make illegal purchases, usually for quick resale. BankAmericard does manage to contain the activities of these professionals sufficiently to keep its operations profitable. But it has never succeeded in eliminating the 'plastics business' altogether. Thus the growth of large-scale social structures not only subjects men to new forms of social control, but also provides them with new possibilities for misbehaviour.

It is by no means clear, then, that the growth in social scale is making men altogether more 'controlled' than before, any more than it is necessarily making their lives generally less private. The changes involved are much too multifarious to afford any such synthetic judgement at this point. What is quite plain, however, is the growing importance of *mass* surveillance and control at the expense of their small-scale counterparts. Broader and broader areas of men's lives are becoming subject to the attentions of corporate agencies of control. The impact on those lives of fine-grained corporate decision-making continues to increase, and the role of mass surveillance in ensuring the vitality of large-scale social structures also promises to grow.

Nor, finally, should one discard the possibility that the development of mass surveillance techniques may, in the long run, lead to something like total surveillance. Men's ingeniousness in devising such techniques, and the profundity of the social forces propelling their application, would only make such an assumption rash. At length, it is possible that the growth of mass surveillance may not only counterbalance the weakening of traditional controls, but also come to replace and even exceed their effects. This would hardly represent a more radical development of mass surveillance than that which has occurred in the last fifty years. For the next several decades, it appears that the totalitarian world envisaged by Orwell is not in store, even in the benign version of total but benevolent surveillance. Beyond that, one cannot say.

The Politics of Mass Surveillance

Discussion has already noted the absence of any inherent

technical or organizational limit to the continuing extension of mass surveillance and control. Systems like those studied here are currently subject to all sorts of limitations of capacity, but human ingenuity promises to keep wearing away at these. The more important limitations are not ones of technique, but instead have to do with people's feeling that unchecked corporate surveillance and control is somehow a bad thing. It is this feeling, of course, which gives rise to the limitation of disclosure of information and cooperation among systems discussed above. The recent American legislation on consumer credit reporting, however modest its impact on the more important credit bureau practices, attests to this same concern. Indeed, this same sort of public sentiment represents the most potent block to the re-institution in Britain of an identity card system of the sort used during the war years. The products of mass surveillance may be beguiling, but they are not so universally and irresistibly beguiling as always to allay deep anxieties about their unlimited application.

For those, like myself, who regard the extension of mass surveillance with distrust, such reserve may be comforting. One would like to believe that the public conscience on such matters represents a potent and durable guarantee against the unlimited development of surveillance capacity. But I fear that no such confidence is justified. It is true that public reactions, and even what one might see as deep-seated values, may block the extension of mass surveillance in specific instances. But these attitudes are both quite inchoate in the present, and highly susceptible to manipulation and even reversal by the force of future events.

The preceding chapter noted, for example, wide differences in policies regarding disclosure of information and cooperation among systems of surveillance. These variations suggest the lack of a clear-cut set of guiding principles concerning the justification and desirability of increasing the scope of mass surveillance. Again, the ethical questions involved are difficult from any point of view. The complexity of such issues may help explain the willingness to accept in one setting measures which would be held intolerable elsewhere. But another explanation certainly lies in the processes through which clienteles become inured to accepting corporate surveillance and control. For it appears that the successful operation of such systems, as *faits accomplis*, itself shapes public attitudes on what measures are acceptable.

The systems studied here, with the possible exception of National Insurance, have evolved gradually to assume their present form and scope. When the British police first began their 'register of habitual criminals', no one could have imagined its growing into the massive police surveillance system of today. When the first blacklists of bad debtors circulated among American merchants at the beginning of this century, no one could have envisaged the modern consumer credit reporting system. Nor, so far as I can tell, have these surveillance operations received a great deal of publicity during the course of their growth. Certainly the organizations maintaining the surveillance have not had much to gain from making the detail of their activities conspicuously public. These systems are now receiving much more publicity than they have previously. But they naturally do so as part of ongoing bureaucratic operations necessary for the provision of services, like social security or consumer credit, to which the public have become accustomed. This sort of 'packaging' is bound to minimize any objections to the record-keeping activities *per se*.

A number of the British civil servants whom I interviewed in the course of this research expressed interest in the consumer credit practices depicted in the American part of the study. Was there not a considerable public reaction against such practices, they wondered? Was not the collection and use of personal information under such commercial auspices the object of general mistrust? These qualms sometimes struck me as ironic, since these same officials were engaged in carrying out vast record-keeping operations in their own right. But one senses that such attitudes are characteristic of public opinion in Britain, where consumer credit itself is much less developed than in America. In the United States wide reliance on consumer credit is a fact, and acceptance of the surveillance measures which accompany it is quite general. On the other hand, it may well be that Americans would resent the sudden imposition of state surveillance measures of the sorts involved, say, in National Insurance. It would be difficult to test these ideas, short of an ambitious study of public opinion. But it seems to me that what people accept in the way of mass surveillance is very much a product of what they see as operational realities. One wonders whether many of the mass surveillance systems in operation today would have received advance approval from their clienteles or from the public at large. One suspects that such advance reactions would resemble more the attitudes expressed towards the first British census, as in the quote at the beginning of this book.

Given the frequently frightening prophecies put forward by writers on mass surveillance, one might expect their pronouncements to end with demands for wholesale curtailment of such practices. Such expectations are not fulfilled. One encounters proposals aplenty for the reform of record-keeping practices, for their regulation by outside agencies, or for wider client access to or control over personal record-keeping. But to my knowledge no one has seriously opposed the *principle* of using personal data in discriminating decision-making processes like those discussed here.*

In fact, it is difficult to do so. Most of those who have commented at length on the growth of mass surveillance have been what I would term liberal intellectuals. By this I mean to designate a category of thinkers solicitous of privacy and personal liberty, but also broadly favourable to the growth of modern social institutions. They are people whom one would expect to support 'progressive' measures like social security or the rationalization and modernization of policing. One would expect them to insist that such measures be carried out fairly and with ample regard for individual rights, but not to advocate 'turning the clock back' in any of these respects. Certainly one would not expect to find them opposed in general

---

* For useful discussions of possible reform measures see Malcolm Warner and Michael Stone, *The Data Bank Society*, London, George Allen and Unwin, 1970; especially Chapters 10 and 11. Also, Alan F. Westin, 'Legal Safeguards to Ensure Privacy in a Computer Society', in Zenon W. Pylyshyn, ed., *Perspectives on the Computer Revolution*, Englewood Cliffs, New Jersey, Prentice-Hall, 1970.

to the application of 'fine-grained decision-making' *per se* on the part of corporate agencies dealing with mass clienteles.

The trouble is, it is this need for fine-grained decision-making which necessitates the use of detailed personal information. If any agency is to take account of important but idiosyncratic differences in the situations of individual clients, it has little choice but to seek authoritative documentation on those differences. This holds *a fortiori* with regard to 'justice' in decision-making. Those who have proposed reform of record-keeping practices have naturally enough sought to ensure that the decision-making based on such records proceeds justly. But justice in decision-making implies and indeed requires the judicious use of relevant information, so as to give each client his due. In consumer credit reporting, for example, it requires that credit-grantors avail themselves of 'the full story' on the client, including extenuating circumstances left out of the credit report. The new American legislation seeks to make provision for this. Or in National Insurance, the requirement for 'justice' in the allocation of benefits necessitates, for example, close surveillance over the status of widows. Much as people may wish to ease the burdens of mass surveillance, they also want these systems to be effective in their discrimination procedures, and above all just. And discrimination, especially just discrimination, requires the collection and use of authoritative personal information.

Lest I be mistaken, let me say that many of these reform proposals seem wholly desirable in themselves. Some have stipulated that everyone should have full access to all records concerning himself, and this is simply indispensable.* Also highly desirable are those provisions for ensuring accuracy of filed data, accountability of decisions based on such data, and some measure of control over the use of data by those to whom it refers. Finally, it is essential that procedures governing *access* to filed information be matters of public knowledge, and that this access be strictly limited and non-discretionary.

---

* Even on this point, however, there are some difficult cases. One would have to be deeply committed to the principle of disclosure to insist on opening to medical patients data on themselves so distressing as to endanger their lives.

But none of these measures, desirable though they are, strikes at what to me seems the most problematic issue implicit in the growth of mass surveillance. This is simply the question of how much of men's lives should be subject to such surveillance, and how sweeping the decision-making based on it should be. How far should corporate bodies go in controlling their clienteles through systematic intake and use of personal information? How is one to weigh the interests of such agencies, or of the public at large, in maintaining such control, against the interests of the controlled, and against the values jeopardized by the exercise of control? These are questions which the 'reform' of surveillance practices, in the narrow sense, cannot resolve. Indeed, ensuring justice, accuracy and accountability may only sharpen these dilemmas by making mass surveillance more efficient and more widely acceptable.

One might clarify this issue by considering a heuristic extreme case. What if one could eliminate *all* forms of undesirable social behaviour through the maintenance of total but entirely benign surveillance? What if the members of a society could agree on a set of social norms which all desired enforced, and a series of thoroughgoing but absolutely just surveillance measures for their enforcement? Some might object that the total annihilation of privacy under such a system, the universal experience of being watched every moment, would make such an arrangement insupportable. But imagine that the surveillance took place with complete discretion, or, better still, by some mechanical device which involved no human intervention unless one did something wrong. Such a hypothetical total surveillance system could be entirely fair, accurate in its use of its data, and non-repressive in that the rules enforced would be accepted by all, or by the overwhelming majority. Would this satisfy all objections to mass surveillance? Would the elimination of all forms of 'bad' behaviour be worth total surveillance under such conditions?

It is easy to object to thoroughgoing measures of surveillance when they work in the service of rules which one holds wrong. The moral problem becomes more complex when such efficient strictures work against those forms of behaviour which one finds most repugnant. Perfectly efficient total surveillance could hypothetically eliminate all forms of crime and other violations of formal norms. But it need not stop there. It could also eliminate much behaviour universally considered undesirable, but which staging problems may make it impossible to control. It is possible to make and enforce laws against physical assault, for example. But at least as much human suffering probably results from what one might term symbolic assault – harsh words, deprivation of basic kindness, failure to honour intimate understandings and the like. Total surveillance might prevent such symbolic cruelty. Or, if these sorts of misdeeds are not sufficiently impressive to the reader, perhaps he can simply imagine whatever forms of social behaviour he finds most reprehensible. Again, would their elimination justify total but benevolent surveillance?

I shall not weary the reader by speculating further about a possibility which is, after all, very remote from reality. The only usefulness of such an exercise is to clarify a matter with the most concrete implications for practice. This is the question of the fundamental objections to mass surveillance. Do these have to do only with *injustice* in the administration of such measures? Or with the failure of such practices to serve 'the public interest'? If these are the only objections, then total but benevolent surveillance as described above should be entirely acceptable. If not, then one must take the position that mass surveillance must at least sometimes simply be a bad thing in itself.

Between Efficiency and Autonomy

Sociological inquiry, at its best, can help men reason and act wisely, but it is not the task of sociology to prescribe wisdom. Sociological thinking and sociological research can clarify and illuminate intellectual and moral issues, but the choices made on those issues turn on more than just sociological insight. What good sociology should contribute is an accurate and pertinent view of how the social world *works*. At most, this can enable men to arrive at an understanding of the true issues facing them, a rejection of inauthentic issues, and a sensitivity to the likely outcomes of different choices of action.

But the business of choosing involves the goals, the values, and the *partis pris* of the actor, all of which interact intricately and even violently with sociological reality. Thus there is no 'sociologically accurate answer' to the questions just posed. The test of such questions is not whether the answers are easy or automatic, but whether the questions themselves succeed in getting to the heart of an important issue.

All sociological thought involves some sort of purely moral choice, overt or implicit, on the part of the thinker. This is just as it should be, provided that there is no confusion between what is and what ought to be. Indeed, the more explicit the sociologist can be about his own values and their role in his sociology, the better. Nevertheless, until now, these discussions have not advocated any over-all, programmatic response to the growth of mass surveillance and control. Partly this has been to avoid giving the impression that the factual material presented here was gathered simply to justify a preconceived argument, which was definitely not the case. More importantly, it seemed that moral and social issues involved were so complex that premature closure might fail to do them justice.

But now the end of the study is at hand, and I have placed all my cards on the table in the way of facts and observations. This is the time to confront directly the moral and social issues implicit in the growth of mass surveillance and control. My position is simply that these practices are sufficiently undesirable in themselves and in certain of their potential consequences that we would do well to curtail them wherever possible. This judgement applies even in cases where systems operate with justice and on behalf of highly desirable purposes. Indeed, the development of popularly-supported, 'just' systems of surveillance strikes me as more worrying in the long run than those against which popular sentiment is capable of being aroused.

There are several distinct reasons for mistrusting the continuing growth of mass surveillance. One is simply the repressive potential which they confer upon the corporate agencies maintaining the surveillance, or upon whoever controls those agencies. I have taken pains to emphasize that the potential for repressive use of these systems is anything but identical with actual repression. On the contrary, discussion has made it plain that some surveillance systems are capable of putting up considerable resistance to 'unauthorized' use of their facilities. Nevertheless, any over-all response to these systems must take into account not only their present impact, but also their future prospects. And this means accepting the possibility that, in the course of other political changes, the intent and political disposition of those who control these systems may change.

Caution in this regard is hardly without precedent in other contexts. Many societies limit access to dangerous drugs, poisons and armaments on the principle that these things are potentially too destructive. Thus even people of unquestioned character and good-will may be forbidden to possess automatic weapons. Similarly, most governments are at least theoretically restricted in the application of police powers, for example, in the arrests of private persons. The implicit assumption is simply that unlimited power of arrest, for example without warrant or accountability, places dangerously excessive power in the hands of the state. The same sort of argument, it seems to me, is applicable to the use of mass surveillance and control. The 'bureaucratic weaponry' represented by these systems is simply so formidable as to require limitation, even in the absence of obvious repressive inclination on the part of any specific regime.

Barrington Moore, Jr, has written:

... it might be tempting to conclude that conformity under a centralization which accomplishes the purposes that human beings set themselves cannot by definition be repressive. Though such an answer draws attention to an important part of the truth, by itself it is inadequate. For one thing it tells us nothing at all about the very strong possibility that centralized decision-making in the interests of all may turn into repressive despotism. I have not the slightest faith in the benevolent self-restraint of any rulers and accept wholeheartedly the liberal insight that power is the only reliable check on power ... Whether or not industrialism contains within it processes that upset this balance is a factual and historical aspect of our question that cannot be answered by the manipulation of definitions. For the past fifty years, the trend appears to have been very definitely in a direction unfavorable to the operation of this balance.*

One imagines that Moore would include the development of mass surveillance techniques as part of this over-all unfavour-able trend. Readers more optimistic than he may feel that the safeguards against repressive use of systems like those des-cribed here provide more than enough assurance. For the present, this is debatable. For the future, to maintain con-fidence in the indefinite forbearance of those who control these systems seems to me to require a political and historical clairvoyance not given to men.

Another objection to the extension even of 'just' discrimina-tion based on mass surveillance has to do with their effects on those discriminated *against*. The object of discriminations like those discussed here, after all, is to achieve the cheapest possible identification of those who have not or will not obey the rules. Often the idea is to exclude these people in advance. Chapter 7 has shown how, with sophisticated manipulations of aggregate data, even tiny and seemingly irrelevant facts can represent significant predictors. The use of such discrimination procedures thus raises the question of what sorts of data should legitimately be usable in decision-making which may, after all, weigh very heavily upon the clients concerned.

Consider an example from consumer credit in America. Many credit-grantors believe that Negroes in general meet credit obligations distinctly less faithfully than do whites. Of course, it is true that being black in America is also associated with a number of other factors predictive of low creditworthi-ness – low income, irregular employment, poor education, and so on. But it is also thought that race in itself, even after correction for these factors, represents a valid statistical pre-dictor. Assume, for the sake of discussion, that this is the case, that Negro-hood in itself does predict high rates of consumer credit default. Should race then figure as a subject of informa-tion intake and use in consumer credit surveillance? If the criteria were the attainment of the most accurate possible dis-crimination procedures and the minimization of default, the

* Moore, *Political Power and Social Theory*, pp. 189–90.

answer would be affirmative. But I am sure that many readers, like myself, would find such discrimination procedures unconscionable. The question is not exactly one of privacy, since a person's race is not ordinarily something which he chooses to keep secret from the world at large. But one feels that there are certain kinds of personal information which simply ought not to bear on decision-making of this sort – no matter how accurate the information or how 'fair' the processes guiding its use.

One has no control over one's race, nor over any number of other characteristics which one may share with people who, for one reason or another, are to be discriminated against. Being black may statistically predict poor payment patterns, but it hardly stands in the same moral light as deliberate failure to pay one's bills in the past. In the latter case, one might argue that a clear-cut 'infraction' of the rules in one instance warrants punitive discrimination in a directly comparable instance later on. But sophisticated surveillance procedures may turn up all sorts of facts about people which, while not *morally* related to the exercise of some form of discrimination, are highly relevant statistically. Administrative rationality, working to maximize compliance and minimize costs, would dictate that all available statistically relevant data be used. But the application of this kind of thinking only promises to tip the balance between individual and corporate interests more and more heavily against the former. With the continued perfection of discrimination techniques like those described in Chapter 8, with the subjection of broader and broader areas of men's lives to mass surveillance, the impact of discrimination based on data so collected is bound to grow.

No doubt everyone holds some assumptions, however vague, about the difference between inherently private personal information and that which is justly subject to public attention. Often, for example, people seem to draw a distinction like John Stuart Mill's between self- and other-regarding actions. One imagines that certain behaviour, like committing and being convicted for a crime, involves the rest of society and hence creates a licence for surveillance, for example, in the form of criminal record-keeping. Other behaviour, such as sexual behaviour among consenting adults, may be considered to concern only those who engage in it, and hence not to justify others' attentions. This doctrine has its problems from a philosophical point of view, but it does seem to support a commonsense distinction of considerable importance. The trouble is that mass surveillance techniques work to erode the very distinction between public and private in this regard. This they do by turning up unexpected connections between highly personal, and hitherto private, data and social behaviour in which corporate bodies claim a legitimate interest. Chapter 8, again, entertained some possibilities for the future development of these connections; many of them involved corporate interest in very private areas of men's lives indeed. Whether these will come to be seen as just matters for institutional concern, and public surveillance, remains to be seen. Certainly there can be no denying that these private matters do bear on the public interest, or that decision-making based on them can provide benefits for society as a whole. But as for myself, I hope that values of individual autonomy and privacy can prevail in these contexts over those of collective rationality.

To be sure, restraint in these respects can lead to some difficult questions, especially where the benefits of surveillance are particularly clear-cut. What if, by collecting data on some extremely private area of people's behaviour, one could predict with virtual certainty the likelihood of their causing a fatal traffic accident in the near future? The predictive behaviour, presumably, would involve no direct and obvious connection with motoring, and obviously would not itself represent an infraction against motoring laws. To this extent, one would be inclined to resist compulsory surveillance over the behaviour in question. On the other hand, if prediction were really virtually perfect, the cost of forgoing it, in terms of lives, would be excruciatingly obvious. At present such discrimination represents nothing more than another heuristic, hypothetical case. But there is no guarantee that this will always be true. The growing sophistication of predictive techniques promises to make the choices implicit in these situations increasingly dramatic and difficult.

There is a final reservation about the growth of mass surveillance, more subtle than the preceding ones, but no less compelling. It has to do with the inherent value of choice in responding to the strictures of control imposed by the social world. These discussions have insisted that some measure of enforced compliance is necessary for the vitality of any social unit. Yet the reader must also feel, as I do, that the business of choosing whether to comply is an essential element of human experience. Total surveillance could theoretically provide limitless benefits in the way of compliance, but only at the expense of watching and controlling people so closely and constantly as to render misbehaviour out of the question. The case studies have shown just how remote is the prospect of total surveillance, so there is no question of its imminent realization on a large scale. But the underlying principle is important. Corporate participation in every moment of every individual's life, no matter how fair or how discreet or how benign, is simply too great a price to pay for obedience. Life in a highly imperfect social world is still infinitely preferable to life in a world offering no opportunities for imperfection.

So much for principles. Is there in fact any realistic chance of combating the undesirable effects of mass surveillance? Measures of reform, as I have said, do not strike at the heart of the issue. In fact, the only means of confronting the fundamental problems described above is to curtail the exercise of 'fine-grained corporate concern' towards members of mass clienteles. This would mean, in other words, abandoning discriminating decision-making based on the details of clients' past histories and present circumstances. For it is this sort of discrimination which necessitates the systematic collection, storage and use of personal information encountered in this book. The reform of such practices, again, can go a long way to making them more just and more amenable to public regulation. But the only way to ease the over-all impact of these practices is to renounce the benefits as well as the drawbacks of mass surveillance.

On the face of it, such drastic measures would seem to preclude many services which are simply too important to forgo. But there are alternative means of attaining certain desirable results of mass surveillance without its disadvantages.

These would entail providing indiscriminately certain benefits currently contingent on corporate surveillance and discrimination. Consider the case of consumer credit. The use of more and more subtle personal data on consumers obviously serves to enable credit-grantors to arrive at increasingly precise discriminations between those who will and those who will not pay their debts. Forgoing this fine discrimination would obviously alleviate the necessity of such thoroughgoing surveillance. It would mean, of course, that credit-grantors would have to accept accounts on the basis of very limited clues as to their creditworthiness. Similar non-discriminatory alternatives exist in the case of social security. These might for example entail the provision of a guaranteed minimum income for everyone. Such a 'floor' under all incomes would relieve the necessity for amassing detailed and often volatile personal information to determine who is entitled to precisely which benefits. Comparable alternatives are also feasible in other operations which now rely on mass surveillance.

There can be no doubt that any such measures would be costly. Discussion has emphasized the profound appeal of mass surveillance systems, both to their managers and to their clienteles, stemming from their ever-increasing ability to reduce the costs of deviant behaviour. Even a limited relaxation of surveillance would reduce this trend and appreciably raise operating costs. Indeed, it could even cause some institutions now dependent on surveillance to curtail their operations. The issue is most clear-cut in consumer credit. Cutting back on discrimination over credit applications would directly lead to higher rates of default, with the inevitable result of higher credit costs. Some credit schemes would probably become unworkable, including especially the most convenient and flexible ones like BankAmericard. For it is precisely the most sophisticated consumer credit systems which depend most heavily on close and thorough surveillance over their clienteles. The costs of abandoning discrimination in social security services should be equally obvious. For there such measures would require providing support to those who do not 'need' or 'deserve' it, while making no special concessions to those in circumstances of extraordinary stringency.

Indeed, the most unpopular result of abandoning discrimination in these settings would not be measurable in cash terms. This would be the inevitable inability of corporate agencies to render 'justice' to their clienteles. People may, as we have seen, sometimes resent the collection and use of information about themselves in processes of mass surveillance and control. But people also expect the agencies involved to deal 'fairly' with their clients, to act with 'just' consideration of the latter's past histories and present circumstances. And justice means careful discrimination. Curtailing discrimination in consumer credit, by reducing the general availability of credit, would limit access to credit on the part of 'good' credit risks. It might well, for example, make it impossible to provide credit privileges now available to impecunious but 'stable' customers. Likewise, curtailing discrimination in social security services would mean allocating public monies to 'parasitic' recipients as well as to the needful – something which the public conscience would probably deplore. There is simply no way of obviating these dilemmas. To deal 'justly' with individual cases means to take account of fine details of clients' lives. And this in turn requires the collection of authoritative personal information and its application in forceful decision-making – in short, the maintenance of mass surveillance and control.

Because of the beguiling appeal of fine-grained decision-making, it is hard to hope for any sweeping curtailment of mass surveillance and control. Certainly it is reasonable to expect public opinion to oppose measures seen as repressive or coercive towards the public at large. Certainly, too, one can realistically hope for the acceptance of reform measures like those already proposed, to make mass surveillance more open, accountable and just. Whether one can expect people to renounce altogether the benefit of practices felt to provide essential personal services is another matter. The benefits forthcoming from the systems studied in this book, from protection against criminals to easy consumer credit, are palpable and easily grasped, while the drawbacks of unlimited extension of mass surveillance are bound to appear abstract and remote. The precedents for choice among such alternatives are not auspicious. In a world threatened by products of industrialism ranging from ecological disarray to nuclear warfare, the Industrial Revolution in retrospect appears as a mixed blessing. Nor, of course, was its advent a universally welcomed trend at the time. But one doubts whether any amount of earnest discussion in itself could have done much to arrest or modify the course of those events once they were under way. So it often is with major currents of social change. Considerations of the desirability in principle of this or that innovation do not readily withstand subjection to the earthy forces which move men in fact. For the immediate future, then, we can probably expect to live with the consequences of more and more effective mass surveillance and control – both for better and for worse.

What is absolutely essential, however, is that we see the alternatives for what they are, that the issues not simply be settled by default. The seductive appeal of mass surveillance makes it all too possible that the public will become dependent on the benefits of these practices before their dangers are apparent. The frequent efforts of the elites who control such systems to conceal their activities and to obfuscate the issues involved conduce to the same sort of effect. I hope that I am wrong in fearing that popular feeling will be insufficient to oppose the unlimited growth of mass surveillance. But I am sure that this will happen if these issues do not become current and clearly understood. If this book has contributed to such understanding, then the efforts involved will be amply repaid.

Appendix

Methods of Research and Verification of Findings

Working on any piece of research over a long period of time, one becomes a sort of connoisseur of friends' and colleagues' first reactions to the project. In the case of this study, the standard, reflexive response was to ask, of the persons and agencies involved in the case studies, 'Will they talk to you? Will they help you with your work?' A variation on this theme, especially common among social scientists, was 'Can you believe what they tell you?' The answer to all three of these questions was 'Yes, but not automatically'. Considerable thought and effort went into creating the conditions under which useful information would be forthcoming, and to ensuring that the conclusions drawn from such information were reliable. The brief glosses at the end of the five case studies have already sketched some of the steps involved in the development of the materials contained there. It remains to add here some more general remarks about the strategy and tactics of the research and about the ways in which conclusions were drawn from the data.

The potential for resistance to this inquiry from the agencies concerned is hardly difficult to understand. During the last five to ten years mass surveillance and related data-gathering practices have been the subject of a crescendo of publicity and controversy. Over-all, such commentary has been more critical than favourable. The managers of the systems under study here, on whom I depended for permission to gather these materials, saw themselves as having more than enough to do simply in running the day-to-day operations of their organizations. They felt, not without justification, that publicity of any kind would only make their jobs more difficult. At best, public criticism would take up their time in responding; at worst, outside pressure might demand the curtailment of practices which they considered essential. Thus the desire to avoid attention from outsiders altogether.

Nevertheless, these were not the only considerations which formed the attitudes of those in charge. In many instances, I am sure, people simply felt on principle that the required information should be released, notwithstanding the consequences. In addition, less purely self-sacrificing motives probably also played a role. Many officials must have felt, for instance, that refusal to help would create more adverse publicity than the provision of limited assistance. To this end, it was important to portray the study in advance as scholarly, thoughtful and fair-minded, so as to make refusal of cooperation *prima facie* less reasonable. The sponsorship of the study by Nuffield College no doubt helped considerably in this connection. Another consideration which seemed to encourage some officials to communicate with me was the desire to gain a hearing for their own point of view. Much of the recent publicity on personal record-keeping has been not only unfavourable but also simply garbled. Consequently, some officials explicitly asked for the opportunity to 'set the record straight'. Here I could offer a sincere determination to do an accurate and thorough job, and the opportunity for official comment on my remarks before they reached print.

In all my efforts at establishing communication with the agencies concerned, time and patience were invaluable assets. There is something about bureaucratic organization which endemically tempts those who work in them to obviate thorny issues by failure to act. It was thus important to assure people, on initial contact, that the study was to take several years, and to fortify this assurance by conscientiously following up ignored communications and other evasive moves. Demonstration of determination and perseverance not only discouraged evasion but probably also helped people to see the proposed investigation as sufficiently serious to justify their efforts to cooperate. This bore fruit initially, and most importantly, in the decision to allow me to gather material within the organizations described here.

The main methods of research were unstructured interviews and direct observation. By 'unstructured' interviews I mean discursive, probing conversations with those having access to the required information. Unlike the common sociological method of administering identical questionnaires to large numbers of respondents, each of these interviews was unique, unguided by a rigid, pre-set formula. By direct observation I mean simply watching the daily work of record-keeping *in situ*. The constraints of the subject matter made reliance on these methods the natural choice. For one thing, the 'reality' which the study sought to uncover was distributed among so many different persons and locations that one could only visit them all, gathering different strands of information from each. For another thing, the information sought was con-troversial and complex. The controversiality and complexity meant that informants were uneven in their willingness and ability to tell me the 'whole story'. No one person knew every-thing I wanted to know about any one system, nor were there many who were prepared to tell me everything that they themselves knew. One thus tried to build every interview on the sum of one's previous information, asking slightly different questions in slightly different ways each time. Finally, the sought-after information was evanescent and proprietary to the organizations involved. The practices which I wished to study were continually changing, and few outside the organiza-tions involved knew about them in detail. Thus there was little choice but to interrogate those involved in record-keeping practices, and to watch them at their work.

There were a few exceptions. Occasionally useful docu-mentary sources were available, and I shall have more to say about this below. Also, in interviewing, it was sometimes possible to rely on people outside the organizations under study who were nevertheless knowledgeable about their practices. In a few cases these were retired persons or other former members of the organizations involved. More com-monly, they were other researchers whose inquiries had led them to develop information on subjects related to those studied here. These informants were invaluable, in that they were free of the organizational pressures which inevitably bore on the information provided by others. I only wish that I had been able to contact more people like this; as it turned out, the great bulk of the sought-after information was available only from members of the agencies under study.

It is probably unnecessary to point out that problems of access to required information scarcely ceased once I received official access to the organizations involved. Members of all these agencies were more or less resistant to divulging certain needed material. The amount of such resistance varied considerably from setting to setting, but was never altogether absent. Frequently the most senior officials were the most chary, no doubt because they realized most clearly the possible public reactions to the information in question. Yet there were also many instances when top officials overrode the demurs of their middle-echelon counterparts. In any event, overcoming the effects of this occasional reluctance to part with relevant facts presented one of the main challenges in preparing the case studies.

In fact, the constraints of the data-gathering situation left the investigator with more resources than one might think for wearing away at this reserve. One must remember that the systems studied here are all very large operations indeed. They are large in two ways. First, they employ enormous staffs in many different locations. Second, the maintenance of surveillance requires the meshing of many detailed sub-operations. The fact that so many different people are involved in running the systems inevitably leads to differences in willingness to disclose sensitive data. Some officials are bound to be especially secretive, while others feel that virtually everything should be explained. Of course, the most responsible figures have their own ideas about how far disclosure should go, and often seek to make these universally binding. But this is not necessarily easy. Most of the surveillance systems studied here were actually congeries of different organizations, often admitting of little direct control from the top. An extreme case in this respect, of course, was the consumer credit reporting system. And even where direct control from the top was theoretically possible, it was often difficult in practice. For one thing, sources of disclosure were not always evident after the fact. For another, the internal complexity of operations made it difficult for those at the top to anticipate what information might be sought, and to warn all possible contacts against discussing it. Once the gathering of material had begun, the burden of limiting disclosure rested on those in charge. That burden was often considerable.

The 'secrets' involved in the operation of systems like these, then, are big secrets. Such big secrets are difficult to keep, especially given a measure of ambivalence about what the secrets are and indeed about whether they should be kept. The investigator, for his part, has the advantage of ample time and considerable latitude in contacting different informants. By talking to many different people, one eventually locates and relies upon those who are especially helpful. Different sources should complement one another, each providing information which the other is unwilling or unable to provide. Indeed, the acquisition of any one scrap of information can often represent a lever for the acquisition of more. If, for example, the investigator catches wind of something important, he may find it useful to ask for amplification on the point subsequently, at a moment when the question is quite unexpected. Under such circumstances, it may be difficult to avoid discussing the point, much as one's interlocutor may wish that it had never been raised. Again, the investigator can make the most of knowing precisely what he needs to know, whereas his opposite numbers may not have thought in advance what they want to conceal. By building each interview on the preceding ones, and by cultivating a multiplicity of sources, one can often learn virtually as much as one's time and energies permit.

Still, it would be wrong to suggest that the hardest work involved in data-collection came in overcoming the resistance of informants. Resistance there was, on sensitive points, but I was actually surprised at how little of it I encountered once the research was accepted in principle. The hardest work came simply in understanding complex accounts related to me sincerely and openly. The typical interview, if such a thing existed, involved visiting someone at his place of work and hearing him explain and demonstrate his job. On these occasions I tried to go as deeply as possible into the daily routines of record-keeping practice, attempting to build a much more detailed picture in my own mind than would ever be presented in the case studies. These routines were often excruciatingly dull, but it seemed essential to learn them in order to understand the over-all workings of the systems involved.

I often found myself, in these situations, playing virtually the role of a new member of the office staff. It is difficult to say whether these experiences represented interviews or participation, since both things went on simultaneously or by turns. I would sit, for example, at a desk where files were being processed, watch the progress of the work, and discuss what I saw with my companions. Sometimes concerns elsewhere would draw the supervisors away from the scene, creating a windfall opportunity to discuss matters with those who actually did the work. Their more uninhibited explanations often added considerably to my understanding. I once began an interview with a manager of a consumer credit reporting agency who particularly stressed how carefully his staff ensured the accuracy of data inserted in consumers' files. Then he took me to the office where this filing was taking place, only to be unexpectedly called away. I was left to chat with the staff engaged in the filing, and found them in a state of frustration. They were unable to interpret the data which they had received from their sources, the member bureaus, and thus were obliged to file it in garbled form. Grateful for a sympathetic ear, they explained that this situation was common.

Again, the hardest work involved in these sessions was simply that of learning the humdrum but often complex routines of information processing. This was a repetitive process of noting down what I had learned, trying to reconstruct it in my own mind, and then relating back to my interlocutors to make certain that I had it right. When I began to be more confident of my understanding, I sometimes attempted com-

plicated exercises with my informants to test my knowledge.
I would pose hypothetical special cases or unusual contingencies,
and then we would speculate together about their possible
outcomes. How long would it take to detect that a particular
sort of file had been mislaid? Could a client cheat the system
in a given situation by presenting a false name? Could a given
datum be misinterpreted in decision-making, and if so what
would be the results? When my interlocutors and I began to
reach similar answers to these puzzles, I felt some measure of
closure in my picture of the systems concerned.

Obviously, the feasibility of this sort of work is bound to
turn largely on *rapport* with one's interlocutors. Persistent
questioning of an antagonistic or resistant contact can sometimes yield valuable information, and so there are moments
when thick skin is a prerequisite. But much of the information
presented here would never have been available without the
pleasant opportunity to develop really cordial relations with
source persons. These were the people to whom I returned
again and again, and who provided voluntarily information
which I needed but did not always know how to ask for. No
doubt investigators are highly varied and idiosyncratic in their
ways of cultivating good relations with their interlocutors.
What seemed to work best in this case was to be friendly and
approachable without revealing a great deal about any of one's
own opinions and attitudes towards matters under discussion.
This seemed to lead people to take for granted the moral support which they basically desired from the interviewer.

Thus I usually found myself striving to say as little as
possible during interviews, trying to formulate questions that
would encourage people to provide the maximum information
without further intervention from me. When it did become
necessary to ask explicitly for sensitive information, one tried
to couch the question in terms most sympathetic to the inter-
viewee. To ask a man, for example, whether he ever violates
the confidentiality of clients' files is to place him in the position
of defending himself. To ask him how he meets the needs of
other agencies for assistance is to pose the same problem as he
feels it impinging on himself. Whatever the details of one's
interviewing techniques, some diffuse acceptance of one's

contacts' world-view seems essential. By minimizing the stimuli of one's own opinions and reactions, one gives the other man the best chance to tell his own story.

It would clearly have been impossible to deal with so much data, collected over such a long period of time, without systematic recording and indexing. For the interviewing and observation, this obviously meant keeping field notes. Taking down notes during interviews encourages people to feel that what they say is 'for the record', which is quite the opposite of what the interviewer desires. Therefore I usually restricted myself to taking mental notes while in the presence of source persons, recording these into a tape recorder as soon as possible afterwards. These recordings were subsequently transcribed for future reference. In cases where the interviewing coincided more closely with writing up the case studies, my note-taking was much less formal. While I was plying back and forth between my contacts and the typewriter, my notes were brief, hand-written memos to myself, and were not recorded and transcribed.

Interviews and direct observation were not the only sources of information, though they accounted for the bulk of the material presented in the case studies. The use of documentation was also essential. In some instances these were documents published by the agencies under study, including press releases and annual reports. Elsewhere, officials prepared statistics especially for inclusion in this study, often going to a great deal of trouble to do so. I am especially grateful for the provision of these statistics, which obviously were available in no other way. In still other cases, the organizations concerned allowed me access to internal documents prepared for the use of staff which outlined standard procedure in areas of interest to this study. These, too, were indispensable, especially for comparison with the accounts given in interviews.

In a small minority of cases, members of these organizations allowed me to examine documents which I was not officially supposed to see. It would be easy to exaggerate the importance of information so obtained, in relation to that made available through more customary channels. And indeed, as I have said, there was frequently either personal confusion or collective differences of opinion as to what should or should not be disclosed. But certainly there were instances in which people showed me papers – or simply told me things – which they realized that more responsible others would not approve. This was the case with the memos cited in Table 3 (page 80), for example. In most instances such documentation served mainly to substantiate information already provided in interviews. This was especially important in controversial areas where my reports might subsequently be contested. One regrettable result of my occasional recourse to 'forbidden' information, however, is my inability to thank by name or affiliation certain people who went to some lengths to provide this help. I can only thank them in general, and express my hope that they find the finished product worthy of their trust.

In at least one case, the official response on learning of my access to forbidden information was that such actions were unfair, that it was unethical to obtain and use data not intended for release. The reader may wish to ponder for himself the rights and wrongs of this question. So far as I am concerned, there do exist morally unacceptable means of obtaining information – thievery, blackmail, and so on – in a study like this one. But I do not find it unethical to obtain from willing informants information which the highest authorities prefer to withhold. I sympathetically understand the strain on members of organizations engaged in controversial activities when those activities are subjected to study by outsiders. But I would place higher value on the right of the public to know about practices which affect a wide range of private citizens so directly and so intimately. Whenever any agency involves itself in the private lives of members of mass clienteles to the extent of these five systems, there is simply no justification for concealment of the practices involved. Certainly there is always an obligation on the part of the investigator to deal fairly and accurately with the resulting material. But this is an obligation which I have tried earnestly to meet.

Every researcher, whatever his field, is obliged to clarify to his reader his steps in moving from recorded *data* to reported *findings* and *conclusions*. This obligation is if anything especially weighty here, where the subject-matter is volatile and controversial. Before reporting any of the information collected in this study, I have tried to subject it to several tests of accuracy. It remains to make a few concluding remarks about these.

The first test of the accuracy of any information has to do with its source. No source, human or documentary, is absolutely impeccable in its own right, but some sources are inherently more authoritative than others. Obviously, the word of someone with direct and evident expertise and acquaintance in a specific area carries more weight than that of someone more remote from the scene. I have, for example, often valued the accounts of junior officials actually engaged in a given record-keeping activity over those of their superiors with less direct contact with the daily routine of office practice. Further, the willingness of any informant to commit himself to a statement before his colleagues or the public at large carried a significant element of persuasiveness. Likewise, the statements of someone who has nothing special to gain by making them, either for himself or for his organization, carry a particular persuasiveness. Admissions of uncomfortable truths, for example, carry more weight than grandiose claims. Finally, the role of any informant within his organization bears importantly on his believability. Some of my interlocutors, for example, were in effect specialists in presenting a bright organizational face to the world – public relations officers, and so on. Others were so remote from the impact of their work on public opinion that they seemed not to realize that there was any. While the former provided much useful and accurate information, the word of the latter counted more heavily in doubtful cases.

Even more important than the source of information, as a test of credibility, has been its internal consistency and its consistency with other findings. Accounts which contradict themselves, obviously, must be rejected. More difficult and demanding is the business of reconciling new information with the sum of data previously accumulated. Two kinds of comparisons are implicit here. First is the question of whether one reported element of organizational behaviour is consistent with other known elements. Is the account of transmission of information from one office for example, reasonable in light of what is known about its receipt elsewhere? Second is the test of consistency with other accounts of the same fact or process. In some cases this may mean checking the account of an informant on one occasion against the same person's previous or subsequent reports. Elsewhere it requires checking one informant's word against that of others, or against documentary sources. Documentation is hardly sacred in its own right, of course, and there were many occasions when personal reports proved more credible than the written word. There, too, the final judgement turned on critical comparison within and among sources. In all instances, matters of special importance or sensitivity called for special efforts of double-checking through all available sources.

The case studies have also received a final review from the principal agencies which supplied the information. The one exception was the Home Office in Britain, which refused comment on Chapter 2; but that chapter received a reading and commentary from members of three other bodies dealing with criminal record-keeping. In each of the five cases, the reviewers provided useful suggestions which were adopted in the final version. The suggested changes ordinarily pointed to discrete matters of factual detail which, if uncorrected, would have flawed the final version. In general, there has been ultimate agreement with the agencies involved on statements of fact in the various case studies, and only an occasional disagreement over matters of opinion or interpretation. I would like to take this opportunity to thank once again those who took such pains to review the case studies and to provide such careful comments on them. My gratitude is especially great to those who conscientiously commented even on matters which they may have preferred not to see discussed in the first place.

In conclusion, I should say that I have tried to observe the principle of methodological conservatism in all statements made in this book. The test for inclusion of any statement has not been simply whether I believe it to be so, but whether the available evidence indicates its veracity beyond reasonable doubt. One result of this policy has been the omission of material which I felt interesting and significant but which I have been unable to double-check. This is a price one pays for presenting to one's readers a study which one hopes they will find not only interesting but also sound and trustworthy.

Index

absconded husbands: use of National Insurance records to trace, 165; use of vehicle registration files to trace, 110; Parliamentary debate on, 316

ACB, 179–81, 202, 203, 210, 212, 222

access to delinquent clients, *see* apprehension of delinquent clients

access to filed information, 333–8; in vehicle registration, 110–11; in consumer credit, 199, 214–215, 219–20; to one's own records, 214–15, 347–8; to BankAmericard files, 256–7; *see also* disclosure of filed information

access to surveillance facilities, 350–1; *see also* symboisis among surveillance systems

accessibility of filed information, 78, 283–7

accident-prone motorists, control of, 324, 354

accountability for decision-making in mass surveillance, 347–8

accuracy of filed data, 213–14, 216, 220, 221, 347, 348

acquittal of police suspects, 67

addresses of clients, currency of, 111, 145; in establishing identification, 207

age of clients, in identification, 207

agency or regime, defined, 23

aggregate date as basis for mass surveillance, 325, 352

Allen, Sir Philip, 95–6

alphabetical index: in National Insurance, 150; *see also* nominal index

American Express credit card scheme, 226

amount of useful information held per client, 38; in police surveillance, 88–9; in vehicle and driver licensing, 117; in National Insurance, 167–8; in consumer credit, 216–18; in BankAmericard, 262–3; growth of, 270–71; in relation to surveillance capacity and scale, 301–2.

anonymity, in large-scale societies, 28; from National Insurance, 146; of mass clienteles, 279

anonymous communications, in vehicle and driver licensing, 106–7; in National Insurance, 158

antecedent history sheet in police surveillance, 51; illustrated, 54; standardization of, 284

apprehension of delinquent clients, 291–4, 299, 312–17; in vehicle licensing, 119; in National Insurance, 123–4, 145; role of cooperation among

Date Due